POLITICAL ADVANCEMENT IN THE SOUTH PACIFIC

A

POLITICAL ADVANCEMENT IN THE SOUTH PACIFIC

A COMPARATIVE STUDY OF COLONIAL PRACTICE IN FIJI, TAHITI AND AMERICAN SAMOA

F. J. WEST

GREENWOOD PRESS, PUBLISHERS
WESTPORT, CONNECTICUT

Library of Congress Cataloging in Publication Data

West, Francis James.
Political advancement in the South Pacific a comparative study of colonial practice in Fiji, Tahiti, and American Samoa.

Reprint. Originally published: London : Oxford University Press, 1961.
Includes index.
1. Colonies--Administration. 2. Fiji--Politics and government. 3. Tahiti--Politics and government. 4. American Samoa--Politics and government. I. Title.
JV412.W47 1984 325.31'0961 84-6745
ISBN 0-313-24533-9 (lib. bdg.)

Originally published in 1961 by Oxford University Press
Melbourne, London, Wellington, New York

Reprinted with the permission of Oxford University Press Australia

Reprinted in 1984 by Greenwood Press
A division of Congressional Information Service, Inc.
88 Post Road West, Westport, Connecticut 06881

Printed in the United States of America

10 9 8 7 6 5 4 3 2 1

CONTENTS

INTRODUCTION

The islands of the South Pacific have been generally neglected by students of colonial administration: indeed their serious study has hardly begun. In part, no doubt, this neglect is the result of their own romantic legend of the South Seas: paradise, by definition, has no problems and therefore little interest. But the greater part of the reasons for this neglect is, no doubt, the relative insignificance of the islands. They are small, distant from the metropolitan centres of administration, politically insignificant for the most part, lacking in economic resources or raw materials; and they suffer because of the attractions which larger and more important colonial areas like Africa and Asia exercise over students. No one can pretend that absolutely the South Pacific islands are of much importance. Still, there is a strong case for their scientific study: the island societies are small; the history of colonial administration there covers a short span of time; it is therefore possible to study that history as a series of relatively clear, isolated problems which in other colonial areas are obscure and much more complex, and possible, too, by examining the Pacific, to obtain a clearer idea of the general processes involved in colonial rule, often in almost classical simplicity. The islands have, of course, a fascination of their own as the legend of the South Seas bears witness, but they are also important as a microcosm of the colonial situation, as an excellent case study of the issues which arise in this situation in other more important or more significant areas of Africa or Asia; their study, therefore, has a relevance to the body of work on colonial problems.

Three island groups are examined in this study: Fiji, a British crown colony, Tahiti and French Polynesia, and Eastern Samoa, an American possession. These islands were selected in order to write a comparative study of colonial practice. All of them, in pre-European times, had a roughly similar system of rank and authority which was characteristically Polynesian; all of them have experienced a very similar history of European contact, to which they have been exposed over a very similar period of time. They offer a basis for a comparison of the effects of the colonial rule of three different powers, each of which has its own traditions and its own practices. This kind of comparative study has not often been attempted, but there can be no doubt of its value in any effort to understand what happens in a colonial situation.

A comparison obviously implies a standard of judgement which should be made quite clear at the outset. This work is *not* an attempt to compare colonial policies and to pronounce one better or more successful than the others: this would be an idle proceeding. Colonial policy is not really a matter of choice open to a metropolitan power, but a natural projection of metropolitan attitudes (which change only very slowly) into a colonial situation. For example, there is really no choice open to the British Government between the kinds of policy which are represented by the words 'assimilation' and 'association': British traditions limit any choices to those of emphasis or method or technique within the latter kind of policy. In exactly the same way, French colonial policy exists within a tradition of assimilation. Approaches to colonial problems are broadly determined by metropolitan values, attitudes and traditions, and any great change in policy is dependent upon change in the metropolitan power. Thus, to say that British colonial policy is superior to French, and both inferior to American, is futile because such a judgement would blame the British for being British and the French for being French. Such a judgement is an arbitrary one which asserts one set of values to be superior to another, and it is based on some ultimately metaphysical standard.

There is, however, another reason for the futility of such a comparison. The word 'policy' is itself misleading: it implies a deliberation and an intention which are rarely present. The occasions on which policy is consciously thought out or debated are rare. More usually it is a matter of the general tendency of a number of decisions which, often in retrospect, add up to a consistent attitude which one calls 'policy'. Here again, there is no choice between different kinds of policy: there is only a decision taken by an individual or individuals who act within the framework of values and attitudes of their own society. When the total of such decisions seems to amount to a consistent policy, it reflects the values of the metropolitan society, and it is therefore to be judged superior to any other only by the arbitrary standard which has no place in a study of this kind. It must be accepted that each of the three colonial powers has exported its own attitudes and institutions into the colonies because these are all that is available for export, and this projection of their values must be taken for granted.

The comparison involved in this work is different. The colonial powers have erected standards for themselves. Within their broad colonial policy, it is possible to discuss the measures which have been taken in relation to the ends which the colonial powers have set before themselves; and to compare their administration in very similar situations in relation to their different colonial traditions. This is a fair standard of judgement because it accepts both the limits within which colonial policy is conceived, and the standards set up by the colonial powers themselves. Each of the powers envisages some form of political advancement for the peoples under their rule, although the interpretation of this end varies. Political advancement in this study is not used to mean political independence or progress towards it: neither the French nor the Americans have accepted independence as a declared aim of policy, but the British have, although in the case of Fiji there has been no explicit declaration. Whether a colony is intended to become either politically independent or self-governing is a matter of that broad colonial policy which has been described as taken for granted. All three powers, however, have committed themselves to the development of local self-government, and this is what is meant by political advancement here: the furtherance of the opportunity and the capacity for local rule and administration by the indigenous people through institutions which the colonial powers have provided to meet local conditions which were originally alike in sharing a common Polynesian type of rank and authority.

'Political advancement', as the term is used in the Charter of the United Nations, is a very general definition of one of the aims of colonial practice. It may legitimately be interpreted as self-government or local autonomy, as distinct from independence, by the wording of Article 76 of the Charter, but such a definition is still a very general one rather than a precise description of colonial practice. For the purposes of this study, political advancement has been tested by three questions. What institutions are available to promote discussion or formulation of policy by the indigenous people? What institutions enable them to execute or control the execution of those decisions? How far do these institutions really fulfil the intention of promoting political advancement? All of these questions are concerned with the exercise of power by which political advancement is ultimately tested, but they imply two premisses which have been taken for granted. The first is that to achieve self-government the political institutions of colonial society must be representative: they must be generally accepted by the people. The second is that such self-government must also, to paraphrase the words of the Covenant of the League of Nations, be able to stand on its own feet in the conditions of the modern world; it must be able to meet the minimum demands of efficiency imposed by the outside world and, implying at least the acceptance of Western technology, of modern science and modern medicine. The questions and the answers are concerned with advancement judged by these two assumptions, but they have also been treated as an aspect of one general colonial problem which is common not only to the South Pacific but to Africa and Asia as well: the question of 'direct' and 'indirect' rule as techniques of colonial government in promoting political advancement.

'Indirect rule' is a term which is often used very loosely in writing on colonial administration and which has now fallen into disrepute. It was originally used to describe the method by which Lord Lugard administered part of Nigeria through the highly developed Muslim emirates, and by extension it has been applied to any colonial government which has employed a system of Native Authorities, nowadays usually termed Local Government. In a popular and corrupt form it has often been summed up in the catch-phrase 'find the chief', and, having found him, use him for administrative purposes. Such a loose usage fails to distinguish the system it purports to describe from 'direct' rule which may also employ the chief in an administrative capacity. What really separates the two techniques is the actual basis of the traditional leader's authority, particularly as it is revealed in the control of revenue, and it is in this sense that the terms 'indirect' and 'direct' rule have been used in this work, for what is discussed here is the relationship between the institutions of leadership and authority in indigenous society and those of the colonial powers. The theme of the book is the way in which each of the three has used or dispensed with the traditional basis of authority for the purposes of modern government, and the way in which their distinctions between legislative and executive authority have operated in the setting of a Polynesian system of rank which knew nothing of them. The three small colonies which are analysed here may serve to illustrate a group of problems which exist wherever colonial rule exists.

Political advancement cannot, of course, be considered in isolation from the particular circumstances in which it must occur.

Within the scope of this book, there can be no exhaustive discussion of economic or social advancement which are directly linked with political in the terminology of the United Nations, but the economic and social background of each colony has been sketched in. Nor can political questions be divorced from their historical setting, and while no complete account can be included, the main historical factors have also been briefly touched upon. This background is the more important because of the general absence of scholarly work on the Pacific region which is only now beginning to be remedied. These considerations have shaped the pattern of the book. Within each section, the background has been supplied, and then the questions by which political advancement has been tested are answered, in the first place by a formal description of the institutions the colonial powers have set up, and in the second by an examination of their actual operation in the conditions of the colony. The final section is a discussion of some general issues of colonial practice arising from the particular discussion of each colony and the more general problems of colonial rule.

The idea of this book originated some six years ago when I had to collect the material for, and to deliver, a course of lectures to advanced students on comparative colonial policy, but its execution had to await the offer of a Fellowship under the Cultural Relations Programme of the South-East Asia Treaty Organization which gave me six months in the islands to collect material without which the metropolitan sources are of very limited value. The Victoria University of Wellington generously gave me leave from my Senior Lectureship to take up the Fellowship. The Australian National University offered me a Senior Research Fellowship which enabled me to write the book. My debts are many: to the people in the islands who gave me kindness and hospitality as well as the material I needed, to the Governments of the territories without whose co-operation I could have done little, to my colleagues Professors J. W. Davidson, O. H. K. Spate, and Dr Norma McArthur of the Australian National University who read the manuscript in whole or in part. My major debt is to S.E.A.T.O., and especially the Cultural Relations Office and its Director who made both the research and its publication possible; in fairness to them I must add that they are not committed by my opinions or errors, which remain my own.

F. J. W.

Research School of Pacific Studies, Canberra

ABBREVIATIONS USED IN FOOTNOTES

C.P. Journal of the Legislative Council of Fiji Papers (with their numbers and years)

J.O.E.F.O. *Journal Officiel des Etablissements Français de l'Océanie,* which became in 1957

J.O.P.F. *Journal Officiel de la Polynésie Française*

NOTE ON PRONUNCIATION

Standard spelling of indigenous names is used throughout, and no attempt has been made to reproduce phonetic forms. The convention is as follows.

In Fiji	*b*	is	pronounced	as	*mb*	in	*timber*
	c	,,	,,	,,	*th*	,,	*thy*
	d	,,	,,	,,	*nd*	,,	*band*
	g	,,	,,	,,	*ng*	,,	*bang*
	q	,,	,,	,,	*ng*	,,	*bangle*
In Samoa	*g*	,,	,,	,,	*ng*	,,	*bang*

CHAPTER I

THE FIJIAN BACKGROUND

1. *Physical Description*

The British Crown Colony of Fiji consists of more than three hundred islands strung like a bow, the convex side facing north, across a quarter of a million square miles of ocean in the centre of the south-west Pacific.[1] Of the islands less than a third are inhabited, and between those that are there is no equality of size or population. Viti Levu is by far the biggest, occupying more than 4,000 square miles, and the next largest, Vanua Levu, takes up more than 2,100 square miles of the remaining land surface; the two islands together make up six-sevenths of the total area of the colony. The rest of the group varies in size from Taveuni and Kadavu, 168 and 157 square miles respectively, to Matuku which is scarcely more than 10. Many of the uninhabited islands are mere specks. It need hardly be stressed that the difficulty and expense of communications inside the colony are serious obstacles to any kind of social, economic and political advancement, and they emphasize what the physical nature of the islands suggests: the dominance of Viti Levu in the life of the colony. Fiji's contacts with the outside world are frequent, and they also stress the importance of Viti Levu. Suva, the capital which stands on the south-east coast of Viti Levu, has a fine deep-water harbour which is a regular port of call for ships *en route* to North America, Australia, and New Zealand; Nadi, situated at the south-west end of Viti Levu, is an international airport for planes flying over the same routes. Difficulties of internal communication aside, Fiji, or, to be more exact, Viti Levu, is a nodal point for traffic in the South Pacific.

The islands of the Fiji group are broadly divided into two types; the 'high' islands of volcanic origin, and the 'low' islands,

[1] The islands lie between latitudes 150° 42′ and 21° 02′ south, and longitudes 176° 53′ east and 178° 12′ west, a distance of 1,100 to 1,500 miles south of the Equator; the 180th meridian passes through their midst; New Zealand is 1,300 and Australia 2,000 miles away. The total land area of the colony is a little over 7,000 square miles.

or atolls, of coral or limestone. This is a distinction which extends to the other Pacific islands. Viti Levu is a 'high' island, with a central plateau, a mountain backbone, hilly uplands, and low-lying coastal plains and river deltas. The mountains are jagged, volcanic peaks which rise to a height of 4,431 feet at Mount Victoria, with other peaks well over 3,000 feet. The valleys which cut into this mountain region are steep-sided, overhung with crags and peaks, through which the rivers of an elaborate drainage system make their way into the sea. Inland, in the wet zone, the mountains and hills are heavily forested; in the dry zone covered with reeds and grass. The coastal plain is in general narrow except at the river deltas where there are extensive alluvial flat lands. There are five major rivers, of which the biggest, the Rewa, drains a third of the island and is navigable by small boats for over sixty miles from its mouth. The others, the Navua, the Sigatoka, the Nadi and the Ba, are all navigable for short distances, and each of them enters the sea through a fertile flood plain. The coast of Viti Levu is surrounded by an extensive system of coral reefs, but the water between the reef and the coast is often deep although requiring careful navigation. There are many good, deep-water anchorages of which Suva is the best, and only in the west of the islands is it necessary to use open roadsteads.

Whereas Viti Levu is roughly oval in shape, Vanua Levu is irregular. It, too, has a high mountain backbone, some peaks of which are again over 3,000 feet. Its coastal plains, however, are lower, flatter and drier than Viti Levu, and on the north side of the island are much larger than those of the south which are really no more than discontinuous slopes. The rivers which drain the northern plains are extensive and follow sinuous courses, entering the sea through swampy mangrove deltas. The larger ones, like the Dreketi and the Gawa, are navigable for more than ten miles. Like Viti Levu, the coast of Vanua Levu is enclosed by barrier reefs to the north, but the south coast has no such massive reefs. Vanua Levu, too, has good anchorages of which only one, Labasa, has been developed with port facilities. Kadavu, like Vanua Levu, has an intricate coastline, but the island itself is simply a chain of volcanic peaks of up to 2,750 feet, heavily eroded and dissected by radial valleys, with no continuous plain between the mountains and the sea. The drainage system is a simple one of numerous small streams. Taveuni is not so irregular in shape, but it has basically the same structure: a high volcanic chain of peaks up to 4,000 feet, heavily wooded steep slopes going down to the sea, little coastal plain, and numerous small streams which are scarcely more than torrents from the high mountains.

The 'low' islands are very different from these. They are limestone or coral, like Wailagilala, an atoll in the Lau group, which is limestone covered with superficial deposits of sand and coral, bearing coco-nut palms and scrub. This particular island, for example, is roughly triangular in shape, about 1,100 yards long and 700 yards wide, with a height of 15 feet. Compared with the 'high' islands, the 'low' ones are of much less importance demographically or economically, but they nevertheless contribute a great deal to the map of the South Pacific. With a dazzling white beach, a blue lagoon, green palm trees swaying in the trade winds, they are the 'typical' South Sea island of European literature.

The differences in physical structure between these types of island have a considerable climatic importance. The prevailing winds which blow over the Fiji group are the south-east trades which often tend to be easterly in this region, but in November, December and January there are north-westerly winds. In consequence, there is a marked difference in rainfall and, therefore, in vegetation, between the windward and leeward sides of the 'high' islands: the windward side during the prevailing trade winds is the 'wet' side of the island, as opposed to the 'dry' side which gets its rain from the north-west. To the east of the islands, therefore, there is heavy rainfall fairly evenly distributed throughout the year; to the west there is still a relatively high rainfall but concentrated into three or four months.[2] This difference has, of course, an important economic bearing especially with a crop like sugar-cane. The 'low' islands are not affected in this way and have a relatively small rainfall on porous soil, which can mean a water shortage of a kind which does not exist in the large catchment areas of the 'high' islands. The climate of Fiji generally is an oceanic one. The temperature differs little at sea-level between the leeward and windward sides, being seldom above 81° F. or below 73°, although it is lower in the interior where it can fall by ten degrees from the coastal level. The humidity can be very high (up to ninety-five or one hundred per cent.),

[2] Suva, for example, on the windward side, has an average annual rainfall of 123 inches; Lautoka, in the dry zone on the north-west coast, has 70 inches, most of which falls between December and March.

and it varies, of course, between the wet and dry sides of the high islands; the average on the windward side is seventy-two per cent. which is greater than to the leeward. While not unbearable for Europeans, the climate can nevertheless be very enervating, and economic enterprises run the risk of damage from high winds reaching hurricane force, of which one or more hit the group each year, during the north-west monsoonal season.

2. *Resources*

Those resources of Fiji which are exploited on a commercially significant scale are primarily agricultural ones, and the colony has basically a two-crop economy. In 1955, for example, the total export value was £F12,542,064, of which nearly one-half came from the sugar industry.[3] Slightly less than one-third came from coco-nut products, mostly in the form of oil. The only other significant export of fruit was bananas, which amounted to only £F376,206. There were some miscellaneous products, like trochus shell, but the only other important export was gold to the value of £F1,027,538, and this represented an asset which has steadily declined over the years. There are probably mineral resources in Fiji, but their development has not occurred and may not be a commercial proposition. The Fijian economy, resting on sugar and copra, is exposed to the fluctuations which affect any primary-producing country. Both crops have been marketed under agreement since the war, and prices have generally been good.[4] Such agreements which prevent the disastrous slumps of pre-war years do not entirely abolish the effects of price fluctuation, and are of course themselves subject to alteration. The increase over pre-war prices must also be set against a general inflation, and the high post-war prices have concealed a considerable drop in productivity per head of the population.[5] In only one year of the five from 1952 to 1956 has Fiji had a favourable balance of

[3] *Fiji Information* (Fourth Series, No. 1, Suva, July 1956), pp. 11-13. A Fijian pound is linked to sterling at the fixed rate of £F111 = £S100. Fijian economic development has been a matter of great concern in recent years, and a number of reports have been prepared, of which easily the most important is that of O. H. K. Spate, *The Fijian People: Economic Problems and Prospects* (C.P. 13/1959); C. O'Loughlin, *The Pattern of the Fiji Economy: The National Income 1950-53* (C.P. 44/1956).

[4] *Fiji Information*, pp. 15-17. In 1942 the price paid for a ton of sugar-cane was on average 19*s.* 2*d.* In 1954 it was 71*s.* 6*d.* and in 1955 70*s.* 10*d.* The same increase is shown in copra prices: £3 10*s.* in January 1941, and £70 15*s.* in February 1954.

[5] Spate, op. cit., p. 2.

trade. This precarious economic situation must always be borne in mind when political development is being considered.

Any discussion of the Fijian economy raises two issues: the first is that the economic life of Fiji is largely non-Fijian; the second is that the land, the basis of that economy, is still largely in Fijian hands. These two facts are crucial in the economic development of Fiji, and they are not less important in its political advancement. Both of them are, of course, closely linked with the demography of the colony, and with its social structure.

When the census was taken in 1956 the total population of the group was 345,737, of which the Indians numbered 169,403 against a Fijian total of 148,134.[6] There were 6,402 Europeans, and 4,155 Chinese. Three-quarters of this population live in Viti Levu, and thirty-eight per cent. of this is concentrated into the province of Ba in the Western Division, while fifteen per cent. lives in the capital city of Suva. There are lesser urban concentrations at Lautoka, Vatukoula, Ba and Labasa (on Vanua Levu). Vanua Levu exhibits the same unequal concentration of population, the greater number living in the single province of Macuata. Within the two main social groups there is one important difference in the distribution of population. The Fijian is spread fairly uniformly over the islands, with a greater density in the coastal villages and along the rivers: there are over a thousand Fijian villages sited in these areas with perhaps an average of eighteen dwellings in each. The Indian is concentrated into urban areas, and especially the six main sugar-cane-growing areas; and it is their distribution, rather than the Fijian, which produces the inequalities which have been mentioned and which gives Viti Levu its dominant position.

Fiji is no longer Fijian in the sense that the bulk of its inhabitants are not the indigenous people who held the land when the first Europeans arrived; it is still Fijian in the sense that most of the Indians were born in the colony and regard it as home: they are not immigrant. The historical circumstances which led to this position will be discussed in their place; for the moment the important point is that Fiji is economically dominated by Indians and Europeans, although in rather different ways. Moreover this dominance will become more marked and not less because of the Indian birth-rate and the age structure of the Indian population. By 1971 the total population of Fiji will

[6] N. McArthur, *Report on the Census of Population* (C.P. 1/1958).

probably be about 548,000 of which 314,000 will be Indian, and their potential increase will continue to be greater than the Fijian.[7] European dominance is not demographic, but that of capital resources and equipment; the Chinese are not significant.

The predominance of these non-Fijian groups is very evident in the economy. The sugar industry is operated by European capital (through the Colonial Sugar Refining Company) and Indian cultivation. Sugar is grown in the dry zones of Viti Levu and Vanua Levu, and the company operates a system of Indian peasant farms in ten to twelve-acre blocks which can be worked by a single Indian and his family.[8] Sugar, the major industry, is an Indian and a European concern from which the Fijians are very largely excluded. In the copra industry, Fijian production is about half the total, and Fijian villages grow about fifty per cent. of the nuts. The remainder comes from European plantations, and this copra is of much better quality. In only one industry—bananas—do the Fijians have a monopoly, and this is a much smaller fraction of the economy. There are crops which can be grown for an internal market, but of these rice is predominantly Indian, and the root crops, *dalo,* tapioca, *kumala* and *yaqona,* although grown by Fijians, are largely marketed by Indian middle-men. The disproportion between the Fijian share of the economy and their numbers can be summed up in the fact that while it is estimated that forty-five per cent. of the acreage of local crops and thirty-two per cent. of that for export crops is cultivated by Fijians, the value of their contribution is far below that of Indians and Europeans in proportion to the land worked.[9]

Yet the Fijians hold the great bulk of the land of Fiji. Land cannot be acquired from them except by lease. Of the total land area of 4,505,000 acres, eighty-three and a half per cent. is Fijian-owned of which 434,799 acres are alienated to Europeans in freehold.[10] The disproportion between numbers, economic activity and these acreages is not so great as the figures suggest, because the alienated land is some of the best in the colony and a great

[7] ibid., p. 17.

[8] *Colony of Fiji* (Suva, 1957), pp. 58-60. In 1957 11,500 small farmers worked 123,986 acres of sugar-cane land which was about ninety-one per cent. of the total cane land of the colony. Fijian cane-growers numbered 1,600 and cultivated 6,900 acres.

[9] Spate, op. cit., p. 3.

[10] *Colony of Fiji*, p. 53.

deal of Fijian land is poor or unworkable. But those good areas which remain Fijian are still not developed as they might be, and as a matter of Government policy they cannot now be bought from Fijians, although they may be leased for short terms. Allowing for purely physical characteristics which make land unworkable, the Fijians cultivate about ten per cent. of the lands they hold.[11] The political implications which this Fijian land position holds in relation to economic effort are of obvious importance, and the relationship between the economy and the landed basis of that economy has a very vital bearing on political advancement; it produces a dangerous lack of equilibrium between political and economic importance, quite apart from the economic and racial tensions which it may create. There is a third factor which comes into play at this point: the policy of the British Government towards the Fijians. The reasons behind the land policy stem from a desire to prevent the disintegration of Fijian society, to honour the obligations which are believed to be implicit in the Deed of Cession. The land must therefore remain Fijian; any development must take place on the basis of existing Fijian society and through its institutions. The interests of the Fijians are paramount. In practice, this means maintaining the authority of the Fijian chiefs and maintaining Fijian village communities, on the land which was secured to them by the Deed.

3. *The People of Fiji*

Fiji is the border between Melanesia and Polynesia, and although more research remains to be done on the elements which make up Fijian society, the more distinctive characteristics seem clear enough. The system of rank is Polynesian in a society which has many Melanesian characteristics; a society whose economy can be described as a subsistence one with a margin for ceremonial exchange and obligations to rank. It is very difficult to generalize about Fijian society because the importance of these different elements varies. In the west of Viti Levu and in the hill country in the middle of the island, the Polynesian influence was weaker than it was in Bau, the home of the Cakobau family, or the Lau group which was very much under Tongan influence. All kinds of local variations exist. Nevertheless, some general points can be made if the qualifications are also

[11] Spate, op. cit., p. 1.

borne in mind, and it also happens that the eastern, Polynesian, characteristics tended to be politically dominant and were accepted as characteristic by the Europeans.

The original social structure no doubt consisted of an agnatic family group which tilled the soil, and the basic unit of society was the patrilineal and patrilocal family or household, except in the west of Viti Levu where some matrilineal forms existed.[12] The family was part of the *tokatoka,* which was a group of related families living in a village or cluster of homesteads. The *tokatoka* was the working unit which actually cultivated the soil, grew the food, allocated the work, and cleared the land (and in some cases was itself the landholding group); it was the smallest unit, the unit of service, in Fijian society. It was part of a larger organization, the *mataqali,* which was a patrilineal and exogamous descent group of relatives. The members of a *mataqali* were lineal descendants of one of a group of brothers who descended from a common ancestor, and *mataqali* developed special functions closely connected with the system of rank.[13] The *mataqali* was an important ceremonial, legal and social unit, and very often it was the landholding group as well. Within each there was a ranking chief supported by lesser chiefs. The specialized *mataqali,* which were often demarcated by a territorial division, together made up a *yavusa,* the most inclusive group which traced descent from a common ancestor. This was the largest social and kinship division of Fijian society, and its leading chief was in theory a lineal descendant of the common ancestor. Apart from the ancestor, the unity of the *yavusa* was expressed in a common set of totems and a war cry. It may also have had some function as the titleholder or guardian of land rights, but its structure was probably looser than descriptions suggest. The *mataqali* and the *tokatoka* seem to have been much stronger and more cohesive groups.

There were two other units which had some political significance without the social or economic significance of those de-

[12] W. E. H. Stanner, *The South Seas in Transition* (Sydney, 1953), pp. 172-8; L. A. Mander, *Some Dependent Peoples of the South Pacific* (Leiden, 1954), pp. 379-81. B. Thomson, *The Fijians: A Study in the Decay of Custom* (London, 1908) is, however, still the best account of Fijian society.

[13] Five kinds were generally distinguished: the *turaga,* the chiefly one from which the ruling chiefs were drawn; the *sauturaga,* or executive one which carried out the commands of, and supported, the chief; the *mata-ni-vanua* comprised of heralds or masters of ceremonial; the *bete* or priestly one; and the *bati* who were the warriors.

scribed. These were the *vanua* and the *matanitu*. The former was a confederation of *yavusa* combined for war or to resist enemies, or a collection of fragments of *yavusa* broken up by war and united under a paramount chief who tried to make his position hereditary. Some *vanua* were further combined into *matanitu* which were kingdoms or grand alliances. Their significance is the capacity which they revealed for political development in Fijian society under European impact; they were not effective social units. Both kinds of organization, the primarily social and the primarily political, show the complexity of Fijian society. It had evolved a highly organized social system, and one which was at all levels closely bound up with a developed and centralized system of rank and authority.

The chief in Fijian society was regarded as of divine origin, possessing *mana* or mystical power. He was the highest of the six classes of men into which society was customarily graded, from serfs to commoners to high chiefs. The chief had the power of life and death over his subjects, and his person was hedged around with *tabu:* no one might stand erect in his presence; no one might touch him or his belongings; no one dared move ahead of him on the march; at first sight of him in the morning the *tama,* a cry of reverence, was given; in the ceremonial drinking of *yaqona* or *kava* he took precedence. Many of the customs which horrified the early Europeans were closely connected with his *mana:* the launching of canoes over human bodies; the use of human beings to support the foundation of his house; cannibalism itself. Apart from such *tabu* and religious sanctions, the chief's position was also supported by economic ones. He could call on the services of his people, not only for ceremonial support like the provision of turtle, but for house-building, canoe-building, and the provision of feasts for the entertainment of visitors. He had the right to a whole range of services under the term *lala.*[14] He might also, if he were a conqueror, exact something more like feudal services from conquered or tributary people. To early Europeans in Fiji, and to some later ones, the chief's position looked absolute. In fact it was not. The chief in a sense served his people: he represented the ancestor from whom they were descended; he was the centre of religious and social life; he protected them and led them out to conquest; he organized economic life by feeding them when they worked for him, and by arranging the use and distri-

[14] Thomson, op. cit., pp. 66-74.

bution of land. The relationship between a chief and his people was a reciprocal one, and the chief at his best was a father to his people with whom, in any case, he had kinship ties. In functional terms, the chief was necessary to Fijian society: he responded to and satisfied the needs of his people; and he was elected to his chiefly title: it was not hereditary. The choice might by preference fall on the oldest brother of the dead chief, but it might also fall anywhere within a certain range of kinship. A bad chief could always be eliminated by direct action; and any chief, however great his privileges or awesome the *tabu* which surrounded him, responded in the last resort to the needs of the people he ruled; or he perished.

The effect of European contact on this system of rank will be discussed presently, but there are three other customs of Fijian society which require mention since they have a direct bearing on its development. The first of these is the custom of *kere kere*. *Kere kere* was the right of borrowing what was needed within a certain range of kinship; it rested on the assumption that the related members of a group had a lien on each other's goods. The custom clearly protected the Fijians against natural disaster to their gardens and helped them socially and economically to maintain themselves when the need arose; it also kept a relatively even distribution of wealth within society as well as providing a kind of welfare insurance. So, too, did the custom of *vasu,* the right of a Fijian to go to his mother's group and take what he wished. The third of these customs, *solevu,* was a method of exchange between different groups which allowed some specialization in products, quite apart from its social, ceremonial and political importance in bringing the groups together. These three customs have an immediate relevance to economic development, and an indirect one to political development, because of the social attitudes they represent, and because they, too, supported and enhanced the authority of the chief who arranged, organized and sometimes manipulated them.

This traditional Fijian society has, of course, been modified by European contact, but many of the attitudes, especially those connected with the system of rank and authority, survive; indeed they have been deliberately preserved. Some customs like cannibalism and warfare have necessarily been suppressed, but others still exercise a strong influence over the behaviour of Fijians; they will be discussed in detail in the succeeding chapters. Still, this traditional Fijian society must always be borne in mind because in its major characteristics it survives in Fiji, and it has shown remarkable strength and resilience under the European impact.

The other racial groups in Fiji are not directly the concern of this work, although they have an obvious indirect importance because their presence means that Fijian political advancement cannot occur in isolation; it must always be seen against the background of the numerical superiority of the Indians and the economic superiority of both Indians and Europeans. Unlike the Fijians, these other social groups have no obvious unity and it is distinctly misleading to talk about the Indian 'problem' as if it represented a compact social group. The Indians of Fiji had no unity in their origins: they came from a wide variety of areas and castes; they had little linguistic unity.[15] The effects of their settlement in Fiji and the attitudes of the Fijian-born Indians are difficult to gauge, but it is unlikely that anything other than a common knowledge that they are Indians as distinct from Europeans or Fijians binds together a prosperous shopkeeper or professional man and the sugar-cane-growing peasant or taxi-driver. The Indians are not a homogeneous community: there are obvious differences of religion, language and economic status. They are probably deeply divided among themselves, and their attitudes are also very different from the Indians of their original homeland. How far some kind of unity is imposed by the nature of their relations with the other groups is obscure, but it cannot be easily assumed that they are a coherent group. They have as yet produced no single political organization and, although their presence is politically important, their chief significance at the moment in their relation to the Fijians is economic. Indirectly, however, the Indians produce one immediate political effect; their presence maintains and emphasizes the unofficial Europeans' preference for the Fijians: an alliance of sympathy which has political consequences. The unofficial Europeans are politically united as a minority which controls most of the capital resources of Fiji, either themselves or as agents of overseas firms. They are united, too, by their attitude towards the government of official Europeans. The latter form a distinct group in Fijian society which is important because the administration is in their hands but, unlike many unofficial Europeans, they, or at least the senior ones among them, are transient: they have no stake

[15] K. L. Gillion, 'The Sources of Indian Emigration to Fiji', *Population Studies*, vol. x, No. 2.

in the colony other than the professional one of a career in the Colonial Service. Yet they, too, have a direct political importance because of the structure of government which is designed to secure the political paramountcy of the Fijians, and they perhaps share some of that European prejudice against the Indians which reinforces their commitment to the official policy of 'Fijians first'.

Nevertheless, there are few signs of a bad social or communal situation in Fiji at the present time.[16] The present Crown Colony constitution provides equal representation in the Legislative Council: five Europeans, of which three are elected, two nominated; five Indians similarly elected and nominated; and five nominated Fijians. The equality is not, of course, a representation in terms of numbers but in terms of economic interest; and it is organized on a communal basis. There is always the possibility that race relations may deteriorate, that the present equilibrium may be upset, and the communal roll perpetuates racial distinctions. It emphasizes the fact that in considering the political advancement of the Fijians, it must always be remembered that Fiji is not a homogeneous society; it has few of the signs of social unity within which British institutions evolved; and the Fijian administration which is to be discussed is based on the assumption that Fijian society must be kept isolated until it can compete on something like equal terms with the other social groups. This policy has a long history behind it and, before the present structure of Fijian administration can be properly understood, it is necessary to examine briefly the factors which have been at work to produce this situation and this policy.

4. *Historical Factors*

The Fiji islands were discovered and visited from time to time in the seventeenth and eighteenth centuries—by Tasman, Cook, and Bligh, for example—but these explorers and navigators did not affect Fijian society. The successive waves of European impact broke over the islands in the nineteenth century, following a course similar to those which reached other Pacific islands. The often sordid details of this history need not detain us, but the effects of European beachcombers, traders and settlers on

16 Notwithstanding the riots which occurred in Suva in December 1959; an analysis of this disturbance may be found in F. J. West, *Australian Quarterly*, vol. xxxii, No. 1.

the one hand, and the missionaries on the other, are important because of the changes they set in motion in Fijian society.

The first wave of European invasion was the sandalwood traders.[17] Earlier European visitors had sometimes had friendly relations with the Fijians, and shipwrecked sailors, such as those from the *Argo* at the very beginning of the century, had been hospitably received; others, such as Captain Barker, were attacked. The sandalwood traders were a different matter. From 1804, and for the following ten years, ship after ship visited Fiji to collect the valuable wood which commanded so high a price in China. The years 1808 and 1809 were the peak of the boom when there was a scramble for quick profits with sandalwood fetching £70 a ton.

This rush of traders obviously introduced into Fijian society new goods, sometimes trinkets but more often highly-prized whales' teeth or *tabua* and European iron goods and tools, while it created a desire among Fijians for this wealth. The traders also introduced European diseases and alcohol, both of which had devastating effects among natives hitherto immune from either. These were major changes but not in themselves a disruption of the social order. More serious was the introduction of firearms, and the part played by the traders in Fijian politics. The traditional warfare of Fiji had been on a small scale, for the forces involved were never large; little damage was done, and aims of such warfare were very limited.[18] Under the stress of this tribal warfare, and also for less dramatic causes, the *vanua* of Fijian life had evolved, but the larger *matanitu* were the consequence of the new warfare of the traders. For the chief who controlled the land on which sandalwood grew could and did demand firearms and European assistance against his enemies. The original trading area was Bua Bay and Tui Bua, a chief of not much traditional importance, became very important indeed. In 1808, for example, he enlisted the aid of armed Europeans in return for a cargo of sandalwood, and with their assistance captured Tacilevu village whose inhabitants he massacred. This was a new style of warfare, and one which spread as other chiefs adopted Europeans both in self-defence and for purposes of expansion. In addition, of course, to gain this European support they drove their people to provide the sandalwood the traders desired. It was one such European, the notorious Charlie Savage

[17] R. A. Derrick, *A History of Fiji* (Suva, 1950), p. 39 ff.

[18] ibid., p. 24.

who was a survivor of the sandalwood ship *Eliza* wrecked on Mocea reef, who became the white man of the Vunivalu, the chief of Bau, while four of his companions were taken to Verata.[19] Savage and his muskets at Bau laid the foundation for the Bauan rise to power which began with his original protector Naulivou.

Such white beachcombers were important to the chiefs because they could use muskets with effect, as the Fijians could not, and once a tribe had a white man and firearms, it was a matter of preservation that neighbouring tribes should try to acquire them too. The use of muskets became general, and their use was followed by that of cannon. Their general effect upon Fijian society was to strengthen the power of those chiefs who could get them, and by 1835 the larger political form of the *matanitu* had clearly emerged. In that year, Fijians thought of thirty-two such units, but there was considerable variation in their power and the Native Lands Commission eventually recognized only eleven as *matanitu*, allowing one other to gain that status after cession in 1874.[20] Among these eleven, some were much more important or influential than others. By 1829 Bau had already reached a dominant position and was face to face with its rival Rewa, although the great Bau-Rewa war, which eventually led to the downfall of Rewa and the predominance of Bau, did not break out until 1843. The Bauans had already gained a loose ascendancy over Verata and Macuata, and the defeat of Rewa left Cakobau, the high chief of Bau, in a dominant position in eastern Viti Levu. But that victory was largely achieved with the help of Tongans when Cakobau's fortunes were at a very low ebb, and having finally destroyed Rewa he was face to face with a much more formidable rival: the Tongan chief Maʻafu who was dominant in the Lau group of islands by 1855 and thence extended his authority over Bua and Macuata in Vanua Levu.[21] He united northern and eastern Fiji into a confederacy which would probably have overthrown Cakobau and Bau had not the cession of Fiji to Britain put an end to his ambitions. The train of events set in motion by the Europeans led to the political consolidation of Fiji into two main spheres of influence, and although this meant little in

19 ibid., pp. 44-5; W. P. Morrell, *Britain in the Pacific Islands* (Oxford, 1960), p. 117.

20 J. D. Legge, *Britain in Fiji 1858-1880* (London, 1958), pp. 11-12.

21 Derrick, op. cit., p. 127.

terms of kinship or social units, politically and administratively it was important because of the strengthening of the authority of certain chiefs who were accepted as rulers of Fiji by the British Government, and it also led to the acceptance of the system of rank, which they so obviously symbolized, for the purposes of that Government.

Such changes as the sandalwood traders brought about were political ones clearly connected with the system of rank and the strengthening of chiefly power by the acquisition of subject people who were conquered. Less obvious but equally important were the changes involved in mission activity. The first European missionaries to land in Fiji were Cross and Cargill who landed in Lakeba in 1835 accompanied by an emissary from the influential and already Christian king of Tonga, Taufa'ahau, who ruled as King George.[22] They were not the first missionaries to Fiji, for Tahitian teachers had been at work on Oneata since 1830 for the London Missionary Society, but Cross and Cargill first reduced the Fijian language to writing and began printing books in Fijian. The political situation, however, affected their teaching, and perceiving that the centre of power and population was in eastern Viti Levu, they first of all tried Bau, which horrified them, and then settled in Rewa under the protection of Tui Dreketi. There were only small numbers of converts, and the high chiefs particularly were conservative, especially Cakobau. Missionary teaching cut at the root of the chiefly position, partly by its insistence on the sinfulness of war and savage customs, more vitally by its denial of the *mana* of divine origin which made a chief; once his connection with the gods was extinguished the very basis of his authority disappeared.

Nevertheless, conversion offered a chief some political advantages, and Ma'afu the Tongan was not slow to pose as the protector of Christians against pagans because in doing so the area of his influence steadily expanded. The first of the important chiefs of Fiji to accept Christianity was Tui Nayau who did so in 1849, followed by the Viwa chiefs and some of those in Bua who also embraced the new faith. Cakobau still resisted the new religion, and certainly intended to destroy it, although he was unable to do so, partly because of the presence of the Tongans, partly because of the support the missionaries received from British naval vessels. By 1852 he had adopted the title Tui Viti; in 1853 he also became Vunivalu in succession to

[22] ibid., p. 71 ff.; Morrell, op. cit., p. 118 ff.

Tanoa. By 1854, however, Cakobau's fortunes were at a very low ebb: he had quarrelled with the Levuka settlers; Rewa was resisting; there was disaffection in Bau itself. And when King George of Tonga, whose support Cakobau counted on, urged conversion upon him, Cakobau agreed, although other Bau chiefs were by no means unanimous in support. He was converted on 30 April 1854, giving his people permission to become Christians, and although his political position did not immediately improve—many still heathen chiefs rallied behind Ratu Mara as the leader of the old ways—the Tongan help finally settled the matter. Cakobau's victory was, in effect, the triumph of Christianity over the old ways, and there were wholesale conversions in Fiji. It is true that by this conversion Cakobau prejudiced his chiefly position by rejecting the divine basis of his authority, but the political rewards of conversion which he reaped to some extent compensated for the change. The chief who was converted sacrificed some of his traditional standing, but when his conversion was associated with political victory, other sanctions were gained: the sanction of physical force, of missionary and European recognition, the sanction of conquered lands and people which strengthened his position by the personal, almost feudal, *lala* which they gave to him.[23] The basis of a chief's authority began slowly to change, but the change, if it were generally perceived at all, was concealed by the new sanctions which were a substitute. Chiefly authority may have implicitly altered in character but it survived and in some respects was enhanced; and whether or not its basis changed, the old forms of reverence and *tabu* continued. As one might expect, the new was interpreted and expressed in terms of the old.

The traders and the missionaries deeply affected Fijian society, but the third wave of European activity involved Fiji more closely with European life and politics. This was the settlers who came to establish plantations. For what the settlers wanted was land for their plantations, labour to work them, and some kind of settled government to give them title and protection. European settlement in Fiji began on a significant scale after Cakobau's first offer of cession in 1859, by which time the era of the small trader was drawing to an end.[24] In 1860 there were thirty or forty European settlers; eight years later there were 1,288; by 1870 there were about 2,000. The early plantations

[23] Thomson, op. cit., pp. 59-60.

[24] Derrick, op. cit., p. 138 ff.

were occupied with coco-nuts but the American Civil War encouraged cotton and after the mid-1860's, cotton was the major export crop to the value of £92,700 in 1870. And by this latter date the cotton plantations were not the small blocks of ten acres run by men struggling without capital but larger affairs of eighty or more acres run by richer men on a larger scale. This growth of a plantation economy also brought with it other Europeans concerned with the mercantile and professional services necessary to run it, and Levuka, on the island of Ovalau, became a thriving pioneer town. Moreover, these new settlers, unlike many of the traders and beachcombers of earlier years, were respectable and law-abiding citizens whose interests required stability in Fijian society.

Part of the instability or lawlessness came from less respectable Europeans, but part came from the very process by which their European plantations had been established. The prospective settlers wanted land, and they got it from Fijian tribes. By 1868 235,000 acres were held by foreigners, and at the time of cession there were claims for 854,000 acres of which 414,615 were confirmed by the investigations of the Lands Commission.[25] The claims, however, did not represent the areas actually cultivated and in 1875 only 16,524 acres were in production. The freehold which was eventually recognized as bona fide purchase from the Fijians was a relatively small fraction of the four and a half million acres of the colony, but in terms of the best land it was a much higher proportion. The European settlement, too, was concentrated into a few of the more fertile, more easily accessible areas of Fiji: Taveuni, the coasts of Vanua Levu, and Viti Levu, especially the great Rewa delta. The localized nature of European settlement limited the areas and occasions of conflict between settlers and natives, but within these limits friction inevitably occurred.

The basic difficulty was the difference between European and Fijian ideas of landowning. It is doubtful if 'ownership' existed as a concept in Fijian society: Fijian land rights were rather 'usufruct' than ownership.[26] Hence the idea of alienation of land was non-existent and the sales which, as the Europeans thought, transferred land ownership, to the understanding of the Fijians transferred land use. A bona fide sale, therefore, could easily lead to friction when the Fijians tried to use or reoccupy land which

[25] Legge, op. cit., pp. 193-4.
[26] Thomson, op. cit., p. 359.

in their view still belonged to them but which a European imagined he owned, and even a bona fide land sale produced little enough money for the Fijians: from 1864 to 1868 in Cakaudrove, the price of land was never more than 3¾*d*. an acre, and on Viti Levu in the same period never more than 5½*d*.; very often the price was as low as 2*d*. Where a land sale was not a bona fide one, the price might be a few trinkets or muskets to the chief. Quite frequently purchasers bought land from the chief alone, over the heads of his people, and in some cases a chief might sell land more than once, perhaps knowing what he was doing but more probably believing that he was selling only the land use. Bona fide or not, a European settler could easily find himself involved in hostility with local Fijians who recognized no alienation and, where land had been sold over their heads by a chief, might drive a settler from his purchase. These land sales provoked attacks by Fijians, and promoted a belief by Europeans in Fijian treachery or dishonesty. Land sales thus created a situation in which the European settlers demanded protection, either by association with their fellows, or by experiments in government, or ultimately by the British Government.

They also demanded labour to work the plantations they had acquired. A certain amount of local labour was available, but it was not adequate and it, too, might involve friction and trouble; if a chief ordered some of his people to work, or protected discontented or rebellious labour, a planter had obvious troubles. In any case a Fijian could support himself relatively easily on the produce of his gardens and had no incentive to work in unfamiliar conditions and to an unaccustomed pace or rhythm. The bulk of the labour, therefore, always came from outside Fiji, either from the Pacific islands or from India. The latter kind of labour was imported after cession as a matter of deliberate Government policy, but the former was part of the notorious blackbirding trade of which Fiji was one of the principal receiving centres in the south-west Pacific. The evils and abuse of the labour trade have often been discussed: they led to the depopulation of certain islands, they produced havoc in native societies, they produced a labour force in conditions not much removed from slavery; most important of all, they led to increasing British intervention in the affairs of the South Pacific.[27]

[27] E. Drus, 'The Colonial Office and the Annexation of Fiji' (*Transactions of the Royal Historical Society*, 4th Series, vol. xxxii).

Land and labour difficulties combined to emphasize the need for some kind of settled government, although in different ways to different people. The settlers had an obvious interest in establishing some authority which could control the relations between themselves and the Fijians, and offer them protection and security. The humanitarians—the missions and some other influential people in Great Britain and Australia—and the Government, had a common interest in law and order and the protection of the natives. These needs, which were eventually satisfied by the annexation of Fiji, initially led to somewhat different solutions. The settlers tried a series of native governments under Cakobau and under Ma'afu, and while the second had some measure of success the first, without exception, failed. Some of the reasons were internal: the weakness of Cakobau's position, and the rivalries of Fijian chiefs; opposition to the policies of the Government; the lawless element among the settlers and traders. Some were external, like the attitude of the British Government expressed in its invocation of the Foreign Enlistment Act.[28] The failure of these native governments, the last one in circumstances approaching rebellion, was part of the reason for the British acceptance of the offer of cession in 1874, but other difficulties pointed in the same direction. Since 1857 there had been a British consul in Fiji, but his powers and jurisdiction were inadequate to meet the situation which existed either in the period of the traders, the settlers or the labour recruiters. To be effective a consul had to exceed his powers, like Pritchard, and run the risk of removal from office, or he had to resign himself to giving advice to settlers and traders which could be disregarded. Either way consular jurisdiction was not enough to control the situation.[29] Internal disorder, the labour traffic and humanitarian considerations thus prompted the British Government to accept the unconditional offer of annexation which was made by Cakobau in 1874, after the report of the two commissioners, Consul Layard and Commodore Goodenough, had strongly recommended acceptance of an earlier conditional offer. The Deed of Cession was made on 16 October 1874 by Cakobau who styled himself Vunivalu and Tui Viti, and twelve other high chiefs of Fiji, including Ma'afu.[30]

[28] Derrick, op. cit., pp. 164-6.

[29] ibid., p. 151 ff.

[30] The text was published in the official *Gazette*, and it is printed by both Derrick and Legge as an Appendix to their books.

The annexation of Fiji led, of course, to the creation of Crown Colony government in the islands, and the effects of this on Fijian society were complicated. Most obviously it 'froze' the existing political order: it confirmed the paramountcy of Bau, and prevented the possibility of Ma'afu's overthrowing Cakobau; it recognized as the provinces of Fiji the *matanitu* which had emerged within recent history. The Deed of Cession itself contained a promise that the rights of the high chiefs should be recognized so far as was consistent with British sovereignty and the colonial form of government. The framework of government which was created both preserved the political order which had emerged and the authority of the high chief. Sir Hercules Robinson, who made provisional arrangements for the Government of Fiji, divided it into twelve provinces which were, substantially, the dominant *matanitu,* and eighty districts which were, in effect, the *vanua* of Fijian political life. Each province was placed under its existing high chief as *roko tui,* and over each district the local ranking chief became *buli.* In addition a European Executive Council was established in the Crown Colony tradition, a general court under one European and one native judge was set up at Levuka, and for native administration, other than the Secretary of Native Affairs in the Executive Council, four stipendiary magistrates were appointed and the colony divided between them.[31] The main outlines of this provisional Government were retained by the first Governor of Fiji, Sir Arthur Gordon, who decisively shaped the pattern of administration and committed his successors to the policy he followed. It is claimed for Gordon that he set up in Fiji an administration based on the principles which later came to be called 'indirect rule'; that is, he created a native authorities system which utilized the old system of rank and other native institutions; and that this system was closely connected with his land policy, which preserved the major part of the land to the Fijians, his native taxation policy and his labour policy which were designed to preserve the essential characteristics of native society.[32] Gordon did not believe in preservation for its own sake; on the contrary he believed in an evolutionary theory of society; but he envisaged change as occurring through Fijian institutions, and the structure of this Government was designed to bring those institutions into the framework of colonial administration. Thus he created a hierarchy

[31] Legge, op. cit., pp. 151-3.
[32] ibid., p. 158 ff.

of councils in the district, in the province, and with the Council of Chiefs, in Fiji as a whole; and a hierarchy of executive officials, the *turaga-ni-koro* in the village, the *buli* in the district, the *roko* in the province, the Native Regulation Board, and finally the Governor. Not all these institutions corresponded to indigenous ones, but the general effect was to attempt to use native institutions for the purpose of Western government, and the Native Regulations as compiled by the Board sanctioned and regulated customs of the Fijians which were not of necessity abolished. The broad effect of Gordon's policy was to distinguish the Fijians from the rest of the colonial society, and by keeping them under the system of native administration to preserve the Fijian way of life.

Gordon's policy has deeply influenced the subsequent history of Fiji, sometimes in a misunderstood form: preservation has sometimes tended to become an end in itself. Under later administrators who lacked his personality or insight the system has often tended to stagnate rather than to be the means of promoting change as smoothly as possible. And this stagnation has led to attack. Early in the century there was criticism of this structure of native administration, and in 1913 the Secretary of State for the Colonies raised the question of abolishing the Native Affairs department and distributing its work among stipendiary magistrates and European commissioners, an action which was taken in 1916 over the protests of the *roko*.[33] Five years later the post of Secretary for Native Affairs was abolished, and the control of native affairs was given to the Colonial Secretary, while the responsibilities of the district commissioner were increased. The Secretary's office was restored two years later, but the department of Native Affairs still had a minor role in the Government apparatus, and the pre-war colony was divided into eighteen magisterial provinces each under a European commissioner. The *roko* were still the nominal heads of the provinces, as were the *buli* in the districts, and the councils still met, but power had passed more and more into the hands of European officials. The background to these changes was preoccupation with the apparently rapid decline of the Fijian population and the necessity for European measures to deal with a complex situation.[34] Even so, Fijian affairs were still dealt with separately from the rest of the colony.

[33] Statement of Sukuna in debate (*Legislative Council Debates*, 1944).

[34] Sukuna's summary of fifty years of Fijian development (C.P. 5/1952).

Apart from 'freezing' the political and administrative situation, the imposition of British control also 'froze' the social and economic pattern. The whole tenor of Gordon's policy was not merely to preserve the native authority system but to retain the essential characteristics of the so-called 'communal system' of economic and social organization. At the same time Government control also meant that the European settlers were preserved as a distinct group, and the land policy followed by Gordon and his successors, with the exception of Sir Everard Im Thurn, not only preserved Fijian lands but also European freehold.[35] More than 400,000 acres of the best land were confirmed with an indefeasible title to European settlers upon whose presence the economic progress of the colony depended, initially through cotton and copra crops but gradually through sugar production. British policy thus preserved the plural society, which had existed at the time of cession, and it introduced a new element when Gordon, partly to protect the Fijians, partly to discharge his duty to the settlers, arranged for the importation of Indian labour.[36] The first shipload arrived in 1879. Knowing the evils which could attend immigrant labour of this kind, it was provided that women should accompany the labourers in the proportion of forty women to every hundred men with the intention that they should enable a stable life to be created. The result was to create another element in the plural society, and eventually to reduce the Fijians to a minority in their own islands, rendering them not merely numerically but economically the weaker group. It was, in fact, to remedy the social and economic backwardness of the Fijians compared with the other groups that in the 1920's more direct administration by European officers was undertaken, with the pushing to one side of the traditional leaders, but the Government's resources in men and material were not enough to make a success of the policy.

Before the war of 1939 Fijian administration was, therefore, in some confusion. The old order was weakening, the new unsuccessful. The Fijians were in an inferior position compared with the other racial groups, although politically their interests

[35] The *Native Land Ordinance* 14 of 1905 allowed land sales and ninety-nine-year-leases instead of the earlier twenty-one years. About 20,000 more acres became freehold in the next five years and a large proportion of long leases are of this date; Spate, op. cit., p. 16. The policy came to an end in 1911, and thereafter the grant or sale of Fijian land except for Crown purposes was forbidden.

[36] Legge, op. cit., pp. 267-8.

were still officially paramount. At the same time Fijian society itself was changing. The system of authority which had been confirmed by Gordon's policy had assumed a rigidity it never possessed in traditional Fijian society, and the basis of that system had in any case changed from the old sanctions to the new one of Government authority. This, combined with the changes set in motion by contact with Europeans, was clearly producing a breakdown which was accentuated by the economic policy of individualism which came with the policy of the 1920's. This is the background against which the reorganization of 1945 must be seen: a confused situation in native administration, and the political consciousness of European and Indian groups which had several elected representatives in the Legislative Council and which were capable of articulate political demands as the Fijians were not.[37]

[37] Before 1904 the Legislative Council was composed of six official members and four nominated ones, but at that date it was reorganized to contain ten officials, six elected Europeans, and two nominated Fijians; the Indians were represented by the Agent-General for Immigration as an official member. In 1916 a nominated Indian was appointed, and in 1929 three elected Indian members were provided for. In 1936 the present arrangement came into effect by which in a council of thirty-one, the Europeans and Indians both have three elected and two nominated members, and the Fijians five nominated; there is still an official majority of one.

CHAPTER II

THE STRUCTURE OF FIJIAN GOVERNMENT

The present Fijian Administration was set up in 1945 after some years of discussion. On 16 July 1943 the Governor, Sir Philip Mitchell, addressed a despatch to the Secretary of State for the Colonies proposing a reorganization of native administration which was in some confusion, to 'broaden the basis of Native support and collaboration, and to give reality to Native responsibility for Native affairs'.[1] These proposals were very similar to those which Mitchell implemented in East Africa, but in Fiji they were influenced by the outlook and opinion of Ratu Sir Lala Sukuna, the most eminent Fijian leader who was the principal architect of the Fijian Administration. Sukuna's career was very distinguished. He was an Oxford-educated high chief, a barrister of the English bar, a former commander of the Fiji Military Forces, and a senior official of the Government of Fiji. A man of great personality and force of character, he was a thoroughgoing conservative who revered the traditions of Fijian society and, while recognizing the fact of change, wished to control and slow down its effects; and he combined with his conservative outlook political ability which amounted almost to genius.

Sukuna's case for the Fijian Administration which was created in 1945 was based on the principles of 'indirect rule' as defined by another British colonial Governor, Sir Donald Cameron:

> The great principles to be followed throughout are those of building on the existing organization and ideas of the people, of leaving it to the people themselves, assisted by sympathetic advice, to devise and develop their own institutions, and of resisting the temptation to play the part of 'kingmaker' or constitution maker: many ideal states have been devised by theorists, but the only true political development proceeds from within by evolution.

Sukuna looked for precedents for the case he wished to argue, and found them in the body of theory which had been evolved by Lord Lugard and his successors, of whom Cameron was the

[1] C.P. 24/1943.

most distinguished. And having invoked the ancestry of his views, Sukuna put forward his own.[2]

> Now some of us regard equality as a sacred thing that should be bestowed on all Communities—social equality, equality of opportunity, equality before the law. So do I: but all in good time when every community has acquired the necessary elements that go to make equality a good.

The purpose of the Fijian Administration, as he saw it, was to train chiefs and people in orderly, sound and progressive government, the better to fit them eventually for the give and take of democratic institutions. Obviously Sukuna did not deny the fact of, nor the necessity for, change, but any change must be gradual, and it must proceed through existing Fijian institutions. In Sukuna's view Fijian society was patriarchal, based on consanguinity and status. The head of the family group (Sukuna's definition of the *mataqali*), with the sanction of the patriarch at the head of the clan (his definition of the *yavusa*), exercised authority over the members of his group, controlling their lands and houses but not their personal property. Society, he said, was held together by common descent, common birth, common interest, and the qualities of shrewdness, tact and forbearance on the part of the chief; loyalty, obedience, and reverence on the part of the people. Such was the society in which Sukuna hoped to 'develop the social and economic and political outlook of the governed through institutions well recognized and having their roots in the people in order to fit them progressively and surely to play an ever increasing part in the development of the country'. What he wanted in fact was development through the old system of rank and the Fijian village system which is loosely, though inaccurately, described as 'communal'. To put the matter in a nutshell, development was to rest on the land which was preserved to the Fijians for ever, and loyalty, which meant obedience to the chiefs. The Fijian Administration which was set up by Ordinance on 1 January 1945 was intended to do precisely this:[3] to preserve chiefly authority and Fijian village society, and through this to bring the Fijians on to terms of equality with other groups in the colony.

[2] In two papers, one of which was his first Annual Report as Secretary for Fijian Affairs (C.P. 22/1944; C.P. 4/1947); and in two major speeches in the Legislative Council, one in 1944, the other in 1948.

[3] *Fijian Affairs Ordinance*, Cap. 100, *Laws of Fiji* (Suva, 1955), vol. ii. Amendments were subsequently published in the *Gazette*.

Lord Hailey once observed that the efficacy of any type of native administration must be viewed not merely in relation to the part it bears in the machinery of government, but in the light of the purpose it is intended to serve in the development of the native population. Since Sukuna was so explicit about his aims and desires, this is a particularly apt standard of judgement. Applying the tests which were suggested in the Introduction, the efficacy of the Fijian Administration's structure may be judged by two questions. Does it in fact afford the opportunity for the Fijians to discuss their own problems and take policy decisions about them in such a way that modern self-government can emerge? Does it afford opportunities to execute such decisions and operate the administrative machinery required to implement them? This is, of course, an aspect of the general question of the degree to which traditional institutions can be used for the wholly different purposes of modern government: the central issue in fact of the whole theory of 'indirect rule'.

1. *The Executive Institutions and Councils*

(a) The Fijian Affairs Board

The distinction between policy making and its execution is not, of course, a rigid one, but it does broadly distinguish the two main forms in which the Fijian Administration is organized: the system of councils and the executive agents. There are all kinds of links between the two, most notably the heart of the whole system of institutions, the Fijian Affairs Board. As it was set up in 1945 the Board was a reconstituted form of the old Native Regulation Board which was created at annexation, but its new position was vastly more important in the scheme of government. Sukuna described it as being in effect a standing committee of the Legislative Council and of the Council of Chiefs, and a link between these bodies and the Executive Council.[4] It was intended to tie together at the top all the strands of government: the councils, the executive agencies and the general Government of the colony.

The Board consists of the Secretary for Fijian Affairs who occupies in effect a ministerial office in the Crown colony and who is *ex officio* chairman of the Board, the five Fijian members of the Legislative Council of the colony, and the financial and legal advisers appointed by the Governor. The Secretary holds

[4] C.P. 4/1947.

an office which is the equivalent of that of Financial Secretary in the general Government, and he is a member of both the Executive and Legislative Councils; the five Fijian members (one of whom is also a member of the Executive Council) are nominated to the Legislative Council by the Governor from a panel of names submitted to him by the Council of Chiefs. The vital position of the Secretary and the Board in the whole apparatus of the Fijian Administration is very clear (and formally it is indeed the link to which Sukuna referred), especially when the enormous width of the power of both the Secretary and the Board is considered.

The Fijian Affairs Board has the duty of submitting to the Governor proposals and recommendations for the benefit of the Fijian people, and considering such questions as the Governor may submit to it; it is the duty of each member of the Board to give his opinion in writing. The Governor *must* submit to it any Bill before the Legislative Council which affects the rights and interests of the Fijians, especially any Bill relating to the chief, the local Fijian authorities, or the land, unless the Governor certifies that such a Bill is urgent. The Board may then advise that the Bill should be submitted to the Council of Chiefs, but if it does not, then it returns the Bill to the Governor with a memorandum which may be discussed in the Legislative Council as if it were part of the Bill; a similar memorandum may also be sent with the Bill by the Council of Chiefs. Thus the Board has considerable powers over legislation affecting the Fijians, but its more important powers are executive ones. The Board may make regulations to be obeyed by all Fijians for their peace, order, welfare and good government; the observance of Fijian customary rights, ceremonies, obligations and communal services; any other matters as required by the Fijian Affairs Ordinance and such other matters as it may be empowered to deal with by resolution of the Legislative Council. Without prejudice to any of the foregoing, it may also make regulations for the provision of public services, the imposition of rates by provincial councils, the jurisdiction and powers of Fijian courts and magistrates, the making of by-laws by provincial and *tikina* councils, sanitation and health, and fishing, although such regulations are not effective until approved by the Legislative Council. The Board may also make standing orders, to the satisfaction of the Governor, for regulating the receipt, custody and disbursement of revenue, for accounting and audit; and similar standing orders regulating the engagement, salaries, conditions of service, dismissal and pensions of those in its service. The Governor, with the advice of the Board, appoints the *roko* of provinces and the Fijian magistrates, but the Board itself may appoint all such other officers as required, and the Governor must refer the matter to the Board for inquiry if he deems that a *roko* or a magistrate has given grounds for removal.

The powers of the Fijian Affairs Board make it the controlling agency of what may, without much exaggeration, be called a State within a State: it controls its own treasury and revenue, and its own courts; it has its own hierarchy of officials; it gives the Fijians a distinctive Government of their own within the general Government of the colony. Its formal position is secured by the section of the Ordinance which requires that it meet at least once every three months with a quorum of three of its members including the chairman. Still, great as the position and powers of the Board are, they are exercised to a large extent by the Secretary for Fijian Affairs who is its chairman. The Secretary is responsible to the Governor for the whole of this native administration. He may address his minutes directly to the Governor through the Colonial Secretary. Undoubtedly his most important legal power is the right to grant provisional approval to any regulation made by the Board if he deems it to be in the public interest, thus anticipating the approval of the Legislative Council. He is also, of course, the permanent head of the Fijian Administration, and its chief executive officer.

The most obvious expression of the Board and the Secretary's powers is the Fijian Affairs Regulations, promulgated in 1948 after the revision of the old Native Regulations of 1876.[5] These Regulations defined the structure of the Fijian Administration, and the institutions which were set up under the Ordinance; they also laid down the ways in which Fijian social services must be performed, provincial funds collected, and how the courts should function. An attempt was made to modify the criminal law so far as it arose out of Fijian custom by providing penalties for failure to observe custom which could not be punished under the ordinary English criminal law. Thus, for example, a girl absenting herself from a village was liable to prosecution; adultery became a criminal offence; killing or taking turtle, turtles' eggs, or young *bêche-de-mer*, were punishable, as well as offences which involved abuses of Fijian custom like

[5] *Laws of Fiji*, Cap. 100, vol. ii.

kere kere above the amount of five shillings. The Regulations further defined the duties of Fijian officials, and the economic and social duties of ordinary Fijians towards their chiefs and their communities. The Regulations bring the power of the Board into every aspect of Fijian life; in theory even a village dance must be approved under them. They are the formal expression of the Secretary's and the Board's control of the whole of Fijian life, because they provide a framework of law under which this State within a State is governed, a framework which the Board or the Secretary may extend by new Regulations. The Board and its Regulations come as close to being an independent Government as is consistent with the existence of a general Government of the Crown colony as a whole.

(b) The Council of Chiefs

Although the legal and actual importance of the Fijian Affairs Board is very great, it is not, of course, absolute. The Board is advised by a hierarchy of Councils which was also reorganized by the 1945 Ordinance. The Council of Chiefs is the most dignified of them, but it is also the one which has a wholly advisory position. It was established in the early days of colonial government, and its position was confirmed in 1945. The Secretary for Fijian Affairs then became its president, and the membership consisted of the *roko* of the fourteen provinces, one representative of each province selected by the provincial council (a number later increased to two from provinces with a population of more than 10,000), one Fijian magistrate and one Fijian medical practitioner nominated by the Secretary (a Fijian schoolteacher was added later), and such other chiefs not exceeding six as appointed by the Governor; the elected members hold office for four years and are eligible for re-election, the appointees as specified at the time of their appointment. The constitution of the Council may be altered by regulation, and the two later changes mentioned were in fact accomplished by the Fijian Affairs Regulations of 1948. It is the duty of the Council of Chiefs, apart from any powers which are specially conferred on it, to submit to the Governor such recommendations and proposals as it may deem fit for the benefit of the Fijian people, and in particular give its advice on all questions or Bills relating to the good government and well-being of the Fijian people which the Governor or the Secretary for Fijian Affairs may submit to it. For this purpose the Council must meet at least once in every two years as determined by its own resolution. The order of its business is prescribed by regulation. Questions which reach the Secretary at least four days before the opening of a meeting should be taken first, then matters communicated by the Governor, then the discussion of matters raised by members, and finally motions submitted to the Secretary at least four days previously. These duties, which are advisory rather than legislative, are reported to the Governor by the Secretary, but the Council during its meeting also nominates a panel, usually of ten names, from which the Governor appoints the five Fijian members of the Legislative Council. The Council of Chiefs was intended by Sukuna to play an increasing part in Fijian development: it was not to be merely an august body which passed pious resolutions;[6] and in the scheme of the Fijian Administration, although it is purely advisory, it has links with the central agency, the Board; its individual members serve on provincial councils, and some of them are also executive agents of the Board. It occupies a central position of some dignity and influence but no real legal power.

(c) The Provincial Councils

The provincial councils share in the advisory functions of the Council of Chiefs through overlapping membership, but by contrast they have some legislative functions in the Fijian Administration. In 1945 the number of provinces was reduced from nineteen to fourteen,[7] and in each of these a council meets annually. Its membership consists of the European district commissioner in whose division the province lies, the *roko* of the province, the European district officers, not more than five chiefs nominated by the *roko* (changed in 1955 by the deliberation of the Fijian Affairs Board to five landowners of the province), all the Fijian magistrates of the province, the Fijian medical practitioners, the *buli* of all the *tikina* within the province, the provincial scribe, and from one to three representatives of each *tikina* elected by the *tikina* council according to the number of ratepayers in the *tikina*. The Secretary for Fijian Affairs or his appointed deputy presides over the meeting, the time of which the Secretary decides on the advice of the district commissioner or the *roko*; the meeting itself makes rules for the conduct of its

[6] C.P. 22/1944.

[7] C.P. 4/1947.

business. Every *buli* must report in writing to the provincial council and reply to questions or answer complaints which any Fijian of the province may lay before the council. In this way the councils exercise control over the administration of a province, but they have more precise legal duties. They may make and pass by-laws for the carrying out of the Regulations, for the good government of the Fijians of the province and for the imposition of rates on the Fijian residents belonging to the province. Such by-laws come into force on the approval of the Fijian Affairs Board. The provincial council is really the governing body of a separate and subordinate native administration, which has its own treasury, its own courts and its own executive officers. The importance of such a council varies with the wealth and resources of the province which it governs; there is considerable variation, but it is through the provincial councils that the authority of the Fijian Board and the Secretary begins to make its impact, especially a financial impact, on the lives of the Fijians.

(d) The Tikina Councils

That impact, however, is most immediately felt through the lowest of the hierarchy of councils, that of the *tikina* or district, of which there are now seventy-six within the fourteen provinces; in 1945 the number of *tikina* was reduced from 184.[8] The councils meet at least twice every year as fixed by the *roko,* and overlap in membership with those above them. The *buli* presides over three chiefs elected by the *tikina* chiefs, the Fijian magistrates, medical practitioners, and field assistants of the *tikina,* three *turaga-ni-koro* or village headmen elected by all the *turaga-ni-koro* of the district, and one representative of each village of the *tikina* elected by a show of hands by every *mataqali* of the village. The *tikina* council may by resolution make orders, which acquire the force of law when approved by the Secretary for Fijian Affairs, to be obeyed by all inhabitants of the *tikina.* The council is also responsible for drawing up the programmes of work by which the communal services required by the Regulations are performed, the programme being authorized by the provincial council. The *tikina* council is the 'grass-roots' of the conciliar system, and to the Fijian villager the nearest of the hierarchy of councils on which the Fijian Affairs Board depends. There may also be a non-statutory, un-official village council,

[8] C.P. 52/1948.

but this depends upon local factors which vary considerably, and such a council has neither power nor a defined form although it may have considerable influence in village affairs. Quite apart from the duties laid down by law, the provincial and *tikina* councils may offer advice or recommendations (the latter only through the former) on the whole range of Fijian life as, of course, may the Council of Chiefs; and through their interlocking memberships they offer every Fijian the chance of a voice in his affairs and the conduct of the Fijian Administration. It has been claimed in fact that 'from the lowest council to the highest, the interests of communities *[vanua]* and federations *[matanitu]* are fully represented in a workable form of political organization based on the Fijian social system and on the principle of the open vote in all its councils'.[9] It may also be said that the membership of the councils establishes very close ties with the executive officers of the Fijian Administration who are members of the councils as much as they are agents.

2. *The Executive Officers*

The three principal executive officers of the Fijian Administration have already been mentioned by name: the *roko*, the *buli* and the *turaga-ni-koro*, who are the administrative officers corresponding to the province, the *tikina* and the village.

(a) The Roko

The *roko* is usually, although not invariably, a ranking Fijian from a landowning unit of the province of which he is head. He is responsible for the native administration of his province to the Secretary for Fijian Affairs through the district commissioner, having executive charge of the provincial funds, expenditure and revenue, and being responsible for the good government of his province, for the maintenance of proper records (such as land registration, births, and deaths) and the observance of the Fijian Regulations. He may also grant annual commutation of the social services required by those Regulations of every Fijian: road and house maintenance, food crops, transport of officials on duty and land surveys. The *roko*, in fact, is responsible for the social and economic life of his province, and he is a very busy man who must travel extensively to exercise proper super-

[9] G. K. Roth, *Fijian Way of Life* (Melbourne, 1953), p. 152. Like so many of Roth's statements, his precise meaning is a little difficult to discover; if by 'open' vote he means a 'public' vote, his statement is wrong and its implication misleading; in fact there is a secret ballot.

vision over his subordinates. This post carries a salary of some hundreds of pounds per year, but in addition he may, if a chief, exact certain personal services which are defined as customary obligations: house-building, planting food crops, making mats and bark cloth, canoe-building, supplying visitors with food, participation in ceremonies for their entertainment, and supplying turtle. The state of a province depends, therefore, very largely on the abilities and personality of the *roko* and upon his capacity to discharge what is an exacting office.

(b) The Buli

The *buli* is also important, but in a slightly different way. Whereas the quality of a *roko* colours provincial life by his force or energy (or lack of it), the *buli* is more immediately responsible for the details of Fijian affairs. His principal duties are the collection of the provincial rate, the enforcement of the Regulations, especially those relating to communal services, and the execution of the programme of work within his district. It is upon the *buli* that the duty of compiling registers of births and deaths actually devolves, and he is responsible for publishing the orders and notices of the Fijian Administration. In other words, the *buli* is the principal agent of the system who actually enforces the Regulations and performs many of the duties for which the *roko* is nominally responsible; he is the chief link between the villages and the Fijian Administration and the most obvious agent of its authority. The *roko* may influence a province by his behaviour, but the *buli* is the instrument he must use and upon which he must rely and, like the *roko*, he is a paid official. In 1945 the salaries of *buli* were low: from £12-£18-£24; but the amalgamation of *tikina* enabled an increase to be made to £50-£100-£150 for three grades of *buli* according to the number of taxpayers in his district.[10] Unlike the *roko*, however, a *buli* cannot call upon customary chiefly services, although he gets a small entertainment allowance; very often, indeed, the *buli* is not a chiefly rank, although he is the principal executive officer of a system which preserves customary and chiefly society.

(c) The Turaga-ni-koro

The third and lowliest of the officials, the *turaga-ni-koro*, is the village headman upon whom the Fijian Administration ultimately

[10] C.P. 52/1948; the three grades in numbers of taxpayers are 1: under 250; 2: 250-500; 3: over 500.

depends. The *turaga-ni-koro* is generally not a chief and is elected by the village. He is responsible for seeing that the Regulations and orders are actually carried out: the 'grass-roots' of the executive system. In particular he must draft the programme of work relating to the growing of crops, and see that the programme, and the social services, are in fact carried out. The effectiveness of the Administration in the last resort depends upon the *turaga-ni-koro* of the 1,100 villages but, unlike the higher Fijian officials, they are for the most part unpaid. Some provinces pay ten shillings a month: most do not; and the *turaga-ni-koro* instead may call for up to six days' work in each year. The position of a necessary official who is at once elected by a village and responsible to the Administration is difficult, but it is with the office of the *turaga-ni-koro* that the elective principle is present in the system of executive offices of the Fijian Administration, and in theory it should be the office which most closely ties the Government to the people.

The connections between the councils and the officials are clear enough; the two strands are closely intertwined with the discussion of provincial and district affairs and the measures taken to implement decisions.

(d) The Provincial Scribes

Between the councils and the officials, the Fijian Administration combines policy decisions and their execution; and to assist these authorities there is a staff of clerical workers and police. The most important of these is the provincial scribe, a man who is in effect senior clerk, registrar and accountant rolled into one.[11] The scribe is usually appointed from beyond the province in which he serves: he holds a paid executive office of the Fijian Administration which is independent of hereditary rank or position. He acts as secretary to the *roko* and as clerk to the provincial council of which he is an *ex-officio* member; and he also supervises the provincial treasury, dealing with salaries, rates, judicial fees, deposits and the records concerning these finances. In addition he is charged with the actual keeping of the register of land, births and deaths, for which the *roko* is nominally responsible. The provincial scribe, especially in a populous province, may have other scribes or clerks to assist him, and much of the efficiency of a province and a *roko* depends upon the skill

[11] C.P. 4/1947.

and capacity of the man who is the chief clerical official keeping the records upon which provincial administration relies.

(c) The Police

In a different way, that administration depends upon the Fijian police. The Fijian Administration police correspond to the provincial, district and village pattern in which both the councils and the executive officials are organized.[12] There are provincial police, two or three of whom are responsible for a group of *tikina*. One of these is usually stationed at the headquarters of the province to carry out the orders of the *roko* and to accompany him on his travels. The others are normally attached to the Fijian magistrate for convenience of administration, and they prosecute cases in both the *tikina* and provincial courts for offences against the Regulations and other orders, as well as serving warrants and summonses. Their general duty is to see that the orders of the *roko* are obeyed, and to investigate offences brought to their notice. They are uniformed men who receive a salary of from £3-£8 per month from the provincial funds. Similarly there are *tikina* police or *buli's* constables, stationed in every district with the duty of assisting the *buli* by seeing that his orders are carried out and of prosecuting disobedience in the provincial or the *tikina* court, although they usually leave prosecution in the former to their provincial counterparts and appear only as witnesses. They, too, can serve summonses and execute warrants for breach of the Regulations, and they, too, are a uniformed body, paid from provincial funds at the rate of 10*s*.-15*s*. per month. The third class is the village police, one of whom is stationed in each village (with rare exceptions) to assist the *turaga-ni-koro* in keeping law and order. They may prosecute in the *tikina* court, but they are not usually supplied with a uniform, nor are they usually paid. If there is any salary it is of the order of 5*s*. per month or payment in kind. Like the village headman and the non-statutory village council, the village policeman operates on a less official level than those men higher in the scale but, like the *tikina* constable, the village policeman does not have a full-time job, and both classes are on duty usually for some specific task. Nevertheless, the village policeman is the basis of the system of enforcement of the Regulations and, like the *turaga-ni-koro*, he is a lowly but necessary

[12] ibid.

official without whom the system would operate with greater difficulty.

3. *The Courts*

The policing of the Regulations leads directly to the question of the legal machinery for enforcing the authority of the bodies and officials who have been described. The organization of the courts naturally corresponds to the administrative structure.[13]

(a) The Provincial Court

There is a provincial court which consists of three members, two of whom are Fijian magistrates and the third of whom may be a European district officer, who meet regularly at least once every three months as the European district commissioner appoints. The provincial court has jurisdiction, where the parties to a dispute are Fijian, in a civil action of from £10-£50 and in prosecutions for a breach of the Fijian Regulations where the punishment is more than a £10 fine or two months' imprisonment. Such judicial profits go to the provincial funds. The court is a court of record and an appeal lies from it to the Supreme Court of the colony; the provincial court hears appeals from the second type of Fijian court, the *tikina* court, in cases where the amount involved is more than £1 or more than seven days' imprisonment in default, or when imprisonment without option of a fine is inflicted.

(b) The Tikina Court

The *tikina* court which sits as necessary consists of a Fijian magistrate sitting alone, having jurisdiction where the punishment is less than £10 or two months' imprisonment, and the civil action for less than £10. It, too, is a court of record but it is open to Fijians only, not to the general public. On an appeal to the provincial court, the *tikina* court magistrate may not sit in judgement.

Both courts enforce the Fijian Regulations, and the provincial court is also a divorce court under the Native Divorce Ordinance. Their jurisdiction, however, does not exclude the ordinary criminal jurisdiction of the colony's courts, which extends to Fijians as well as to other races. The records of both courts are submitted to the legal adviser of the Fijian Affairs Board who has the power to alter or revise them. These courts complete

[13] ibid.

the system of the Fijian Administration because they enforce Fijian custom as the law under which the Fijians live, and although this custom is not repugnant to the general laws of the colony, nevertheless it prescribes for the Fijians a code of conduct which distinguishes the Fijians from the rest of the colony, being in effect a separate legal system just as the Fijian Administration constitutes a separate social and economic one.

There are, however, two exceptions to the separateness of the Fijian Administration which must be mentioned: there is a small number of 'exempted' Fijians, and a system of European district administration. The former are Fijians who, for payment of a commutation fee, have been allowed to contract out of the communal obligations prescribed by the Fijian Regulations; they are few in number and, whatever their economic importance, they are not really a significant modification of the pattern of Fijian life under the Fijian Administration.[14] The latter is a system of supervision which exists beside the Fijian officials and institutions we have been describing. Fiji is divided into four districts: the Central, Northern, Eastern and Western Divisions, each under the control of a European district commissioner, assisted by a number of European district officers.[15] This administration is responsible for a great deal more than Fijian affairs—it deals with Indians and Europeans too—but the district commissioner is the deputy of the Secretary for Fijian Affairs within the provinces comprising the division. The *roko*, for example, is responsible to the Secretary through the district commissioner, and is expected to consult him and take his advice, for the district commissioner is charged with the efficient administration of his division including Fijian affairs. It follows that the district commissioner is required to keep check on accounts, on Fijian courts, and on the apparatus of government within each province. He is also responsible, because his range of functions is wider than Fijian affairs, for co-ordinating them with general

[14] It is possible for a village to be 'exempted' from a *tikina*, either to work under authority or do its own work, although there are not many examples, especially of successful ones; Spate, op. cit., pp. 83-4. More usually the exempted Fijian is an individual farmer. Officially his desire to be a peasant farmer is encouraged, but in practice under the requirements of Regulation 6, he must pay a commutation rate and maintain a certain size of holding as well as produce a defined amount of produce and income. The conditions do not encourage the independent farmers; at best they are tolerated; Spate, op. cit., pp. 87-91.

[15] C.P. 4/1947.

Government activity, including specialized departments like Agriculture and Health which have an obvious interest in the Fijians. The district commissioner is the most important link between the Fijian Administration and the general Government of the colony and for this purpose he has some of the authority of the Secretary deputed to him, but his subordinate district officers, upon whom the work of supervision and co-ordination falls at a more local level, have no such clear authority.[16] They are required to supervise the records and the accounting by regular and frequent inspections, to preside in Fijian provincial courts and to act as school managers. Officially they are required to use their discretion and to abstain from giving direct orders to Fijian officials. If some obvious action is required, they must pass on the information to the district commissioner. A district officer is expected to be on close and good terms with the Fijian officials within his area, for he is in the very difficult position of having supervisory power without executive power in Fijian affairs; and Sukuna's advice on his duties may be characterized as 'indirect self-effacement' for which the reward was in Heaven.

The structure of the Fijian Administration certainly embodies Mitchell's and Sukuna's views on the best method of political advancement for the Fijians. Apart from the special circumstance of Fiji in which the Fijians are threatened by the economic predominance of other races, and the long tradition of paternal government moulded by Sir Arthur Gordon, Sukuna's own chiefly rank and temperament and both his and Mitchell's knowledge of the theory of 'indirect rule' all combine to provide a form of government whereby Fijian society might be preserved. The Fijian administration involves a belief in slow advance, and it expects it to occur through the adaptation of traditional institutions for modern ends. The modern end is the creation of a parliamentary democracy of the British type in which a sovereign elected assembly, responsible government and an impartial civil service combine those values of justice, efficiency and honesty which are characteristic of Great Britain. To achieve this Fijian institutions must, of course, be adapted, but the theory has been that a system of elected councils and a hierarchy of chiefly executive agents correspond to institutions of indigenous society while they also represent an approximation to the ultimately desirable form of government. The iso-

[16] *Fijian Administration Circular No. 15* (1945).

lation of the Fijians until these adapted institutions work well and naturally is a necessary corollary to this belief. They are in theory transitional: when the Fijians reach the promised land of equality with the other communities in the colony, their distinctive institutions will no doubt be merged into those of the general Government of Fiji to achieve a multi-racial society having but one form of government, and that of the British type, which is accepted by all the people of Fiji. This approach to political advancement has a respectable ancestry in colonial practice. Lord Lugard used it in part of Nigeria, Sir Donald Cameron introduced it into Tanganyika and revivified it in Nigeria. Sir Arthur Gordon was the precursor of the theory in Fiji itself, and there can be no doubt that the structure of the Fijian Administration represents a version of 'indirect rule' in an elaborate form; in a small colony, there is a large apparatus of government to promote a slow change from the traditional to the modern. The question is how far, by the tests which were suggested in the Introduction, it succeeds in its purpose of promoting the political advancement of the Fijians.

CHAPTER III

POLITICAL ADVANCEMENT IN FIJI

1. *The Executive Institutions and Councils*

The organization of the Fijian Administration makes a general distinction between advisory (or legislative) functions, and executive ones. No rigid line can be drawn because some officials belong to both kinds of organization, but the institutions within which policy may be discussed and, within limits, formulated, and the executive agencies are distinct enough with the major exception of the Fijian Affairs Board, the apex of the whole pyramid of the Fijian Administration.

(a) The Fijian Affairs Board

The Board, which was intended to give the traditional rulers of Fiji a chance to lead, enables the leaders of Fiji to discuss policy at the highest level and to see to its execution. The membership of the Board is essentially that of the five Fijian members of the Legislative Council who are nominated by the Council of Chiefs, of whom the majority have always been the high chiefs of Fiji.[1] In 1950 the membership included two commoners, of whom one, however, had been a *roko*.[2] Two years later, the Board was Ratu Ganilau, Ratu Tuisawau, Ratu Mara, Ratu Vuiyasawa and Ratu Edward; and in 1956, Ratu Mara, Ratu Edward, Ratu Ganilau, Ratu George Cakobau and Semesa Sikivou, the last being the only commoner.[3] There have been changes in personnel, most obviously when the younger chiefs like Mara, Ganilau and Edward Cakobau came back from military service or over-

[1] C.P. 10/1945; C.P. 21/1947; C.P. 48/1948. In 1944 the Board consisted of Ratu Vuiyasawa, Ratu Tuisawau, Ratu Toganivalu, Ratu Edward Cakobau and Ratu Lalabalavu. When the membership changed at the next two-yearly meeting of the Council of Chiefs, Ratu Mataitini replaced Edward Cakobau, and this was still the composition of the Board in 1948.

[2] C.P. 29/1950. It was then made up of, in this order, Ratu Tuisawau, Ravuama Vunivalu, Ratu Toganivalu, Joeli K. Ravai and Ratu Edward. Joeli K. Ravai in 1946 was acting *roko tui* of Tailevu. The commoner, Vunivalu, was a clerk in a Government department.

[3] C.P. 31/1953; C.P. 42/1956. The commoner Sikivou was a schoolteacher. None of the members in 1956 was a *roko*; they were predominantly younger Fijian chiefs.

seas training, but membership has generally changed among the same smallish group of Fijian chiefs, and at least three of the Board and usually more have always been the high chiefs of Fiji. Superficially, therefore, the leaders of the Fijians are still the traditional ones, especially when the powers of the Board in the machinery of the Fijian Administration are considered; and the inclusion of one or two educated commoners like Sikivou and Vunivalu might be held to include in that leadership a modern leaven which links the past and the present. Undeniably the Fijian Affairs Board does offer the old rulers of Fiji the opportunity to lead, and it also offers a chance to a new type of leader in Fijian society, but it is very doubtful if the opportunity is being grasped or could be under present conditions.

The meetings of the Board are not so frequent that it can exercise continuous control over policy and administration. In 1945, for example, there were five meetings in the year, and they were equally infrequent in 1946; in 1948 there were again only five meetings.[4] In the following two years the number of meetings doubled, and thereafter the Board met on anything up to eight to twelve occasions.[5] A major part of the reasons for infrequent meetings, and the low quorum of three, is the difficulty of regular attendance, which is sometimes a matter simply of physical communication and movement but more often of the offices held by members of the Board. Those who are *roko* have exacting offices perhaps in distant provinces; all of them have a number of other offices which demand attention. In 1959, for instance, one member of the Board was also: Economic Development Officer Northern Division (and therefore responsible for the whole of Vanua Levu and Taveuni), *Roko Tui* Cakaudrove, a member of the Legislative Council Standing Finance Committee, Fijian Development Fund Board, Central Road Board, Macuata Road Board, Taveuni Rural Authority, Taveuni Hospital Board of Visitors, Taveuni Native Land Trust Board Local Committee and the Taveuni Liquor Permit Committee.[6] Thus, attendance at meetings of a Board which does not meet frequently may be low.[7] The membership of the Board and the other duties

[4] C.P. 7/1947; C.P. 18/1948; C.P. 27/1949.

[5] C.P. 2/1951; C.P. 5/1952; C.P. 5/1953; C.P. 12/1954; C.P. 38/1954; C.P. 29/1955; C.P. 38/1951; C.P. 10/1957.

[6] Quoted by Spate, op. cit., p. 41.

[7] C.P. 38/1956. There were, for example, eleven meetings in 1955 of which Ratu Tuisawau attended nine, Ratu Edward Cakobau eight, Joeli K. Ravai eight, Ratu Mara six and Ratu Vuiyasawa two.

of its members place restrictions upon its place in the scheme of the Fijian Administration, and tend to concentrate its sessions into the periods when meetings of the Legislative Council bring its members to Suva on other business. These are the mechanical or constitutional difficulties in the way of regular and frequent meetings which affect Sukuna's intention that the traditional rulers of Fiji should lead their people through the powers of the Board.

There can be no doubt that the issues discussed in their meetings are important ones for the Fijians. The Fijian Affairs Regulations were debated there, the standards of Fijian education, the Ministry of Food copra contract, the resettlement of Indian farmers whose leases had not been renewed by the Fijians, Fijian banana schemes, native agricultural authorities, the Fijian Development Fund, the possibility of a Fijian income tax, the financial administration and defalcations or corruption, the examination for Fijian magistrates and the appointment of officials within the Fijian Administration. And it is precisely because these matters are important, and some of them urgent, that the powers of the Board have also been limited in practice.

The difficulties of regular attendance and the urgency of some of the matters under its control have enhanced the power of the Secretary for Fijian Affairs who, in any case, has a strong legal position in relation to the Board and the Fijian Administration. The Secretary has always been at the centre of things, and when the first Secretary was a man of the personality and calibre of Sukuna, who held the office from 1945 to April 1954, it can be said that the real power in the Board lay with the Secretary. The subsequent secretaries have been Europeans, but even when they have not cared to exercise to the full their potential authority, the office still represents the real power of the Board. The necessity for this was recognized very early in the life of the Fijian Administration. In 1946 the Secretary was explaining that the urgency of decisions made it difficult to work through the Board except by the circulation of papers, and the Secretary, or a Deputy-Secretary who was then provided for, was given power to approve rates and by-laws.[8]

The power of Secretary was further enhanced because his office is the executive agency of the Board, the link with the executive branch of the general Government, quite apart from

[8] C.P. 18/1948.

any other offices the Secretary has held, such as the chairmanship of the Native Land Trust Board or the Native Land Commission. Both institutionally and practically the Secretary has tended to overshadow the Board, and even if his office did not by itself tend to do so, there are few signs that the Fijian members choose to assert their position or exercise what influence is open to them. In a real sense, therefore, the Fijian Affairs Board, unless the Secretary be a Fijian, does not fulfil Sukuna's intention that the traditional rulers of Fiji should lead and thereby promote the political advancement of their people. The Deputy-Secretary for Fijian Affairs, who has always been a Fijian when there is a European Secretary, is not enough to enable one to say that the Board constitutes Fijian leadership, especially when the European inherits a tradition of benevolent paternalism from the past history of the Fijian Administration. The Board certainly offers the Fijians the chance, through their chiefs, to discuss policy and to supervise its execution, but for the reasons which have been discussed there are few indications that the opportunity is being taken.

Nor is a similar opportunity taken, which is available to the members of the Board, to discuss and perhaps to influence policy by their membership of the Legislative Council of Fiji. In general the Fijian members say little, and when they do speak seem part rather of the Government's official majority than independent representatives of the Fijians. Frequently they have given the impression of being asleep. Sukuna was exceptional, and justified and defended the Fijian Administration with great skill and eloquence, but his fellow Fijians' contribution even to debates on the very existence of the system and its Regulations has been slight. In 1948, when the Fijian Affairs Regulations were introduced, Sukuna gave a brilliant review of the history of native administration and a justification of custom as a necessary protection for the Fijians. Edward Cakobau's contribution was a statement of the different mental growth of races whose interests had little in common. The others said nothing. In 1948 there was a debate on a proposal to amend the constitution to provide an unofficial majority, including six elected Fijian members, which involved an attack by some unofficial Europeans on the concept of a Fijian Administration.[9] It was opposed by Ratu Vuiyasawa who said that the time was not ripe, that the people were not ready for change; by Joeli K. Ravai, who argued

[9] *Legislative Council Debates,* 1948 (September session).

the same case because of the absence of education among the Fijians; and by Ratu Tuisawau, who defended election by the Council of Chiefs as the best available method. None of the speeches was long, and that they happened at all was something of a rarity; on other than Fijian affairs, the Fijian members contribute little or nothing.

(b) The Council of Chiefs

Too often the purpose which Sukuna had in mind for the Fijian Administration shades off into another: preservation of the *status quo*. This attitude probably accounts for the reluctance of the Fijian members of the Board to assert their potential authority, and it certainly reveals itself as a prevailing attitude in the Council of Chiefs as well as in the Legislative Council. The former was probably closer to Sukuna's heart than any other of the institutions of the Fijian Administration, and it represents the traditional rulers of Fiji as no other does. He intended it to be not merely an august body which passed pious resolutions, but a body which played an increasing part in Fijian development; it was also intended to include some of the educated Fijians from whom leadership might be expected to come: schoolteachers, medical assistants and university graduates. In theory such leadership, as distinct from the chiefs, might have a majority, and the Council has been claimed as the 'House of Legislature' to which the Fijian people look because it represents the changes in Fijian society as well as its traditional aspects.[10] Nevertheless, the Council of Chiefs represents a chiefly attitude. This is true in terms of numbers,[11] but these are less important than the fact that the influence of the chiefs is paramount. This is obviously reflected in the nominations submitted to the Governor for Legislative Council membership, still more obviously reflected in the debates and discussions in the Council, epitomized by Ratu Loco's question in 1956. 'For a long time now there have been members of the Council of Chiefs who are not Chiefs. Why? Is this not a Council of Chiefs and if so, is it not right to change this?'[12]

10 Roth, op. cit., p. 152.

11 C.P. 21/1947; C.P. 29/1950; in 1946 there were twenty-six members present of whom twenty-two were chiefs; in 1950 there were forty of whom twenty-five were chiefs.

12 C.P. 42/1956.

The Council of Chiefs is conservative; its membership, where it is not chiefly, nevertheless still preserves traditional attitudes towards chiefly rule. The usual procedure at a meeting is an opening speech by the Governor, followed by the Secretary and perhaps some special speaker such as the Co-operative Adviser or the Conservator of Forests. This is followed by resolutions of members of the Council communicated previously to the Secretary, and then by a report from the latter on the action taken in reference to resolutions of the previous meeting. After this members may raise matters in the form of question and answer. The procedure is fluid and not precisely laid down, although some attempt was made to define the order of business in the Regulations of 1948.[13] In fact the Council of Chiefs can raise and discuss virtually any matter it chooses so far as the Fijians are concerned. There is scope for initiative if the Council chooses to take it, and the Governor's speech often invites such initiative, as well as offering a report on the work done since the last meeting and advice for the future.

In 1946 the Governor explained to the Council in detail the working of the Fijian Administration: the amalgamation of provinces and *tikina,* the Native Land Commission and the Native Land Trust Board, agricultural policy, education and the Ten Year Development Plan; all of them issues which were further elaborated by Sukuna in his speech as Secretary.[14] Two years later the Governor was discussing medical services, copra crops, the Co-operative Ordinance and education, and the Secretary took up the question of pastoral development, forestry policy and education.[15] In 1952 the Governor talked about the Fijian Development Fund, the Fijian Banana Venture, the conservation of forests and the question of land reserves, and the Secretary talked about the importance of copra.[16] In 1954 certain questions were put squarely to the Council by the Governor.[17] He concerned himself with increased production from Fijian land, and discussed the development programme together with the proposed appointment of officers to forward this, which he asked the Council to consider and comment upon. He then went on to discuss the Native Land Trust Board which it was pro-

[13] *Fijian Affairs Regulations,* No. 5(4).
[14] C.P. 21/1947.
[15] C.P. 48/1948.
[16] C.P. 31/1953.
[17] C.P. 25/1954.

posed should acquire ownership or perpetual lease of Crown Land from which it should receive and control the revenue—powers which were necessary for development. And he coupled these proposals with another: that the Fijians should elect perhaps two members of the Legislative Council by direct suffrage as the other racial groups did, because he had heard from a number of sources that Fijian commoners felt they should have the vote and he thought that the chiefly system must move with the times. It is clear that at each meeting of the Council of Chiefs the Government and the Fijian Administration have stressed the necessity of economic development to raise the Fijians to an economic level comparable with the other races, and the consequent necessity for the technical agricultural measures, education and medical services which were implied in this advance. The Government has consistently urged the chiefs to use their influence towards these ends: to lead in a modern as well as a traditional sense as a matter of great urgency for the future of the Fijian people.

What response has there been from the traditional rulers of Fiji? What has the Council of Chiefs advised after discussion? In reply to the particularly forceful speech of 1954 it agreed that the Native Land Trust Board should control the revenue of Crown Land, be prohibited from selling land except to the Crown for public purposes and that the expenditure and control of the profits should be exclusively for the benefit of the Fijians as a whole; it agreed that development officers should be appointed and thought that development programmes should be drawn up in consultation with those responsible for social services and the co-operatives. In reply to the suggestion of directly elected representatives in the Legislative Council, it resolved that the existing system be maintained, and it rejected a further idea of a standing committee of the Council of Chiefs to advise the Government in the long interval between meetings on the grounds that the traditional representation of Fijian public opinion should be maintained. The discussions of 1954 illustrate two points about the Council of Chiefs: the initiative in such proposals comes from the Government; the proposals which are accepted are conservative ones.

The Council's own initiative is displayed in the questions which are raised by its members, questions which may properly cover the whole range of Fijian life for there are no restrictions on its discussions. Many of the issues raised in Council naturally relate to the everyday concerns of the Fijians. In 1944, for example, the Council considered the question of absentee's fees paid to the villages from the commutation rate paid to the *tikina* and the provinces in lieu of service, and it discussed the question of the independent farmer who paid such a fee to contract out of communal obligations in order to work his own land; the precise details of this cultivation in terms of quantities of produce were laid down. This is an important matter and the Council's discussion, although conservative in the sense that it was preoccupied with the preservation of traditional society and the conditions necessary to maintain it, was nevertheless a responsible decision. The matter was familiar to its members because it represented a daily problem of Fijian life and no doubt the Council was reflecting the majority opinion within Fijian society. Naturally (and rightly too) the Council may be expected to concern itself with those questions which immediately affect Fijian life. In 1956, for instance, the Council asked that Crown Land near Suva be allocated as an area for settlement of the Fijians who were permanently employed in Suva, and similar land in other centres, for example, Lautoka, Ba, Labasa and Nausori.[18] It also asked that the Native Land Trust Board should be authorized to deduct twenty-five per cent. of the rents obtained from leases of Fijian land for the social and economic development of the landowning units from whose rent the deduction was made, and it recommended a levy, similar to the existing copra cess, on sugar-cane, bananas and timber, for social and economic development. The kind of development the Council had in mind may again have been conservative, but at least the discussion was an attempt to grapple with the serious problems which face the Fijian people; perhaps with a little private, unofficial pressure, the Council of Chiefs has discussed questions of policy in this way. Its solutions may be open to question, but the opportunity to take policy decisions is there and use has been made of it. To promote the capacity for public discussion does not necessarily imply that the decisions taken must be right; it does, however, imply a sense of responsibility and some breadth of vision.

The Council has often failed to grasp the opportunity to influence policy on important matters because of its preoccupation with petty details raised by its members which neither reveal much ability to discuss policy responsibly nor show much ability

[18] C.P. 42/1956.

to rise above very local and sectional interests. Joeli K. Ravai in 1952 asked: 'Would it not be advisable to exclude Indians from the Forest Guards?'; a question which reflects a real fear for Fijian land and resources. Or again: 'Can the Government be approached with a view to providing the money for two bulldozers solely for work in Fijian districts?', which reflects some consciousness of a weak economic position. The Council of Chiefs must naturally be concerned with its own genuine anxieties, but they tend to block the kind of leadership for which Sukuna looked, by concentrating on devices intended to maintain the *status quo,* by restrictions on other racial groups rather than positive measures for promoting Fijian advancement. And at worst, the Council of Chiefs can demonstrate failure in leadership and vision by such questions as Ratu Moceletu's: 'Is it correct to allow work and play on Sundays in Fiji?' Or Ratu Latianara, *roko tui* of Serua and Namosi who asked: 'Is it possible for the areas sold by our forefathers to be returned?'[19] Such questions reveal a failure to grasp the opportunity to advise on responsible policy decisions, and they are all too frequent in the Council. Local problems are a natural and often desirable preoccupation, but over and above this there are few indications that a wider view is emerging which can discuss policy in the context of the Fijians in Fiji; and this is the kind of leadership which is needed and which the Council of Chiefs has the chance, if it is taken, to provide.

One of the reasons for the failure of the Council to rise to Sukuna's expectation has been mentioned: the conservative character of the body dominated by the chiefs. Sukuna had in fact projected his own virtues, intelligence and ability through all the members of his class. Recognizing the fact of change himself, he accepted the conclusion that the chiefs must adapt themselves, but his perception has not been generally shared by his fellow chiefs. The reciprocal relationship between chiefs and people with which Sukuna justified the paternal Fijian Administration has been undermined. Many of the old chiefly characteristics survive, although some have obviously been eliminated; others, like the *lala* or ceremonial precedence, have been preserved by administrative action, in some cases giving the chief more authority than he would traditionally have had.[20] The basis of the chiefly position altered: it has been in the

[19] C.P. 48/1948.

[20] Thomson, op. cit., p. 66 ff.

past, and is now, one of governmental authority; it is independent of the needs of the people in that a bad or inefficient chief cannot now be eliminated in the way in which he might have been at an earlier time, and he no longer needs to respond to the desires or wants of his people. It is this changed position which makes the part played by the chiefs so difficult: the formal attitudes survive when the reciprocal relationship has been impaired. And the degree to which the chiefly position can be made to serve modern political or economic ends is plainly dependent on modern education and training. Some of the high chiefs, Edward Cakobau and Mara, for instance, are Oxford graduates; most are not, and they are trying to cope with an exacting situation for which their traditional attitudes do not fit them. In their position, it is all too easy to fall back upon the conservative position to resist all change, certainly to deny its urgency. Trained leadership being spread very thinly amongst the ranks of the chiefs, the predominant sentiment of the Council of Chiefs is the preservation of the traditional order so far as possible, and a general disinclination to change. This position is possible partly because the attitude of Fijian commoners towards the chiefs is generally the traditional one, partly because such higher education as there is, is to a great extent, but of course not completely, confined to the high chiefly families. There is, therefore, as yet little challenge to the traditional leaders from an educated class of commoners, and there is no educated class at all apart from those in Government service.

The conservatism of the Council of Chiefs represents the survival of traditional attitudes in an 'un-traditional' situation, and obviously plays a major part in the failures of the Council to occupy the modern role envisaged for it. Still, there is another important reason for these failures, and this is the function assigned to the Council in the whole framework of the Fijian Administration. It meets too infrequently to have any decisive influence on policy even when important Fijian matters are involved. Its status is purely advisory and its advice, although listened to, need not be taken. The resolutions of the Council may be rejected, noted, heard with interest, considered or acted upon, at the discretion of the Governor on the advice of the Secretary for Fijian Affairs. In other words, the actual power of the Council is dependent upon the personalities and abilities of two officials, and any degree of influence which it attains is in this way informal. It has power to advise and discuss, but it has no responsibility for executing the decisions taken by the Government upon its advice, nor does the power which it has necessarily have any consequences at all. The formal position of the Council thus reduces its value as part of a programme of political advancement, because the degree to which it can influence policy by its resolutions is limited, while its insistence on the *status quo* means that it may become merely an august body. It does not, in fact, link power and responsibility in a way calculated directly or decisively to promote political advancement, although it undoubtedly enables Fijian leaders to discuss important matters if they wish and to attempt to determine policy. Neither opportunity has really been grasped in the sense that the Fijian chiefs have not recognized the urgency of the problems which confront the Fijians, although in relation to the *status quo* the Council has no doubt grasped the opportunity to decide and influence policy; hence the initiative in policy discussions is largely that of the Government which must recognize and attempt to regulate those social and economic changes which are occurring in Fiji.

If the Council of Chiefs suffers from its advisory status, the same is not formally true of those other councils which offer Fijians the chance to take policy decisions, albeit within a narrower field. The provincial and *tikina* councils operate within local limits, and their position is to this extent stronger: they discuss the issues which immediately and visibly affect Fijians, and they are closely connected within the machinery which will implement those decisions. Hence power and responsibility are more closely associated.

(c) The Provincial Councils

The provincial council is the principal local government body within the Fijian Administration, and the biggest link in the chain of communication up and down the structure of councils. It also has its advisory, policy making and legislative functions, with some control over the provincial executive officers. Its most important single function is the provincial budget and the striking of the rate, partly because of the financial control it gives, but also because the use of the money involves the council in discussing and deciding social and economic matters within the province. The subjects in the council business paper are usually under four heads: domestic affairs, matters connected with them, crops and the budget. The latter is usually the last business and both it and the provincial rate (in fact a head tax) are arrived at by setting out the recurrent expenditure, adding all special expenditure. A schedule of revenue is then produced from named items and the rate is assessed on the difference between total revenue and total expenditure from all sources, with five per cent. allowed for failures to pay the rate.[21] The work of the provincial council is closely connected with this budget and the rate. Between provinces there is considerable variation because they represent the old *vanua* of Fijian life, and there is no equality of resources or population between them.[22] Rich provinces like Ba or Tailevu may have over 4,000 ratepayers and an annual revenue of (for example in 1956) more than £11,000 and £14,000, while a poor province like Serua and Namosi may have only a few hundred ratepayers and a revenue of one or two thousands.

But however rich or poor the province, the part played by the provincial council depends upon the revenue at its disposal for social services. If, as is often the case, most of the revenue goes towards meeting the cost of actually collecting it and maintaining the provincial administration, then the council is committed to this expenditure with little possibility of initiative or discussion. A council may decide that a constable's wage should be increased by ten shillings or that the *per diem* allowance should be increased,[23] but, necessary as such decisions are in local government bodies, they do not enable the council to discuss wider matters of policy, nor to take the initiative in the development of the province, both of which activities require discretionary control of available money. There is seldom a surplus from provincial funds, and more usually a considerable short fall in the rates,[24] in spite of a Government subvention (in 1956 it was £89,075) to pay for the salaries of central staff, *roko*, magistrates, *buli* and provincial scribes. The provinces have

21 The whole question of the finances of the Fijian Administration was discussed in a report by R. S. McDougall, an English County treasurer (C.P. 35/1957). He made recommendations to replace the head tax with a proper rate, graded in broad categories according to income.

22 C.P. 18/1948. In 1946 the annual rate varied between £1 17*s.* and £2 15*s.*; two years later the lowest rate was £2 7*s.* and the highest £3; by 1956 the average rate was £4 8*s.* 3*d.*

23 These were two decisions of the Lomaiviti council at which the author was present in 1958.

24 C.P. 35/1957. From 1951 to 1956, the short fall between the estimated collectable revenue and actual receipts varied between 12·7 per cent. and 26 per cent. (in 1955).

barely enough money to keep their administration going, and certainly very little for promoting social services or economic development in their area.

The lack of funds is crippling to provincial development, and it reduces the usefulness of the provincial council which is the obvious body to discuss and take decisions about local development. In consequence, a provincial council meeting, although it can be lively, is often apathetic. At the Lomaiviti council in 1958, the *buli* presented their reports, but the only discussion of questions came from the other *buli*. Then the resolutions of last year's council meeting were reported upon by the district commissioner, and the council was told of the action taken and the commissioner's recommendation. Then the council passed resolutions on provincial affairs for the current year, some of which obtained no seconder. The meeting was quiet, and the people who spoke were usually officials, in spite of the fact that an important report on the Fijian Administration finances came up for discussion and approval which made certain far-reaching recommendations in the method of taxation. Not every meeting is quiet, but the general tendency is for a council to be aware of severe financial restrictions on its activity, and also of the fact that its decisions need approval by the Secretary to be effective. Here again, initiative was crippled by the final power being taken out of its hands, although this position has recently been changed, and a council's resolutions do not now all require approval before they are effective. The councils, in fact, have suffered from something of the same trouble as the Council of Chiefs; they have some statutory functions, but under the limitation of approval or disapproval by an outside authority.

Thus, in spite of their statutory authority, the provincial councils are in effect advisory: their resolutions may not be approved, their budget may be adjusted; but even if these limitations were removed, there are still other reasons for their somewhat apathetic appearance. One of them may be mentioned here, although it is not necessary to elaborate upon it: amateur helplessness in the face of specialist problems like agricultural and economic development; the present resources are not enough to overcome a sense of frustration. Another (and for our purposes more important) factor is the Fijian system of rank. The membership of the councils ensures that the chiefs of a province are well represented, and although commoners may be sent to the council from the *tikina*, they are usually silent in the face of traditional leaders flanked by officials like the district commissioner, the *roko* and the *buli*. Apart from any feeling among commoners that economic or social change cannot come about rapidly under such authorities and such a system, there is the natural reluctance of the Fijian to disagree with or contradict a chief for whom he preserves the traditional forms of respect; a tradition emphasized by the *yaqona* ceremony with which a council opens, and further emphasized by the view of some chiefs and officials that the Council of Chiefs is the only proper place for the discussion of policy. In theory, the provincial council is the place where policy can be thrashed out at the effective local level, but in practice it happens only to a limited extent.

Policy is discussed in these councils. Between 1944 and 1946 the councils discussed a recommendation of the Council of Chiefs, on the initiative of Sukuna, for the amalgamation of areas having kinship affinities into new *tikina* and new villages, the *tikina* for more efficient administration, the villages to provide a proper division of labour and more time for cash crops.[25] These discussions were not smooth. Entire policy had tended to encourage parochialism by its insistence on the maintenance of traditional groupings and, in Sukuna's words, 'narrow tribalism . . . became deeply entrenched'. The forces of reaction led by the chiefs, as he put it, were not easy to dislodge, but eventually the provincial councils accepted that social and economic improvement were more important than inherited sentiment or sectional feeling. In fact, the amalgamation of *tikina* was carried through, but the village amalgamation policy failed, showing the limitations of agreement reached by discussion in the provincial councils which agreed to it. Thus, the advice of the councils is not necessarily an indication of feeling in the villages on matters which affect the structure of Fijian society. Nevertheless, the advice of the provincial councils is valuable to the Board, because they are the principal units of Fijian local government, and they provide the opportunity, even if it is seldom taken, for any Fijian to express himself. It is the hope of the Board, too, that not only will it maintain contact with the Fijians through the councils, but that communication should operate in reverse. It was hoped that, when the provincial councils had grasped what crops should be grown and how economic development should proceed by the advice which expert offi-

[25] C.P. 18/1948.

cers could give to them, an immense amount of good would be done. No doubt the councils do operate to make communication up and down the system effective, but the combination of Fijian social attitudes and some defective machinery impairs the use which could be made of a theoretically admirable system.

(d) The Tikina Councils

The lively discussions which occur in the provincial councils are no doubt due in part to the size of the province; some of the *tikina* which it includes may be old rivals, and their representatives prepared to speak plainly about others. At all events, the province is sufficiently big for kinship obligations or respect for chiefs not wholly to stifle or impede discussions. This is not true of the *tikina* council. This has none of the financial power of the province, nor is it large enough to discuss policy on any general scale, but it is the effective unit for actually implementing social and economic policy. Meeting more often than the provincial council, it is, therefore, important as the body which can give Fijians a voice in the drawing up of the programme of work and determining the steps to be taken to implement policy, to this extent, of course, allowing discussions and decisions on matters of development. There may be some outspoken comment in the *tikina* council from village representatives, the more so since the amalgamation of *tikina* has combined old rivalries within the new administrative units, but here again social attitudes and mechanical difficulties have the effect of reducing it to apathy. The Fijian Administration seems to place stress rather on the guidance a *buli* can give to the council, and not vice versa, so that with an energetic *buli*, especially if he is a chief, discussions in the council may be limited to agreeing with him. The issues involved are local ones and primarily economic: the actual crops grown, techniques of agricultural production, priorities among cash crops. This emphasis was further demonstrated in 1956 when the economic development officers were given authority to preside at meetings of *tikina* councils when development was discussed, together with delegated power to approve resolutions on those subjects on behalf of the district commissioner.[26] Thus a *tikina* council might very well initiate such projects as rice or cane-growing, or the marketing of bananas, and in some *tikina* the councils have really taken the lead in such development.[27] Nevertheless, respect

[26] C.P. 10/1957.
[27] Spate, op. cit., p. 33 ff.

for a chiefly *buli* or a high chiefly development officer may lead simply to obedience or passive agreement rather than enthusiasm, and it is all too often the case that the council acquiesces rather than guides or leads. The *tikina* council, more than the provincial one, is working inside the Fijian communal system and system of rank, and traditional attitudes are generally admitted to be the biggest obstacle to that economic and social development with which the councils are principally concerned. The very concept of the 'programme of work' by which the *tikina* proceeds, is a legacy from the past: it is part of the amateur approach to specialists' problems, and it sets a limit to *tikina* discussions or initiative.[28] And this is quite apart from the mechanical difficulties by which *tikina* council resolutions get lost on the way to, or in, the annual provincial council; even if a *tikina* council were to meet regularly, frequently, and with good attendance, the infrequency of a provincial council meeting would impose a limitation.

Part of the difficulty may also be the actual resources of the *tikina*. A provincial council, however poor, can draw upon financial resources over a wide area, but a *tikina* council may find its resources dramatically reduced. For example, Labasa *tikina* in the past sold over 7,000 acres of land and in 1948 had leased a further 11,000 acres, most of this the best land in the *tikina*.[29] All that could be done to improve social and economic conditions was to reserve the leases as they expired. The inevitable result was that villages of this *tikina* had poor, small blocks of subsistence crops, and its council could do little or nothing. Such a situation may be extreme, but in addition to the other factors which operate to reduce the initiative of the *tikina* council, it contributes the further difficulty of actual shortage of material resources. The plain fact is, of course, that the functioning of this machinery of councils is closely linked with economic development; and the use of the 'communal system' for that purpose reinforces the traditional attitudes which obstruct the intention to have a hierarchy of councils which would enable the Fijians to discuss matters affecting them and to take decisions with some assurance that action may be taken on them. The machinery of discussion, consultation, and communication might be improved by removing some of the obvious blocks, but the social attitudes and the economic situation can

[28] ibid., p. 43.
[29] C.P. 27/1949.

only be changed much more slowly; and these are the more serious limitations upon the success of the system of councils. The point can be succinctly made by the non-statutory village council, which a *turaga-ni-koro* will, if he is wise, consult but which has no assurance that its advice will be sought at all, or if sought, be heeded or acted upon. The frustration which this produces in a village is paralleled all the way up the chain: uncertainty that any discussion or any decision will be welcomed or heeded. And this uncertainty, a combination of constitutional, social and economic factors, is basically that of trying to use institutions having some roots in Fijian society for modern political and economic ends. The hierarchy of councils, which should, and is intended to, promote modern Fijian leadership, is interpreted in traditional terms by the Fijians, and it owes any success it may have primarily to individual chiefs and officers, rather than to the Fijian public opinion it is designed to channel and express.

2. *The Executive Officers*

(a) The Roko

With the councils' effectiveness in political advancement thus reduced, the executive officers of the Fijian Administration, who by intention and necessity must give a lead to the councils, have the more vital role in political advancement. The *roko* is obviously the most important of them. As a matter of general policy, the *roko* is a member of a landowning unit of the province of which he is head, and it is claimed that in this case, as indeed with appointments of other executive officers, merit, experience and qualifications for this job are the criteria, irrespective of whether he is a chief or not.[30] It is usual to point out that for some years now, four of the *roko* have been commoners. Since the war there have always been non-chiefly *roko*, partly because the high chiefs of certain provinces who filled the offices were away on military service.[31] In 1945 there were

[30] Roth, op. cit., p. 146.

[31] C.P. 4/1947. In 1945, for example, the *roko* of six provinces were in the Forces, and two retired, one after thirty-six years and eleven months' service although he was temporarily reappointed. The absent *roko* were Ratus Tuisawau, Lalabalavu, Vuiyasawa, Toganivalu, Edward Cakobau and Nanovo. The retiring *roko* were Ratu Tawake, who could not immediately be replaced, and Ratu Tana, an acting official who was a retired *buli* appointed temporary *roko* of Lautoka and Yasawa which were amalgamated under the reorganization, Ratu Tana then being appointed acting *roko* of Ba.

three non-chiefly *roko*, one of them in the important province of Tailevu and in 1950 there were still three, one of whom was holding the same office in Bua as he had five years earlier; four years later still, the same three commoners were in office in the same provinces together with another commoner who was appointed to the poor province of Serua and Namosi.[32] The commoners who are *roko* are a constant group who have tended to remain in the same provinces. The larger group of chiefly *roko* has also remained reasonably constant, but there has probably been a greater tendency to move them to new provinces where they also have kinship or landholding connections. The point is that a *roko* who is not a chief still has to act inside a chiefly society, and the advantages of a chiefly, preferably a high chiefly, appointment are therefore considerable, in terms of his mobility, his influence and his prestige.

The duties of the *roko* demand that he should be a man of influence and prestige because, apart from the technical responsibilities of keeping records and sitting as a magistrate, the social and economic life of a province depends upon his energy and initiative: his office demands high qualities of leadership. These duties are not nowadays traditional ones. If, for example, a *roko* is to ensure the social services of his province, this means that he must encourage road construction, good sanitation, water supplies, medical treatment, and proper house construction, according to the Fijian Regulations, and to exercise control over these services he must not merely rely on his subordinate officials, but make himself familiar with conditions in his province by frequent journeys. If he seeks the economic development of his province, he must be aware of the possibilities of cash crops, of the marketing situation, of facilities for transport, of capital equipment, as well as the more technical agricultural services implicit in such development. He must, in fact, be a man whose standards are European ones quite as much as Fijian if there is to be any social and economic development and not just the preservation of the traditional way of life. But, in addition, he may also have to combine this office with others: perhaps as economic development officer for a group of provinces, perhaps as a member of the Fijian Affairs Board and the Legislative Council. He can be sure, in fact, that his position will thrust upon him a whole range of duties which require considerable training as well as energy and initiative. The qualifications for traditional

[32] C.P. 21/1947; C.P. 29/1950; C.P. 25/1954.

leadership, therefore, must be supplemented by modern skills, some of which are those of a specialist in economic matters.

There are extremely able, energetic and competent leaders among the Fijian chiefs and commoners who fill the office of *roko*; two of them are university graduates, and others have had experience overseas as military officers or on colonial administration courses; but these men are a handful. The majority of *roko*, whether they are chiefs or not, are appointed in traditional terms: they have to work in what is still largely a customary society. Ratu Penaia Ganilau, *roko* of Cakaudrove, has had considerable success in the economic development of his province, which is often used as a model, but this success is primarily due to his traditional standing and his personality; his activity is personal rather than institutional. The same may be said of other *roko*: in traditional terms they can lead, but such personal and traditional standing cannot compensate for the absence of modern training, and when such a *roko* resigns or is transferred his work may stagnate. The present leadership can keep Fijian society going, and perhaps even advancing, but it cannot cope with major problems of economic and social development, and its attitude is, as the Council of Chiefs shows, basically conservative; it advocates maintaining the *status quo* or slow advance in traditional ways. This is quite as much true of the non-chiefly *roko* as of the chiefly ones: they, too, attempt to operate in traditional ways and they do not represent a new type of leadership qualified by modern training because university education, for instance, has generally been confined to the high chiefly families. A commoner who is a *roko* must still attempt to lead as if he were a chief.

Since Fijian society is largely customary, there is a great deal to be said for the appointment of a ranking chief as *roko*. He can represent the former paramount chieftainship in a province, although the amalgamation of provinces may make this difficult in some cases. If he does, he will be accorded the traditional respect, and his advice will carry weight. But in as far as he relies on these traditional sanctions, he is committed to a considerable extent to preserving the kind of society which supports them: if that society changes, he loses the traditional basis of his authority and must rely simply on his Government office which may not in itself carry weight enough to fulfil his duties. Any changes must, therefore, be slow, and the office of *roko*, as an institution rooted in Fijian society, must correspond with the nature of Fijian society or lose a good deal of its *raison d'être*. The office itself, and the men who in general are appointed to fill it, in practice commit Fijian society to slow development, to patient rather than dynamic leadership.

(b) The Buli

The difficulty of combining traditional and modern leadership is perhaps even more marked in the case of the *buli*, upon whom the *roko* must depend both for his information about many aspects of provincial life, and the effectiveness of his own leadership.[33] The *buli* is the most conspicuous officer of the system so far as the Fijians are concerned and his position is, therefore, vitally important. A *buli* is in practice appointed on the recommendation of the *roko* with a preference for the ranking chief of a *tikina*, although many *buli* are not of chiefly rank. Since the reduction of the *tikina* from 184 to 76, it follows that the *buli* cannot be the chief of all the old *vanua* within a *tikina*, and that there will be, therefore, other chiefs of equal or greater traditional standing. Whether the *buli* is a chief or not, he may encounter difficulties. If he is a chief, his appointment may impair his relationship with the chiefs of other *vanua* within his *tikina;* if he is not, his lack of traditional standing may place him at some disadvantage in the face-to-face relationships in which he is involved. And these difficulties are entirely apart from the fact that the office is not well paid and does not, therefore, attract able or ambitious men. Of course, there are many good *buli*, but there are many slack or officious ones, and it is in any case the post which, as the principal executive agent of Fijian administration, draws upon itself any odium which may be felt in the villages: the chief scapegoat for Government interference or Government neglect or, in some cases, both at once.

(c) The Turaga-ni-koro

Like the *roko*, the *buli* is required by his duties to operate on two levels: the traditional one which is intended to build on the institutions of Fijian society, and the modern one which is

[33] In 1956 the Fijian Affairs Board revised disciplinary measures to improve the standards of work of these two grades of officials. One *roko* was then reprimanded, three had increments in their salaries withheld because of their failure to reach a degree of efficiency. Six out of seventy-six *buli* were not allowed to pass the promotion bar, compared with ten who passed; six were reprimanded, and twelve had increments in salary withheld for failure to carry out their duties satisfactorily (C.P. 38/1956).

concerned with social and economic welfare on European terms. His training and experience may equip him for the former but even less than in the case of the *roko* does it equip him for the latter; even his formal education may be too low for the demands made upon it. Thus, in practice, the success of a *buli* depends upon his personality and/or his traditional standing: it is essentially personal and not a result of the system; with the additional complication that he is responsible to the *roko* who may not himself be equal to his office. And, conversely, the *buli* himself must rely upon the unpaid *turaga-ni-koro* whose office is still more difficult to fill adequately: the man who accepts it, if he seeks to enforce all the Regulations and the programme of work, becomes unpopular with his village, and if he fails to enforce the Regulations, he becomes unpopular with the *buli* and the *roko*. Hence the appointment is not sought after, and the turnover is rapid. It is again a matter of personality. Some *turaga-ni-koro* are energetic and forceful men who do fine work, but it is a matter of chance, not of the system of administration. The formal education of such a man may be very low, he may or may not be a chief, and his position is an unrewarding one. Many *turaga-ni-koro* are for these reasons nonentities who exercise neither traditional leadership nor the kind of modern leadership for which Sukuna looked in his system of Fijian administration.

3. *The Judiciary*

Trained leadership is spread very thinly among the ranks of Fijian chiefs and officials, and its absence accentuates the tendency towards preserving the *status quo*, but it has another and more obvious symptom: the prevalence of Fijian custom over the more technical duties of an official. Most obviously this appears in the legal and accounting activities of the Fijian Administration. The Fijian magistrates administer the Regulations which are based upon Fijian custom; they operate within well-known and defined limits. There are usually about twenty-five Fijian magistrates for the fourteen provinces, excluding the *roko* who is one within his own province until there is a sufficiency of other suitable men.[34] When the Fijian Administration was set up in 1945 it was recognized that magistrates needed special training; it was not enough to appoint a man well versed in

[34] C.P. 4/1947.

Fijian custom, but a man who knew European legal procedure, rules of evidence and so on. And in 1945 and 1946 no such training could be given. The two urgent needs were then described as a handbook in Fijian on procedure and a course of instruction,[35] and until these were available the educational background of Fijian magistrates was weak and the range of choice for appointment narrower. It was not until 1951, in fact, that the handbook was issued and a regular system of examinations for magistrates instituted. The weakness of the early appointments was most obvious in the number of cases which the legal adviser had to alter or revise, which were very frequent in the early years, and equally reflected in the examinations held in July 1951, one magistrate being so far 'below par and beyond hope' that his appointment was terminated.[36] In September the annual examination for serving magistrates and for new appointments was held. The most striking feature of the result was their very poor idea of procedure.[37] The syllabus on which they were tested covered criminal and civil court procedure, knowledge of the Regulations and of the standing orders relating to accounting. Some of the bad results may be attributed to the revision of the Regulations in 1948 which caused confusion among magistrates accustomed to the old regulations, but most of the failures were due simply to lack of background, a lack for which experience and the revisions of the legal adviser seemed to be the only remedies. The rate of failures was sufficiently alarming for more positive action than a handbook to be taken, and in 1955 the most experienced magistrate, Ratu Joni Misikini, was appointed to a supervisory position, examining the monthly returns before the legal adviser, and also training his fellow magistrates who then numbered forty-one, including thirteen *roko*.[38] A further remedy was also introduced. Even if a magistrate passed the examination, he was required to undergo an interview with the Secretary or the Deputy-Secretary for Fijian Affairs to test his suitability of character. The

35 C.P. 18/1948.

36 C.P. 5/1953. Five probational magistrates sat, of whom two passed, although two of the failures were marginal enough to be allowed to take the examination again.

37 C.P. 12/1954; C.P. 38/1954. There were six passes among twenty-seven candidates, and only one of four serving magistrates qualified for promotion. In the following year five out of thirty-two passed, and in 1953, eight out of twenty-five.

38 C.P. 38/1956.

general standard was in fact beginning to improve a little, but in the next year for the two magistrates who passed the promotion bar, two failed.[39]

The judicial arm of the Fijian Administration was thus afflicted in the same way as the executive: lack of training. Nevertheless, the weaknesses were procedural ones; technical failures arising from European institutions. In its purpose of enforcing the substance of the Regulations, there was probably a large measure of success, reflected in the number of cases tried before the provincial and *tikina* courts. The latter are, of course, the most immediate sanction of the Fijian Administration, before which the most common breaches of the Regulations are tried. In 1948 there were more than 8,000 cases before the two courts, by far the largest number before the *tikina*.[40] The majority of them concerned failures to perform the social services required by the Regulations, partly because the new Regulations caused some confusion and uncertainty and there was a tendency to interpret the new in terms of the old.[41] Many of these cases had to be reviewed by the legal adviser. The figure continued to rise, and the large number of prosecutions in itself was no doubt responsible for demonstrating procedural weakenesses,[42] but it also demonstrates the degree to which the courts are an inevitable adjunct to the minute and perfectionist Regulations prescribed by the Fijian Affairs Board: it is easy to break one of the numerous Regulations, perhaps unwittingly, because their very complexity promotes infringements. And the nature of the cases prosecuted is in itself a reflection of the lack of trained leadership on the part of the executive officers who are responsible both for the collection of rates and the performance of social services. The large number of cases of dereliction suggests failure in instruction and example on the part of *roko* and *buli*; failure, that is, to rise to the present situation, not necessarily to the traditional one.

39 C.P. 10/1957.

40 C.P. 27/1949.

41 C.P. 2/1951. Payment of rates thirty-eight per cent., communal services thirty per cent., health fourteen per cent.; and in 1949 the number of cases, in roughly the same proportions, reached 11,000.

42 C.P. 5/1952; C.P. 38/1954. In 1950 there were 12,000 cases before the *tikina* courts, mostly failures to pay rates and perform social services, and 200 before the provincial courts, for maintenance, adultery, drug addiction and the like. Three years later the number of cases was respectively 16,297 and 360.

4. *Finance*

This conflict of modern and traditional values is even clearer in the financial apparatus of the Fijian Administration. The revenue comes from two sources: an annual Government subvention which is used mainly for the purpose of paying the salaries of senior Fijian officials and the central staff, travelling expenses, costs of printing and stationery and the maintenance of district tracks throughout the colony; and the provincial rate which pays the salaries of minor officials employed by the provinces. In 1945 a new accounting system was set up in all provinces with the object of concentrating all items of revenue and expenditure on a single form to be submitted monthly to the Central Fijian Treasury, but the form was too complicated for the Fijian officials, the provincial scribes, who had to handle it, and a revised and simplified one was provided;[43] a columnar system of accounting was introduced at the same time. Both, however, were still beyond the grasp of the officials, and there were other difficulties which arose when the provincial scribe was absent from headquarters. The assistant provincial scribes were, therefore, to undergo the same course of training as Fijian clerks in the Central Treasury. A further check was introduced by the monthly returns and regular inspection of provincial accounts by the accountant and his staff. A system of examination for provincial scribes was also introduced, and with rather better results than the magisterial examination; on a syllabus which included the Fijian Affairs Regulations, standing orders on accountancy, and the registration of landowners, nine sat for the examination in 1952 and all but one passed; in 1954 four candidates passed out of twelve.[44] Nevertheless, in 1956, there were still complaints by the director of audit about carelessness and slackness among officials whose training was still at an elementary level.

Such were the usual technical difficulties which arose from lack of training, but the more obvious ones involved actual defalcations. In 1946 a total of £894 was found to have been embezzled from provincial funds, and seven criminal charges were laid against a number of *buli,* all of whom were convicted of embezzling sums of from £8 to £680.[45] The year following,

43 C.P. 4/1947.

44 C.P. 12/1954; C.P. 29/1955.

45 C.P. 18/1948.

eight more *buli* were dismissed for the same reasons, although full restitution avoided any actual financial loss. In 1948 there was more than the usual number of similar offences, and a general complaint by the Secretary that slackness was rife.[46] Most of the offenders were *buli,* but in 1949 a *roko* and a provincial scribe were sent to prison, in 1950 the provincial scribe of Rewa suffered, and in 1953 a Fijian magistrate went to prison for embezzlement, followed by another one in the next year. In 1956 these financial offences were still worrying the Fijian Administration; three provincial scribes were removed for inefficiency, and embezzled sums were written off in Cakaudrove and Naitasiri. Such devices as card records of the visits of *buli* to deposit money in the provincial treasury were introduced, regular and surprise inspections of provincial funds were also used, and the district commissioner was given additional authority to inspect financial records. Strict control, however, was made impossible by inadequate supervisory staff, and some defalcations continue each year; more, probably, than reach the stage of investigation and conviction. A lack of technical capacity to keep good records is responsible for allowing such embezzlements to occur, but the measures taken to improve the system show clearly enough that the root of the trouble is not technical but arises from Fijian social attitudes which are at variance with European standards of administration.

Fijian society has always placed a marked emphasis on generosity, or wealth used for social obligations, for *vasu* and *kere kere;* thrift is not a virtue. Any financial official working inside this society is thus exposed to social pressures to distribute money under his control, especially if he has customary obligations which his salary is not really adequate to fulfil. Many defaulting officials plead, and with a large element of truth, that their offences were caused by the high cost of entertainment, and requests by people to whom they have traditional obligations of assistance. The *buli* is particularly exposed to this kind of social pressure. If he is a chief, or even if he is not, he must entertain, must display Fijian generosity, or lose pres-

[46] C.P. 27/1949. In Nadroga and Navosa province a *buli* misappropriated £85 and was bound over for three years and ordered to make restitution; in Ba, another received nine months' imprisonment for misappropriating £118 13*s.* which the people of his *tikina* made good; in Rewa, the defaulting official got six months for an offence involving £53, some of which was recovered; and there were incompletely investigated offences in Lomaiviti, Macuata, Ba and Ra.

tige, and since even with the improved salary rates that amalgamation made possible, his wage is still low, the temptation to maintain his prestige by misappropriating the funds he collects is considerable. A provincial scribe may err by refusing to report the failures of a man of high rank. The defalcations show the extent to which a *buli* (or a scribe) may succumb, and the extent to which his action is condoned by Fijian public opinion is shown when the people of his *tikina* make good the deficiency which their social expectations have helped to bring about. The financial administration demonstrates more clearly than most other aspects of the Fijian Administration, that where custom clashes with administrative rules, procedures and standards, custom is likely to prevail.

From this detailed examination of the Fijian Administration, it is abundantly clear that both the legislative or advisory bodies, and the executive agents, work primarily under the impulse of Fijian custom, and that the conflicts which arise between the demands of customary society and those of modern government are most easily resolved simply by maintaining the *status quo*. By themselves the institutions are not enough to promote political advancement, and whatever slow influence they exert upon the Fijians is easily outstripped by the advance of the other communities.

Sukuna's case for this method of colonial government was the same as that used in other colonies than Fiji. Unless the indigenous people are protected from outside economic forces, their customary society will break down and they will be left helpless; law and order, the satisfactions and restraints that enable them to face life will vanish, they will become 'detribalized', and there will be no basis of political advancement. The end, in Fiji, would be a colony that is no longer Fijian. It follows, on this argument, that the Fijians must be kept isolated within their own Government until they have achieved the capacity to resist such destructive force, to hold their own, and it follows also that the institutions with which they are provided, those institutions which have their roots in customary society while bearing European grafts, are expected to produce this equality. The foregoing analysis of their working suggests that they will do no such thing. They have indeed helped to preserve Fijian society (their great strength is that they are Fijian and probably generally accepted by Fijians), but this very preservation creates a vested interest in resistance to change. A Fijian chief will hardly be enthusiastic for changes in the basis of his authority which would eliminate it, and, dominating the councils and the executive offices, the chiefs have a vested interest in the *status quo* from which their authority derives. Since the successes of the system have depended upon individual personalities, this general outlook of the chiefs assumes the greater importance.

The institutions *could* be the instruments of political advancement, but whether they are depends upon independent changes in Fijian society; in its turning, for example, from the 'communal system' to individual peasant proprietorship, in the willingness of Fijian chiefs, through education and foresight, to exchange the traditional basis of their authority for one of modern leadership as Sukuna exhorted them to do. Without these changes the machinery of political advancement will not work at the speed which is necessary if the Fijians are ever to compete on anything like equal terms with Indians and Europeans. But those economic forces which are already at work in Fijian society to produce individual enterprise in the countryside or an urban proletariat may cause the machinery to grind to a halt, by creating a gap between traditional leaders and their people of a kind which has come into existence in other colonies using a government of the Fijian type. This is the dilemma of the Fijian Administration, as it is also that of other colonial governments: the slow process of political advancement achieved by institutions becoming accepted and working naturally is likely to be overtaken by events, but quicker progress may sap the very basis of those institutions by the crumbling of customary society. And the dilemma is made the more urgent in Fiji by the development of the other communities: there is very little time for the Fijians to develop, and their position is comparatively getting weaker and not stronger. The institutions for political advancement have been provided, but they await the winds of change to breathe life into them.

CHAPTER IV

THE TAHITIAN BACKGROUND

1. *Physical Description*

The colony which is called French Polynesia (until 1957 the French Establishments in Oceania) is made up of a number of island groups in the eastern south-west Pacific which stretch over two million square miles of ocean:[1] the Society Islands (both Leeward and Windward), the Tuamotu or low archipelago, the Austral Islands, the Mangareva (formerly the Gambier) group and the Marquesas. The total land area of the colony is not accurately known, but the official figure is 1,544 square miles. The islands are widely scattered and some of them are mere coral specks hardly deserving the name; together they number something over 100. Like the Fiji group, they vary widely in size. Tahiti is by far the largest island, and it dominates the colony geographically, economically, socially and politically, to the point at which the noun Tahiti or the adjective Tahitian is loosely applied to the colony as a whole. The main island is about 402 square miles, and its nearest rival is the adjoining island of Moorea which is 50 square miles. The Marquesas, with a dozen islands, measure 459 square miles; the Tuamotus, made up of 76 low islands and atolls, measure 319; and the Mangareva group 11. There is, however, a lack of detailed and accurate information of this kind, and for many of these groups the figures can be taken as close approximations rather than precise statistics.

Unlike Fiji, the island groups of French Polynesia have no recognizable pattern: they are much more widely scattered, much smaller in size, and the difficulties created for internal communication are correspondingly greater.[2] Nor, in the case

[1] It comprises all the French islands which lie south of the Equator and east of longitude 155° west. San Francisco is 3,660 miles away; New Zealand 2,000.

[2] These small land units are spread over an area quite as great as Europe: from the Marquesas, corresponding to the Baltic area and Finland, the colony stretches down almost to the north coast of Africa represented by the island of Rapa.

of French Polynesia, are external communications so good or so regular as those of Fiji. Papeete, the capital town which stands on the north coast of Tahiti, has a fine deep-water harbour, which is a port of call for the Matson and Shaw Savill lines, as well as the terminus of a Messageries Maritimes route, but the vessels calling are not so frequent as those at Suva, since in general they call only on one leg of a voyage. Papeete's position, although similar in the internal life of the colony to that of Suva, is not that of a focal point of South Pacific sea traffic. Papeete was also the terminal of a flying-boat service (now discontinued) from Fiji once a fortnight, and it has recently acquired an aerodrome. Land-based aircraft can also fly into Bora Bora, one of the Leeward islands, where a landing ground was constructed by American forces during the last war; and a French airline operates a weekly service from Paris; from Bora Bora a shuttle service is carried on by a flying-boat to Papeete. Air communication with the outside world is limited, and, compared with Nadi, Papeete and Bora Bora are quiet backwaters. French Polynesia is in fact relatively isolated, although such communications as there are reinforce the dominance of Tahiti itself in the life of the colony.

French Polynesia exhibits the same broad division into high and low islands which is characteristic of Pacific island groups. Tahiti itself is a high island of volcanic origin. It is roughly hour-glass in shape, oriented north-west and south-east, and consists of two major volcanic cones. There are individual peaks like Orohena, 7,321 feet, Roniu, 4,341 feet, Aorai, 6,773 feet and Le Diadème, 4,362 feet. The interior of the island is extremely rugged and mountainous, penetrated by deep radial valleys. Near the coast there is a continuous and fairly fertile slope towards the sea, and in some areas of lava flow, like Faaa, the angle of descent is even less than these slopes, but in others there are precipitous rock walls, such as those at Hitiaa, which drop into the sea, while in most there are volcanic cliffs varying in height from 50 to 100 feet separated from the sea by a belt of flat land a few feet above sea-level. The coastal flats which are rich, fertile land, are only a small fraction of the total area. They are widest on the western side of the island, and in the districts of Papara, Mataiea and Papeari, are 1,000 yards wide and several miles long. The river valleys tend to be deep gorges cut into the mountains, rarely more than a mile wide, and overhung by rocky buttresses. The rivers radiate out from the centre in short, straight courses, with flooding and erosion common on the lower levels. Alluvial fans are common at the mouth of the rivers and these, too, are fertile areas. The whole island is surrounded by a barrier reef, cut by deep-water passes which are navigable by large vessels. There are many good anchorages, but only Papeete is a port in the sense that it has facilities.

Moorea, lying nine miles west of the north-west point of Tahiti, is another high island, also of volcanic origin but of older formation than Tahiti. Its valleys are broader, its crags more broken and fantastic in shape than the larger island. The backbone of Moorea is a chain of rugged mountains up to 3,975 feet, through which, on all sides but the north, the valleys plunge steeply to the sea. The north side has two larger valleys which drain into two fjord-like bays, Papetoai, and Paopao (or Baie de Cook). There is the usual coastal rim of flat land which is only a few hundred feet wide on the south (except near the main valleys), while on the other sides the flats are wider. Moorea is also surrounded by a barrier reef, pierced by passages, but the lagoon is a shallow one, and only three of the passes are navigable. The other high islands of French Polynesia display the same general characteristics as Moorea; with the exception of a few islets the rest of the Society group is high, so are the Marquesas, the Australs, with the exception of Maria, and the Mangareva group, with the exception of Temoe. The extensive low group is the Tuamotus. These are seventy-six low-lying coral atolls with scarcely any point more than thirty feet above sea-level. They are typical in structure: a long coral reef, more or less circular, enclosing a lagoon, with a small land area of coco-nut palm, scrub, coral detritus and dazzling white sand. They are dangerous to navigation, and good anchorages are rare. The one exception is Makatea which is an upheaved coral formation of crescent shape, about five miles long and two miles wide, of a plateau-like elevation of 190 to 220 feet; the highest point is 372 feet above sea-level. The island is bordered by cliffs with a narrow reef and some white sand at their feet; there is no barrier reef. The reason for Makatea's importance is the high-grade phosphate deposits in its interior.

The contrast between these high and low islands is more visibly marked in French Polynesia than elsewhere in the Pacific: some of the contrasts are startling. The vegetation on the high island is luxuriant, the soil is very fertile; on the low island it is simply palm trees. The mountains of Tahiti, the Marquesas and Moorea are very high; the atolls of the Tuamotus are sometimes awash by the sea. And again there are climatic differences. The prevailing easterly trade winds create important differences even within Tahiti itself, the wet and dry side of the island being very clearly marked, although precise statistics are hard to obtain. Temperatures here, and in other similar islands, are high: in five years' observation at Tahiti the ranges were 61°F and 93°. Humidity is also high, with the mountain tops often shrouded in cloud.[3] In the low islands the climate is hot, with no pronounced variations of temperature, and there is a water scarcity difficulty because of the porous soil throughout the Tuamotus. The whole of French Polynesia is exposed to hurricanes, but the Tuamotus are particularly subject to them. Nevertheless the climate as a whole is probably less enervating for Europeans than that of Fiji.

2. *Resources*

The economy of French Polynesia, like that of Fiji, is an undiversified one. Agriculturally it depends upon copra; industrially upon the phosphate deposits of a single island, Makatea; the two products together constitute the major part of the export value of the colony. In 1952, for example, of a total export value of 500,952 thousand francs, copra provided 271,327 thousands and phosphates 136,040 thousands together making a combined total of about four-fifths of the exports.[4] Four years later, the value of phosphates exported slightly exceeded the value of copra, but the two together were still two-thirds of the total export value.[5] French Polynesia has virtually a two-crop economy, and the only other significant export is vanilla, usually a long way behind in value. The economy is thus exposed, as is that of Fiji, to severe effects from price fluctuations, and it also faces the certainty that in a relatively short time the phosphate deposits will be worked out. The well-being of the economy will then depend upon the improvement which is planned in communications tapping the American tourist market. Mean-

[3] At Papeete the mean average rainfall is 72·3 inches, and in the wet side of the island about a third as much again: 106·7 inches in Papeari.

[4] *J.O.E.F.O.*, 1952, Supplément Statistiques Douanières. The currency is French Pacific francs, of which the value has been roughly five times that of a metropolitan franc.

[5] *J.O.E.F.O.*, 1956, Supplément Statistiques Douanières.

while the Tahitian economy has experienced the same kind of history as the Fijian. In the years immediately following the war, there was in general a favourable balance of trade, but since 1949 imports have consistently exceeded exports in value by an appreciable margin, and the terms of trade have not been good. Tahiti has in effect depended upon a French subsidy. Moreover, there is an additional complication for the Tahitian economy. Because of French policy, there is a much closer assimilation of the colonial economy to the metropolitan one than exists in Fiji, but in spite of this economic assimilation only 29·3 per cent. of the imports in 1955, for example, came from France, and a high proportion of the remainder came from the dollar area; while France took much more than 50 per cent. of Tahiti's exports. French tariff policy has imposed an additional strain on the local economy because of lack of correspondence between import and export markets. Here, again, an American tourist industry would help to remedy matters.

The most important difference which exists between the Fijian economy and the Tahitian one relates closely to the demographic and social structure of the colony: it is the absence of communal divisions of the Fijian type. When the census was taken in 1956, the total population of French Polynesia was 73,201, an increase of sixteen per cent. over the previous census of 1951.[6] Of these 63,666 were described as French of Oceanic origin, and 2,298 as French not of Oceanic origin. The only significant foreign group was the Chinese, who numbered 6,748. These figures emphasize the dominance of Tahiti in the life of French Polynesia. The town of Papeete alone has 17,247 inhabitants and the rest of the island another 19,079, a combined total of 36,326 or nearly half the total population, to which the administrative dependencies of Moorea and Makatea add another 5,858. The other commune of Uturoa contains, by contrast, only 1,980 people. This unequal distribution of population has a broad resemblance to the pattern in Fiji, but with one striking difference: the population has a social unity which Fiji does not possess. The classification in the census distinguishes between two classes of Frenchmen, those of Oceanic origin and those not, but both groups are legally French citizens. The distinction between them is not a legal one, nor is it based on

[6] *J.O.P.F.*, Année 106, No. 11, published the provisional statistics, although there is some doubt about the reliability of the figures, especially those relating to the Chinese.

colour, and it seems to be a subjective distinction: it is what a man *says* he is and how he chooses to live. There are few 'pure' Polynesians left. Many, perhaps most, have anything up to a half European or foreign blood, and the ancestry of those who would call themselves French not of Oceanic origin, where they are local families as distinct from metropolitan French, is part Polynesian. No clear line can be drawn between predominantly Tahitian and predominantly French families: the two shade off into each other as a result of intermarriage and interbreeding over a century and a half. The French policy of assimilation has meant that socially and legally Tahitian society is homogeneous, and thus economic distinctions cannot be equated with racial or social ones so far as the bulk of the population is concerned. The metropolitan French are a distinct group, usually comprised of administrators serving a tour of duty in the islands, but still legally of the same status as local people. The Chinese are the distinct foreign group, who cannot now easily gain French nationality. In general they live as a communal group and do not marry with the Tahitians, although there are a number of half-Chinese children by Tahitian mistresses who are brought up as Tahitians not as Chinese. The pure Chinese population has had an *apparently* negligible increase since 1951, and demographically they are relatively insignificant, even allowing for dubious census statistics and some fraudulent 'adoption' of Chinese children by Tahitian families.

Tahitian society has, therefore, a unity which does not exist in Fiji, and this is reflected in the economy. The phosphate company is financed by British capital, but its labour, and the labour which produces copra, is Tahitian. Because it is so difficult to draw a line between Tahitian and French among the local families, much of the commerce of the island can also be said to be distinctively Tahitian, and even in the case of the Chinese it cannot be said to be 'foreign' since the Chinese, although often not legally French citizens, are nevertheless permanent residents. The economy, with the exception of the retail trade, does not support or emphasize communal divisions, and even here there is a large local French element in Papeete which may also be described as Tahitian; the Chinese dominance becomes marked only in the outer districts and islands where they have a monopoly of trade stores. The economic distinctions which exist in Tahitian society exist within a social, legal and political unity which is quite different from Fiji, and with the modification required by the retail trade, they are not communal or racial distinctions but those which exist in European societies: a distinction which may crudely be put 'have' and 'have-not', or between capital and labour, employer and employee. And these European-type distinctions are the less serious because there is no significant part of the population which is dependent wholly on wages for their subsistence. Most Tahitians can easily support themselves otherwise, and there is as yet no problem of over-population to complicate the economic pattern.

3. *The People of French Polynesia*

Tahitian society has been frequently referred to in the foregoing pages and some of its general characteristics have been mentioned. A more detailed analysis presents some difficulties. The general points can be made with some confidence, but there is an absence of that detailed anthropological or sociological research which would enable one to be equally confident about particular points. The crux of the difficulty is that although the old Tahitian society of pre- and early European days is reasonably well known, that society has been drastically changed by the European contact which will be described in the next section. Over one hundred and fifty years the Tahitians have interbred and intermarried, while the French policy of assimilation has replaced their institutions with French ones, so that Tahitian society has changed out of all recognition. It is this process of change and its results which has gone unstudied, until the position has been reached that more is known about Tahitian society two hundred years ago than today. The Tahitians now are deeply influenced by French culture (using the word in its anthropological sense), but the precise elements of French and Polynesian society, the emphasis upon them, their inter-relationships, need a great deal more research. Still, the outlines of the picture can be tentatively sketched in, although they may need some alteration, and the detail must be left to later study.

Tahitian society originally was characteristically Polynesian, although it seems probable that there were two quite different phases, in the last one of which conquerors imposed their rule on the previous inhabitants.[7] When the first Europeans arrived the population of Tahiti was probably about 50,000, living by agri-

[7] E. S. C. Handy, *History and Culture in the Society Islands* (Bernice P. Bishop Museum Bulletin 79, 1930), p. 7. The view is not undisputed.

culture and fishing and using comparatively simple equipment.[8] Except on the low islands, the physical basis of their existence was abundant, and the islands impressed the travellers with their fruitfulness. Moreover, there were extensive irrigation works in the valleys of Tahiti and the Marquesas, and some impressive stone buildings which testified to their skill as craftsmen. No doubt the basic unit of society was the agnatic family group, but when Cook landed there were quite different grades of society, although each had a firm family organization of which the symbol was the stone *marae* or temple.[9] There was a broad social division between the *hui arii,* the chief or ruling class (including their patrilineal relations, the *iatoai)* and the plebeian or landless commoners, the *mana hune,* who were the great bulk of the population. These two classes were further divided.[10] There were the *rangatira,* landed proprietors who may very well have been the result of intermarriage between the overlords and the superior families of the old population. Among the chiefs themselves, the *arii rii,* or little chiefs, occupied a place just above the *rangatira,* then came the *arii* or chiefs, and finally the *arii nui* or *rahi,* the important high-ranking chiefs. At the other end of the scale, among the *mana hune,* there was a group, not a social class, called *teu teu,* who were the hereditary retainers of the *arii,* always living with or near them; and there was a further class, despised by all, which provided the human sacrifices needed for ceremonial occasions: the *titi,* the mean or evil people.

This carefully graded society was held together by the genealogies of its chiefs and by their stewardship of the land and sea resources of the island.[11] Both land and the title of rank were controlled by the sub-chiefly families, although a high chief might depose or banish a sub-chief without affecting this control. Some of the tools of production were made under a chief's orders and

[8] The precise size of the population has been a matter of dispute, and guesses of early visitors varied widely; the suggested figure seems a reasonable conjecture; J. C. Beaglehole, *The Journals of Captain James Cook* (Hakluyt Society, Cambridge, 1955), vol. i, pp. clxxiv-clxxvii.

[9] R. W. Williamson, *The Social and Political Systems of Central Polynesia* (Cambridge, 1924), vol. ii, p. 60 ff.

[10] The social classes of Tahitian society, their inter-relationships and their nature, are not altogether clear, and scholars have disagreed about the interpretation of evidence. The picture presented in the text is based on Williamson, op. cit., vol. ii, p. 356 ff.; Handy, op. cit., p. 42 ff.; M. D. Sahlins, *Social Stratification in Polynesia* (American Ethnological Society, Seattle, 1958), p. 37 ff.; Teuira Henry, *Ancient Tahiti* (Bernice P. Bishop Museum Bulletin 48, 1928), p. 229.

[11] Sahlins, op. cit., p. 38.

were under his control, as were communal and craft production, while the sub-chief organized and supplied communal labour. There is no indication, however, that the chief controlled household production. Nevertheless, a chief could requisition from his inferiors at will in a way which suggested arbitrary force with the sanction of banishment or human sacrifice, although, as in Fijian society, reciprocity existed in the chief's organization of large-scale distributions of food and feasts, religious ceremonies and entertainments by the *arioi*. The chiefs derived their subsistence from their role in distribution, and were probably not horticulturalists themselves; and, of course, their importance and the area of their influence was closely connected with their genealogies and the nature of the country they controlled.

There were three clans which could claim some social primacy in Tahiti: Vaiari in the south-east, Punaauia in the west, where *arii nui* could wear the *maro-ura* or girdle of red feathers, and Papara in the south where *arii nui* wore both this girdle and the *maro-tea* of yellow feathers.[12] Nevertheless the politics of power cut across and complicated these divisions. The first political division was Teva, in which the *arii nui* of Papara dwelt, the second was Oropaa, which included Punaauia, and the third was Aharoa on the north coast, which was a loose alliance in which there was no powerful chief nor any strong organization, although in the district of Te Porionu there was the *arii nui* Tu whose father had married an *arii* of the sacred and historic island of Raiatea, held by some to be the cradle of Polynesia, and whose *marae* had risen in prestige by this connection. The social and religious honours accorded the *arii nui* did not necessarily imply political dominance, however, and among the *arii nui* themselves there was some kind of social equality and autonomy. The insignia of chieftainship did not in themselves represent the realities of political power nor, necessarily, the realities of a good deal of social life.

Many early observers stressed the arbitrary nature of chiefly power, symbolized by the large guest houses, the size of a canoe, the feather girdle, and more concretely by the *tabu* which surrounded his person.[13] Everything the high chief touched, the ground he walked on, the house he entered, became charged with

[12] Beaglehole, op. cit., p. clxxx ff.; Williamson, op. cit., vol. i, p. 170 ff.

[13] Sahlins, op. cit., p. 41, reviews the differing views of those observers who thought the chief absolute, and those who stressed the extent to which a chief's power was restrained by his dependence on sub-chiefs.

his *mana;* commoners did not stand erect in his presence; he was borne on the backs of special bearers. He might lay a *rahui* on his district preventing the use of the produce of land or sea, perhaps for his own convenience, more probably in preparation for some great festival or rite such as the birth of his child, and sometimes for the general welfare in the maturing season or when the fish were spawning. Yet, as in Fiji, there were limits to this chiefly power. Some of them were the limits of his district, both geographical and social. A sub-chief enjoyed considerable autonomy and this in itself was a limitation on the power of the *arii nui,* which made it necessary to take decisions with the consent of a council of sub-chiefs, and on such a council the sub-chiefs might speak freely. There might also be more public councils, in which the distinction between a chief and a commoner operated, although the same general point can be made about this Tahitian society as about Fijian: however absolute-seeming the chief, in fact he served his people, and in the last resort had to respond to their needs. The relationship was a reciprocal one, resting primarily on supernatural sanctions which gave considerable power to a class of priests, and only secondarily on physical sanctions. This Tahitian system of rank is also the general pattern of authority in the other islands of French Polynesia, although there are some differences. In the Marquesas there was the same broad division between chiefs and commoners, but many of the tribes as a whole had a much greater degree of authority, nor was the system of rank so much 'differentiated' as in Tahiti itself.[14] The chief organized large-scale production activities and also received surplus food and goods, and he possessed the general powers of *tabu* that the Tahitian *rahui* reveals, but most observers agreed that Marquesan chiefs wielded limited powers compared with Tahiti, and their position showed not absolutism but rather a patriarchal quality, buttressed by a council of elders. Nor was the *marae-tabu* power so complex. In the Tuamotus, where the physical basis of life is rather different, the system of rank also varied, but the low islands were generally settled from Tahiti and reproduce its essential features; the Pomare family in Tahiti had a Tuamotuan origin which they tried to conceal or ignore.

Tahitian society has been drastically changed in ways which will be discussed in the next section, although the degree of change has probably been less in the Marquesas, and perhaps in

[14] Handy, *The Native Cultures in the Marquesas* (Bernice P. Bishop Museum Bulletin 9, 1923), p. 59; Sahlins, op. cit., p. 72 ff.

the Tuamotus, than in the main islands of the Society group. The old Tahitian society is nevertheless important in political advancement principally because of one survival, kinship, which still operates strongly in Tahitian life, and also because the forces which worked on that society to break it down, if they succeeded in their purpose also left a legacy which colours the general attitude towards the Government and towards the French. Much of the present political situation in Tahiti can only be explained by its history: it has coloured what, for want of a better and more precise term, can only be called the 'climate of opinion'. Still, the end result of this breakdown has been to produce a society in which the old system of rank has gone, the old religion disappeared and the sanctions and *tabu* have vanished.[15]

The present Tahitian society is still horticultural. Even with the large urban concentration in Papeete which is dependent in part on wage labour, the countryside is important. Many Tahitians live in the villages scattered round the coast of the islands (in this differing from the older, more dispersed homesteads) where they can still maintain themselves without much difficulty on the produce of their gardens and the lagoons. There are probably few Tahitians in Papeete who do not either have land themselves or relations who can support them in the villages if necessary. Apart from wages, any desire for cash can be satisfied by the sale of copra, the preparation of vanilla and the sale of garden produce or fish in the markets; and the latter activity, especially, is sometimes organized on a communal or kinship basis which survives from the old social organization. There may be few 'pure' Tahitians, but this old village life underlies the urban settlements and, although the rank and religion (except for some superstitions which still operate) and social and political groupings may have disappeared, present society retains many Polynesian characteristics. It is also, of course, deeply influenced by French culture, although the precise intermingling and interaction of the two has yet to be studied.

If Tahitian society is at present unstudied, there is an even deeper ignorance which attaches to the Chinese community. It is

[15] N. Robson, 'French Oceania Takes Stock', *Pacific Affairs*, vol. xxvi, No. 1, pp. 42-3, states that the Tahitians still pay royal honours to the Pomare family and do not regard as chiefs the official chiefs of the districts. I could find no evidence for the first part of this statement which I believe to be erroneous, a view confirmed by anthropologists, like Dr Bengt Dannielsson and Professor D. Oliver, who have worked in the islands.

generally agreed that the Chinese control the retail trade, especially of the outer islands, but of their communal organization very little is known. Because of their legal (and therefore political) status they form a distinct group, but what Chinese customs rule their behaviour, their religion or their attitude to money it is impossible to say. Their rate of increase is not greater than the Tahitian as a communal group,[16] and their importance is chiefly their economic position and the degree of rural indebtedness which may exist (no one knows to what extent) to give them social and even political importance.[17] The predominantly French local families are, of course, deeply influenced by French manners, leading a life not very dissimilar from that of a provincial Frenchman, with its attitudes and values, but they, too, are difficult to distinguish from some predominantly Tahitian families whose ancestry is similar. Between a Tahitian villager and a French *entrepreneur* or lawyer the distinction is clear enough, but there is a whole range in between where it is less easy to draw. The metropolitan French are again a distinct group, transitory settlers usually serving a term of duty with the administration who will return to France or depart for some other colony. Their importance, other than the fact that they control the senior posts in the administration, is the degree to which both predominantly French and predominantly Tahitian local families may unite against them; an important point when one is considering anti-French sentiment, which usually means anti-metropolitan French. Even including the Chinese, Tahitian society has a unity which is imposed by fairly general acceptance of French language, French education and French manners, although it is important to remember Polynesian survivals, especially in the countryside.

4. *Historical Factors*

Tahiti was first discovered by the English Captain Wallis in 1767, and his enthusiastic reports of its fertility and the friendliness of its people led to its being selected for Captain Cook's observation of the transit of Venus in 1769. Bougainville paid an intermediate visit. The general agreement in their reports about this paradise of an island made it widely known in Europe: indeed

[16] According to the census figures it is less, but these should be accepted with reserve. The mortality rate among the Chinese is certainly lower.

[17] In addition to rural indebtedness which gives the Chinese some power over Tahitians who trade at their stores, there is probably a good deal of outright bribery of French and Tahitians by the Chinese.

it is more responsible than any other for the romantic appeal of the South Seas. But these early contacts were brief. In 1774 two Spanish priests from Peru spent a year there: Bligh spent five months in 1778-9 and his mutineers later returned there. There were a number of other visits but, again, they were brief. Nevertheless they happened to coincide with an alteration of the balance of power in Tahitian society.[18] The Papara family of Amo and his wife Purea, with their son, Teriirere, who was the high chief, had some claim to greatness in the Hapape district (where lay Matavai Bay, the anchorage of the visitors) through Purea's family. The father and mother were especially ambitious for the son for whom they built the vast *marae* at Mahaiatea and imposed a *rahui* on an unprecedented scale. Purea's female relations could not, or would not, stand this pride and challenged it, shortly after Wallis's visit, by ceremonial visits calculated to break the *rahui,* and subsequently by a military challenge headed by Vehiatua, *arii nui* of Seaward Teva, and a brother-in-law of Purea, Tuteha of Atehuru or Paea. This alliance marched on Papara from both sides, and Cook found the bones of the Papara men still strewing the sea-beach. Papara lost its political position although Teriirere still remained its *arii nui* and retained the yellow feather girdle, while Tuteha carried off the red to his own *marae,* an act which was confirmed by the defeated when they conceded the girdle to the young Tu. The latter was still a relatively insignificant *arii nui,* but the downfall of Papara removed one who overshadowed him. The successful coalition broke up after its victory when Tuteha quarrelled with Vehiatua, but was killed in the defeat of his own attack. Tu got reasonable peace terms, and more important, the peace left him still with the red feather, the sacred *marae* stone from Raiatea which he had acquired by his marriage, and one rival less. He was, in addition, in the best geographical position for trade with Matavai Bay and, therefore, to monopolize the European visitors, especially to obtain muskets from the *Bounty* mutineers. Thus the earliest European contacts, although they did not vitally or radically affect Tahitian society, coincided with political strife and offered the technical means by which the traditional order could be subverted by an ambitious chief. By 1790 Tu could be regarded by the Europeans as 'king' of Tahiti, and even Cook had already assumed that he had some such position; being treated as a king he was encouraged to behave like one.

[18] Beaglehole, op. cit., p. clxxxiv ff.

The muskets and the prestige of Europeans at Matavai Bay may have been the foundation of Tu's (later called Pomare) rise to power, a rise which itself began to upset the traditional system of rank and prestige, but the missionaries were quite as important in the changes which affected Tahitian society. Pomare's physical force might prevail to give him prestige, but his authority might never have been generally accepted had the old system of rank maintained its strength: Pomare's position was made secure by the breakdown of Tahitian society under, especially, the impact of Christianity. In 1797 the newly formed London Missionary Society established in Tahiti the first Protestant mission in the Pacific; they settled at Matavai Bay. Unlike the early navigators they were less impressed by the 'paradise', but saw rather that Tahiti was 'the very seat of Satan' and, with notable exceptions like Nott, consistently misunderstood social and political institutions.[19] In the first eleven years the mission twice came near to failure; the first time in 1798 when the captain of the brig *Nautilus* refused, on their advice, to barter muskets, resulting in four of the missionaries being set upon by an angry crowd. A number of the others thereupon withdrew in the brig, leaving only seven of their brethren who felt that not much progress was being made. Three of them left, for different reasons, the defections being offset by new workers in 1801. Slow progress was made with preaching and a school, but the real grounds for conversion no doubt lay in the change set in motion in Tahitian society by European material goods and the corresponding effects in social and political institutions.[20]

Pomare learned to associate the spreading of his political power with European friendship and the goods it brought, the settled missionaries being the principal agents in both; as interpreters and mediators they smoothed contacts with other Europeans. For Tahiti was beginning to have a trade in hogs, which the missionaries encouraged by making Matavai the safest port in the Pacific. They realized that they could not prevent the trade in muskets, and so made sure that these weapons passed safely into the hands of their protector, Pomare, and his son, Pomare II, who succeeded his father in 1803. The pretensions of the Pomare family strengthened resentment among other traditionally im-

[19] A. A. Koskinen, *Missionary Influence as a Political Factor in the Pacific Islands* (Helsinki, 1953), pp. 36-7. (The missionary kingdom is also discussed by Morrell, op. cit., p. 39 ff.)

[20] ibid., pp. 26-7.

portant families but, in 1802, when these resentments provoked a crisis, the Europeans joined Pomare's expedition with the support of the missionaries. A fresh attempt by his rivals to destroy Pomare in 1808 led to their abandoning the station while Pomare's fortunes fluctuated: he himself made his headquarters for a time in Moorea. These years of disorder, which made Tahiti unattractive to traders in general, led those who came to trust only Pomare who in the end was victorious. Tribal loyalties remained after his victory, but tribal independence was at an end.

Whites and traders had visited the island in considerable numbers, often remaining ashore for considerable periods, and after 1820 a number of reputable traders settled there, but missionary influence was dominant and it created a Tahitian 'kingdom'. At the end of the war in 1815, Pomare had already become a Christian, and after his victory wholesale conversion followed with, of course, drastic effects on the old institutions. The missionaries supplied an answer to the crumbling away of the old order, as another of their brethren had in Griqualand, by calling together an assembly of chiefs to prepare a code of laws.[21] Pomare refused such an assembly but himself drafted a simple code which was promulgated in 1819 in the course of the annual meeting of the Tahitian mission. The code proved unworkable in less than three years, but Pomare's death and the succession of an infant removed the barrier to co-operation from other chiefs who now met to constitute a parliament and prepare a further code which would define their own relations and provide them with a law to replace with revenue the tribute system which had vanished. The parliament consisted of the adult male members of the royal family and the families of principal chiefs who were hereditary members, together with two elected representatives from each district of Tahiti and Moorea. Of this assembly Nott became president. Forty laws were promulgated, the last eight concerned with administration and revenue, the remainder constituting a moral code to ensure Sabbath observance, moral laws and the like. These political changes also coincided with an increased interest in trading by the chiefs themselves; together the two things completed the disruption of the old system of rank. By these changes, the basis of the chiefs' authority had been sapped, with the result that the people who were less involved with either politics or trade began to seek their leadership elsewhere, notably among the whalers and beachcombers. In 1827 an organization

[21] ibid., p. 55 ff. (Also *see* Morrell, op. cit., pp. 42-3.)

was formed to oppose the new society by justifying the old order in moral terms.[22] It was crushed; but in 1830, as the *Mamaia*, it seized its opportunity to encourage the queen to demand homage of the chiefs according to ancient custom. By 1831 the island was on the verge of civil war; in 1833 an actual clash occurred when the *Mamaia* areas disavowed their representatives' consent to the queen's remarriage. This revolt was also crushed, but its defeat had the effect of causing and accentuating the rejection of the new moral code, and increasing prostitution and drunkenness, a tendency aided by some European residents and visitors. It was checked by a temperance society, a prohibition law rigidly enforced by the Government and compulsory church attendance, which in turn provoked further revolt, a focus being found in the arrival in 1835 of two French Roman Catholic priests. The danger was recognized by the chiefs and the missionaries who forcibly removed the intruders, an act which brought to Tahiti a French frigate under du Petit-Thouars to demand reparation.[23] His arrival occurred when the Government was again losing its authority, with a breach between the royal family and the chiefs reviving old rivalries and expressing itself in the parties formed in parliament. The growing lawlessness and the collapse of the Government were conditions present when du Petit-Thouars introduced the factor of international politics.

Law and order in Tahitian society had been a problem every time a whaling boat arrived, met to some extent by the appointment of consular agents like Pritchard and Moerenhout, but the failure of such jurisdiction raised, as it did in Fiji, the question of a protectorate or annexation. French trading interests were negligible compared with British and American, yet there was a vociferous French group; all of them were clamorous for European justice and for some security, although not necessarily for a firm measure of control. The divisions within Tahiti provided chiefs in opposition to Pomare with the need for French support and, in 1841, Moerenhout's treaty began to take on the proportions of a request for political protection from France at a time when some of the newer missionaries were beginning to think desirable a separation between church and state. In 1842 France annexed the Marquesas which had long had a Catholic mission but which were relatively untouched by the factors influencing Tahiti itself;

[22] ibid., p. 102 ff.

[23] Ph. Rey Lescure, *Histoire de Tahiti (Abrégé)* (Société d'Etudes Océaniennes, 1958), p. 58; Morrell, op. cit., p. 71 ff.

and in the same year du Petit-Thouars arriving in Tahiti was presented with a resounding declaration, organized by Moerenhout, for French protection, which he accepted, the administration to be carried on by the queen and French officers. The British Government accepted the protectorate. The first Governor, Bruat, had ruled the Marquesas as a naval base under martial law which was extended to Tahiti in 1845 after the provisional Government broke down because of the queen's hope for British protection fostered by Consul Pritchard. The fighting and confusion which followed lasted for three years, Tahitian resistance concentrating in the valleys of Papenoo, Punaauia, Faaa, Pare and Arue, their camps being considered by Bruat as the nucleus of English hostility to the French and the regular visits of English warships being interpreted as encouragement to the rebels. The French victory in 1847 led to Pomare's taking her place under the protectorate, while the chiefs were in general maintained in their titles. The corner-stone of the state set up by the Convention of 1847 was the Tahitian Assembly, elected by district landholders, and a Tahitian judiciary nominated by the queen and the Governor; it was never ratified by the French. By 1848, the French administration was in fact limited to the supervision of European and Tahitian justice and control of the main ports; its finances were weak. The power of the Governor meant that his decisions became law after publication in the local gazette. By 1860, the administrative framework needed readjustment.

French policy was guided by the belief that French principles and institutions were superior to Polynesian, both technically and ideally, and that therefore they were desirable wherever the natives could be forced or persuaded or taught to accept them. The collapse of the protectorate led in 1880 to annexation, and in 1885 to the provision of a constitution, the Organic Decree of 28 December, which endeavoured to consolidate and extend the policy of assimilation which had been followed piecemeal in the previous years.[24] The general effect was to accelerate the pace of evolution from the old chiefly rights to a centralized authority and a formal number of district office holders. Institutions of French government were introduced to represent both the white and the native population. Economically, a change from a subsistence to a surplus economy was encouraged, with an attempt

[24] *J.O.E.F.O.*, 1885. The annexation of the other island groups now included in the colony was also piecemeal, F. J. West, 'French Polynesia', *Encyclopaedia Britannica* (1961).

also to ensure the transfer of land to Europeans by individualizing all land holdings. The policy was assimilation of the islanders to French culture, and the replacement of traditional institutions by French ones.[25]

Assimilation implied a number of things: legal assimilation to the obligations and penalties of French civil and penal codes; the extension of French education, language, customs and values; economic assimilation by the extension of metropolitan tariffs to local trade; the liberal donation of French nationality to the Polynesians; it also implied, of course, that there was a limit to any eventual local aspirations towards autonomy and that ultimate political control was in Paris. From 1883 the naval officer who had administered Tahiti and the other islands which had been welded into the colony was replaced by civil officials under the Organic Decree. Full military and naval power was vested in the Governor (as a representative of the President of the Republic) who had five principal officials: the director of the interior, attorney-general, chief of naval administration, medical superintendent, and treasurer-paymaster, all of whose powers were defined. The colony was given an elected General Council of eighteen members, with clear but limited duties; the Governor *had* to accept their opinion only on the revision of electoral lists, purchase of property by the administration, transactions with private companies, public charities, pensions, and taxes apart from customs and wharf fees to meet the expenses of the colony.[26] The Council's control over expenditure was limited to optional as distinct from obligatory expenses. A commune of Papeete was created by this Council in 1890, consisting of a mayor and fourteen members.[27] District administration was also by local council in each district under a chief, by French administrators posted in administrative divisions and by the colonial *gendarmerie.*[28]

With one important exception, these institutions existed in Tahiti up to the Second World War. The exception was the General Council which ended in a series of tedious wrangles and personal feuds, especially over the colony's finances; the Council

[25] S. H. Roberts, *History of French Colonial Policy* (London, 1929), p. 512 ff.

[26] *J.O.E.F.O.*, 1886, p. 140. Elected four from Papeete, six from Tahiti and Moorea, four from the Tuamotus, two from the Marquesas, and two from the Gambiers and the Australs.

[27] *J.O.E.F.O.*, 1890, p. 499.

[28] The *Annuaire* (Papeete) of 1905 contains a description of this local administration.

became a safety valve for local settlers (since the Tahitians were excluded by the language qualifications from membership) without sufficient power to move the administration.[29] In 1895 a demand was made for complete fiscal and administrative autonomy which was ignored, and the Council preferred dissolution to ineffectiveness. It was ended in 1903, the old Administrative Council being revived in its place, consisting of the Governor's nominated Privy Council, two nominated residents, the mayor of Papeete and the five administrators of the outer groups. The main cause of the Council's troubles was the consistently weak financial position of the colony which ran up a considerable colonial debt, but even had it worked, it touched very little upon the bulk of the population, still living in its settlements or villages under the system of district administration. The district councils laboured under difficulties. They could not be made into municipal bodies while they were incapable of handling finances and while few could speak French or understand French legislation. There were, too, conflicts of authority between the appointed chiefs who were presidents of the district councils, the *gendarmes*, and the pastors of the Tahitian church. In general it may be said that these councils worked badly or not at all, and affairs in the districts were more and more influenced by party politics at Papeete (which led to competition for votes in the districts) and by the local *gendarme*.

Before the Second World War, French Oceania was administered by a Governor, assisted by a Privy Council of eight official and nominated members, but the Administrative Council had been replaced, after enlargement to twenty in 1930, by the *Délégations Economiques et Financières*, a representative body which was set up in 1932.[30] The *Délégations* consisted of six nominated members: the mayor of Papeete, the presidents of the chambers of agriculture and commerce, the Administrators of the Leeward group, the Gambiers and the Marquesas, and seven members elected by the council of Papeete, the chambers of agriculture and commerce, the municipal commission of Uturoa, and the district councils of Tahiti, Moorea and the Tuamotus. Six years later a permanent commission of five members resident in or near Papeete was created to discharge the *Délégations'* functions of advice on economic and budgetary matters while

[29] Roberts, op. cit., p. 53.

[30] *J.O.E.F.O.*, 1932, p. 568; the Privy Council, which had been merged in the Administrative Council in 1912, was also set up anew in 1932.

they were not in session. The major powers were all in the hands of the Governor, including fiscal and budgetary matters, so that although the *Délégations* ought to be consulted their function was in fact advisory. In any case, it was in effect a nominated body, representative of a fairly narrow range of interests. The logic of French colonial policy centralized power in Paris, which worked through the Governor and metropolitan officials on the spot, while specialist services like education and health were run by the corresponding departments in Paris through officials in the colony appointed by them. But the logic of assimilation did not, before the war, offer Tahitian representation in French constitutional bodies: Oceania sent neither deputies nor senators to the Assembly, although it had a member in the High Colonial Council which was an advisory body of experts. Such outlet for political energies as there was was confined to an advisory body, a municipal council, a municipal commission and whatever could be made of the district councils which were in effect official rather than representative organs.

Assimilation in practice was not a matter of institutions, although these were the necessary formal instruments of it, but of the actual influence of French values on the Tahitians. The early history of the colony before the French protectorate had led, especially in Tahiti and more slowly elsewhere in the islands, to the almost complete breakdown of the old system of rank and authority. In theory, this had been replaced by French institutions, but until such difficult questions as land tenure, literacy in French, individual economic effort and the low calibre of many French officials had been solved by education, development and the simple passage of time, these institutions could not work well when they worked at all. In the early stages assimilation was hampered by missionary education (which, while taken over by a French society, remained Protestant), Polynesian indifference in their state between the old world and the new and the persistent tendency of the French to use Tahiti as a 'dumping ground' for bad officials (the turnover in governors was particularly rapid). Polynesian life was nevertheless slowly penetrated by French values and attitudes, and French institutions began to be accepted into Polynesian life. After the Second World War assimilation had created a society which was homogeneous in a very real sense, and it is with the institutions and developments within that society that the next chapters will be concerned.

CHAPTER V

THE STRUCTURE OF TAHITIAN GOVERNMENT

When the *rapporteur* of the Brazzaville conference declared in 1944 that 'we conceive the Empire in the Roman sense of the word not the Anglo-Saxon',[1] he was reasserting the assimilationist tradition of colonial policy which, apparently modified by doctrines of 'association' and 'federation' in the first draft constitution of the Fourth Republic, dominated the constitution which was actually accepted in 1946. The Empire was still France Overseas, with all that implied in colonial practice, and the colonies must conform to the model of France herself. But if the tradition was reasserted, some concessions had been made, and as well as metropolitan forms the local circumstances had also changed, less in Tahiti than other parts of the Empire but still significantly. The French Establishments in Oceania had been among the first colonies to declare for General de Gaulle, but only after a *coup d'état* which removed the pro-Vichy administration; this division of opinion still has effect in political life. Control from Paris ceased, and the colony was thrown upon its own resources together with whatever could be spared from the allied war effort. Tahitians served in the French Pacific battalion. The general result was the opening up of wider horizons for the Tahitians and the beginning of a movement which may loosely be called 'nationalism' although, as will be seen, the term has a peculiar Tahitian connotation. Thus, at the end of the war, when the time came to re-create normal colonial government, the changes in French institutions found new conditions in the colony. Such local conditions had in themselves little or no influence upon metropolitan ones which, when they produced discussion of colonial policy and practice, did so with the African colonies in mind, but the logic which sought to provide a constitution for the Empire as a whole also applied to Tahiti. The

[1] C. A. Julien, 'From French Empire to French Union', *International Affairs*, xxvi, No. 4.

colony shared common institutions, but their actual operation was peculiarly Tahitian.

1. *The Representative Assembly*

The first reorganization in Tahiti was carried out under the Provisional Government of General de Gaulle which assumed that the first draft constitution of the Fourth Republic would be accepted. On 31 August 1945 a decree set up a Representative Assembly in the French Establishments in Oceania, elected by universal suffrage with considerable power in local affairs, and modelled upon the General Council of a metropolitan French department.[2] The *conseil général,* under both the Third and Fourth Republics, has been a local elected body with considerable control over departmental affairs, especially in budgetary matters, and to which the Prefect has been responsible for departmental matters distinct from state ones. In one capacity the Prefect has been the chief executive officer of the *conseil général,* which has usually contained many men eminent in national political life as well as those who have predominantly local interests. In another capacity the Prefect has had tutelary powers which he exercises as an official of state responsible to the Minister of the Interior and the national Government. The creation of a Representative Assembly marks the assimilation of colonial practice to this metropolitan form and the Governor occupies a position analogous to the Prefect. The Tahitian constitution, therefore, represented the projection of departmental organization into the colony, and the administrative services follow the same pattern in distinguishing between territorial ones and those of the state.

The Representative Assembly consisted of twenty members,[3] elected by direct universal suffrage of French citizens of both sexes in one electoral college, following the method of *scrutin de liste* in constituencies where there were two seats. Candidates could be citizens of either sex, domiciled in the constituency, more

[2] B. Chapman, *Introduction to French Local Government* (London, 1953), pp. 63-79.

[3] *J.O.E.F.O.,* 1945, p. 277. Elected by *circonscriptions* distributed as follows: four to Papeete, two Tahiti West, two Tahiti East, one Presqu'île and Taravao and one for the other dependencies of Tahiti; five to Leeward Isles (one each to Tahaa, the commune of Uturoa, Raiatea, Huahine, Bora Bora and Maupiti and its archipelago); two to the Tuamotus (Tuamotu North and Tuamotu South including the Gambiers); two to the Marquesas (North and South) and one to the Australs.

than twenty-one years of age, living in the colony for at least three years, who could read, write and speak French, and who were not officials or members of the Privy Council. Members of the Assembly were unpaid, but might claim transport costs and a daily indemnity. To be elected they must obtain an absolute majority with a total poll equal to at least a quarter of enrolled electors. The *Conseil du Contentieux Administratif* might judge cases of irregularity or annulment. The life of the Assembly was to be four years unless it was dissolved by order of the Ministry of France Overseas. During that time, it should meet twice a year, in May and in November (for the budget session) on the summons of the Governor who could also call a special session either on his own initiative or at the request of two-thirds of the Assembly. The Governor or his delegate opened the session, whereupon the Assembly elected a president, vice-president and two secretaries, who organized its business and discipline, and a Permanent Commission of five members, analogous to the *commission départmentale,* to sit between sessions; the quorum was half the members. The proceedings of the Assembly were published as soon as possible.

The Governor had the right of entry to all sessions, in which the secretary-general of the Government, or another delegated official, represented the administration, while the heads of the departments of the administration were authorized by the Governor to address the Assembly on matters within their competence. Foreign affairs or the internal affairs of France could not be discussed, but within those limits the Assembly could discuss any questions relating to the colony, all economic questions and all questions of general administration. It might take final decisions on a range of matters: the management of buildings and real estate of the colony, roads and other public works on the local budget, the granting of forestry and mining rights except to foreigners, encouragement of production, loans and financial guarantees entered into by the colony on the basis of its own resources, the organization of savings banks, endowment and allocation of travelling scholarships, housing and co-operatives, tourist activities, infant and social welfare charged to local services and control of local stamp revenue. There were further matters upon which the Assembly should be consulted without having the power of final decisions, such as the administrative organization of the territory, of education, property, labour and social security, local prisons, regulation of land and property rights and civic procedure except the judiciary. It might also, within the local system of tariffs, impose import and export duties and other levies.

Its most important power, however, was its voting of the budget of the colony, raised from indirect taxation by duties, which was prepared by the Governor in Privy Council, with the sole right reserved to him of proposing revenue. As in the old General Council, the budget was divided into *dépenses obligatoires* and *dépenses facultatives*. The former category included expenses of the Governor and his establishment and secretariat, salaries and allowances of officials appointed within the framework established by legislative measures, maintenance of the services of justice, police, security, and customs, education, public health, debts of the colony, superannuation, special funds, expenses charged by law to the local budget, and public works and social measures already debated by the Assembly. If the obligatory sections were not passed, or if insufficient funds were provided, the Governor in Privy Council could raise the necessary money by reducing the optional section, using 'free' funds, or by credit assigned to the local budget by decree on the report of the Ministry of France Overseas. The Governor could not alter the optional section of the budget except for the preceding purpose, or if the amount exceeded the ordinary resources of revenue after the obligatory section had been discharged; and the Minister for France Overseas finally decided on all such changes or modifications. If the Assembly failed to vote the budget at all, the Governor might fix it by decree at the previous level. Any supplementary estimates were to be discussed by the Assembly and ordered by the Governor in Privy Council, but operations financed by the French Overseas Development Fund (FIDES) did not come under their scrutiny. Even with such limitations, the Assembly could exercise considerable control and influence over local affairs and administration, and in addition it might address non-political observations to the Minister in Paris.

This limitation upon political discussion did not deprive French Oceania of a voice in political life, for the constitution of the Fourth Republic, when it was accepted by referendum in October 1946, provided the colony with a deputy in the National Assembly (the old Chamber), in the Council of the Republic (the old Senate), and in the Assembly of the French Union (a new body). These representatives might express themselves on political questions. The constitution of the Fourth Republic also brought changes to Tahiti itself by modifying some of the provisions of the provisional Government's decree. On 25 October 1946 a new decree relating to the Representative Assembly was issued.[4] The life of the Assembly was extended to five years, the age of candidates was raised to twenty-three, the date of the budgetary session was changed to July or August. More important changes were that the deliberations of the Assembly on taxes and customs were only to be applicable after approval by the French cabinet, and that such approval ought to issue in a decree within eighty days of the arrival of the deliberation of the Assembly at the colonial ministry; if within this period no decree had been issued, the deliberation should be deemed approved and effective. It was also provided that the initiative in the budget belonged to both the Governor and the Assembly. The general effect of the changes was to strengthen control from Paris as part of the reassertion of assimilation against federation in the draft of the rejected constitution. Further changes were made when the term of office of the first Assembly expired in 1951. A draft Bill, supported by all political parties in Tahiti during a visit of a French parliamentary committee, was before the Assembly in Paris, being introduced by the leader of the party with which the Tahitian deputy voted.[5] The new legislation made some important changes. The composition of the Assembly, now called Territorial not Representative, was to be twenty-five members,[6] and other important changes related to the qualifications of candidates, who needed no longer to be resident in the constituency for which they stood, must have lived for two years in the colony not three, and needed only to speak French not to read and write it. The second Assembly in Tahiti was elected in January and February 1953, and it lasted until November 1957 when new elections were held, but once again under a new constitution.

From 1953 onwards, the Ministry of France Overseas had been considering plans for the Union which modified assimilation by greater decentralization and increased local autonomy, and in April of the following year the Minister declared in the Assembly

[4] ibid., 1946, p. 56.

[5] Robson, loc. cit., p. 34.

[6] *J.O.E.F.O.*, 1952, *Arrêté* of 22 October promulgating Law 52-1175 of 2 October 1952, elected from nineteen constituencies as follows: Papeete five, Tahiti West two, Tahiti East two, Presqu'île and Taravao one, Moorea and Maiao one, Makatea one; in the Leeward Isles no change was made from the five earlier members; nor to the representation of the Marquesas; but the Australs got two members instead of one and the Tuamotus and Gambiers four instead of two.

that 'the hour has come to envisage decisive reforms for the future of the French Union'. Nothing was done until 1956 when, Indo-China having been lost and colonial nationalism creating difficult problems, Gaston Defferre developed these plans into the *loi-cadre*. On 23 June 1956 the National Assembly in Paris passed Law 56-619 authorizing the Government to put into effect reforms and measures to ensure the evolution of overseas territories, a law prompted entirely by the affairs of the great African colonies, by virtue of which the Governor of French Oceania promulgated, on 10 August 1957, a further law of the National Assembly passed on 22 July previous, reorganizing the Territorial Assembly of what was now called French Polynesia. The membership was increased to thirty,[7] elected by proportional representation by the method of *scrutin de liste*. These were technical changes, but the actual powers of the Assembly were also extended with its size. It was empowered to make resolutions about territorial laws in matters of the general status of agents of territorial services, civil procedure (except judicial), the regulation of the *état-civil* within the framework of the laws which organize it, the land of the territory, real estate, internal commerce, syndicates and co-operatives, agriculture, forests, inland waters, soil conservation, animal husbandry, fishing, production, certain exports, internal transport and navigation, hygiene and public health, beverages, delinquent children and the mentally sick, tourism, urbanism, first- and second-stage education, and professional and technical instruction except syllabuses and examinations, scholarships in the territorial budget, libraries and cultural centres, sport, social assistance, the penitential system, the expenses of justice, foreigners exercising certain professions, and agreements with the State over radio and television programmes. The resolutions of the Assembly in these matters could be passed notwithstanding any earlier laws but under the limitation of international conventions, and they had the force of territorial laws which the Assembly could repeal or amend. The Assembly might also resolve on the local operation of the plan of equipment and development of the law of 30 April 1946, and on all matters affecting the 'patrimony' of the colony and public works established by the Governor or the Council of Government. Again, under the limits of international conventions and certain French laws, it might resolve on

[7] *J.O.P.F.*, 1957, pp. 443, 446, of which sixteen came from *circonscription* of the Windward Isles, six from the Leeward, two from the Australs, two from the Marquesas, four from the Tuamotu-Gambiers.

financial matters raised by any project of the Council of Government relating to levies, taxes and dues, to the profit of the local budget, concessions, rights of occupation in domanial land, creation and suppression of territorial public services and public institutions, the territory's participation in the capital of State companies or even private ones concerned with economic development, loans and the use of budget funds in measures for the encouragement of production. The Assembly must be consulted on all of these affairs and especially upon orders in the Council of Government dealing with the overall organization of public services, their officials' conditions of pay, service, leave, pensions and so on, and the question of administrative divisions and boundaries. It must also be consulted on the regulation of the price index and the representation of the colony's economic interests. The Governor was also under the necessity of informing it about administrative accounts in the budget and the annual financial situation, and its observations were to be forwarded with a copy of the accounts to Paris. The resolutions of the Assembly were to be put into effect by an order of the Governor who, if he wanted to have such a resolution annulled by the Minister for France Overseas, had to inform the Assembly, after he had asked that the resolution be considered a second time, that he considered this to be in the general interest or for good administration, such action to be taken within thirty days of the first resolution. The grounds for annulment by the Minister were excess of power by the Assembly or violation of the law.

2. *The Council of Government*

The *loi-cadre* represented a liberal reform which still was based upon French models. The Assembly's power was enlarged in a way which brought it closer to the *conseil général,* and the increase in its power and competence brought the office of the Governor closer to that of the Prefect in his relations with the Assembly, but in another aspect it marked an advance on metropolitan practice. The creation of a Council of Government introduced an executive body which had been foreshadowed in French departmental government but never achieved, and it introduced a chief executive beside the Governor, although not replacing him. The Council was composed of six to eight members having the title of Minister, elected by the Assembly. The minister elected at the head of the list had the title of Vice-President of the Council because the Governor, styled *chef du territoire,* was *ex-officio* president; the former presides in the latter's absence. The Council could resign if it felt that it no longer had the confidence of the Assembly, and each minister had to answer questions within his competence put to him by members of the Assembly. To qualify as a minister, a man must be a French citizen of at least twenty-five years, but he need not be a member of the Assembly. The election was by a list of candidates, or a choice between several lists, which must be chosen or rejected in their entirety; and if no list had obtained an absolute majority on the second vote, the third might be elected by a relative one; new lists might be put up after each vote. Those elected held office until they resigned or the mandate of the Assembly which elected them ran out; they might not remain in office after the end of the Assembly by which they were elected, although they might carry on until a new Council elected by a new Assembly replaced them. The ministers must regard their discussions as secret, and they might not also be members of the Government of the Republic, President of the Territorial Assembly, or President or member of the Permanent Commission of the Assembly; if they were in this position, they must make a choice between their offices. Provision was also made for the Vice-President to propose the dismissal of a minister to the Governor, and such a vacant seat could be filled by an election by absolute majority of the Assembly; several vacant seats involved a new Council elected by list. The ministers received a salary and expenses voted by the Assembly in the territorial budget.

The functions of the Council of Government were both individual and collegial. As a group, its members were collectively responsible for the measures ordered by it, and all proposals about business of territorial interest which were to be submitted to the Assembly or its Permanent Commission had to be taken in the Council; and then handled by the minister for the particular department affected. The Governor must make his orders in the Council relating to the regulation of economic and commercial life, prices, weights and measures, fairs and markets, production, administrative divisions and posts, rural collectivities, territorial services and their conditions of service, primary education, and the application of the labor code. The heads of the territorial service departments were placed under the authority of ministers and were nominated by the Governor in the Council on the proposal of the relevant minister. The Council might discuss all questions of territorial 'patrimony' and public works, but only after the resolutions of the Assembly. In case of urgency, however, the Governor in the Council might make immediate orders to suspend or reduce duties affecting articles of production, but such orders must subsequently be submitted to the Assembly or its Permanent Commission if the former were not in session. If the Council exceeded its powers in the opinion of the Governor, or seemed to be a danger to public order or security, he might secure the annulment of a decision by a report to the Minister for France Overseas, who must take the opinion of the French Cabinet and reach such a decision within three months. The acts of the Council might also be challenged before the cabinet as a *cour du contentieux;* any act of the Council taken without the presence of the Governor, his deputy, or the Vice-President, was invalid. Each year the Vice-President, consulting the Council, was required to submit a report to the Assembly on the general work of the Council, and the progress of territorial services.

Individually, a minister was charged, by delegation from the Governor after consultation with the Vice-President, with the handling of one or more departments of the territorial service. He then became responsible to the Council for its functioning and for the administration of the affairs relevant to the department, and had to keep them regularly informed. He must take all decisions about the progress of departmental affairs, with the exception of those assigned to the Council as a whole or to the Assembly. To assist him, he might, within the limits of the budget voted by the Assembly, appoint a secretariat, and he should direct the service itself by officials to whom he delegated power as necessary. All projects and reports belonging to his department had to be presented to the Council as well as to the Assembly where he had to conduct the discussion of his departmental business under direction from the Council, assisted perhaps by an official of the service in question. Such officials were appointed by the Governor on the proposal of a minister, as were the agents of the service. Any minister in these individual functions must observe the same professional secrecy as the officials of the service.

This new constitution or *loi-cadre* came into effect in late 1957. It provided the institutions by which the citizens of French Polynesia could both discuss policy and take decisions, and it also provided an executive agency for carrying out those decisions while itself having considerable influence upon them. It provided, in short, legislative and executive organs which bore a strong resemblance to the National Assembly and the cabinet in France itself, although it reserved final power to the Governor, as the representative of the President of the Republic, who was in any case the medium by which decisions and resolutions were put into effect. The final power was not intended to be used often, however, and the whole structure imposed the closest co-operation on the Governor. The *loi-cadre* offered the chance of considerable local autonomy, with the possibility of development into responsible government, and provided institutions by which political advancement could occur in an orderly manner; it also represented a considerable degree of decentralization from Paris, and some real power in local affairs. In essentials, this *loi-cadre* still exists in French Polynesia, having survived a political crisis at the time of the de Gaulle referendum in September-October 1958, and being retained when the Assembly came to vote on its future under the de Gaulle constitution; it voted for the *status quo,* with the difference that the individual functions of ministers were abridged in favour of the collegial functions of the Council of Government.[8]

3. *The Communes*

Perhaps the most striking fact about this framework of government is the extent to which it is central development: the recent constitution, marking considerable decentralization from Paris, has emphasized a centralized administration in Tahiti itself and left the local government untouched. Unlike Fiji, for example, where the Fijian Administration has developed local authorities, in French Polynesia local government has always been relatively unimportant. The most significant local agencies are the communes. Before the war Papeete had a mayor and council elected by the citizens of the town and since the war Uturoa, formerly a municipal commission, has become a commune too. The constitution for Papeete was approved by a decree of 20 April 1890, which established a mayor and fourteen councillors who were to meet four or five times a year to execute sales, approve leases, make decisions on municipal works and have in charge the police, the port facilities, the *octroi de mer* and public buildings, within the defined boundaries of the commune.[9] To finance these works, the council

[8] *J.O.P.F.*, 1958, *Arrêté* 1090 of 9 October, in the interests of public order suspended the Council of Government until a new one was set up; *Session Extraordinaire de l'Assemblée Territoriale*, 14 November 1958.

[9] *J.O.E.F.O.*, 1890, p. 499. The other commune of Uturoa was created in 1945; *J.O.E.F.O.*, 1945, p. 184.

prepared and voted a budget, which was then submitted to the General Council. This, with some modifications, is still the function of the commune, but since 1953 the communes have had their own budgets, and power to levy small taxes for local purposes. The commune set certain limits to the power of the Assembly, and in doing so it raised the possibility of squabbles over jurisdiction. Its existence, however, established another local elected body which offered the citizens of Papeete some control over their own affairs, and it also represented the commercial interests of the town as a unit capable of exercising political and economic pressure on the Assembly itself. Uturoa, being more distant, is less capable of this kind of pressure, although it, too, represents commercial interests.

4. *The District Chiefs and Councils*

Just as the communes represent urbanization in political life, so the district chiefs and councils represent the countryside. In 1852 it had been proposed to formalize the appointment of district chiefs, hitherto selected after consultation with the local families, into an electoral system, while specifying that they should be chosen from the family whose member left the vacancy if there were a suitable candidate; if not the queen or the Governor appointed. In 1855 the Council was defined as the chief, the judge, the *mutoi* (Tahitian policeman) and two elected landholders, and its business was defined as the provision of labour for the upkeep of roads, tax collection, registration of births and deaths, and the registration of contracts concerning land, all decisions requiring the Governor's approval. The chief and the districts were regarded as administrative units, and in 1877 their functions were largely transferred to the *gendarmerie*, leaving only the responsibility for hearing land cases. Since 1897 the composition of the district councils has been five members (plus two supplementary ones), including a president and an *adjoint*, all elected by universal suffrage and *scrutin de liste*.[10] They are unpaid, but for special functions the president may be allowed expenses. A district council is elected for four years and is renewed at the same time as the municipal ones; they may be suspended by the Governor. The president is charged with publishing the Governor's orders, the upkeep of buildings and roads and yearly amendments to the census and electoral lists. The

[10] *J.O.E.F.O.*, 1897, p. 363.

council may propose improvements in the district to the administration. The president is further charged with postal surveillance and the upkeep of the police duties. The district councils have very little power or initiative in deciding policy within a district, because the whole tendency of administration has been to use them as official instruments, not so much for the execution of policy as to exercise a loose kind of supervision over very limited aspects of government: they are in fact dependent on the central administration, and represent its views and wishes rather than existing in any representative capacity for the Tahitians in the villages.[11]

5. *The Chambers of Commerce and Agriculture*

There are two further bodies which must be noted as offering the chance to discuss policy within certain limits, and to offer advice to the Government: these are the Chambers of Commerce and Agriculture which may express their opinion on measures for the benefit of local commerce and local agriculture and cultivation.[12] Both organizations stand outside the local government structure. They consist of certain officials and other members elected by their registered members who, in the one case, are those practising in commerce and in the other the agricultural population. They should be consulted on measures within their sphere of interest, but their status is purely advisory. They do, however, constitute two additional pressure groups which, with the existence of an elective Assembly, can, if they choose, exercise some influence upon policy, especially since they, too, tend to represent the views of people living in or near Papeete and, therefore, at the centre of power.

Such are the institutions which, in differing degrees, offer to all Tahitians the chance of discussing policy so far as it applies to the internal development of the colony, and in the case of the Council of Government since 1957 some executive control of the territorial services. It remains, therefore, to ask what are the institutions of primarily executive significance. Since Tahitian society draws no legal or social distinction between its members, posts in the administration are open to Tahitians equally with French, if they have the necessary educational qualifications.

[11] In 1932 an *Arrêté* of 7 October created a special official to supervise the chiefs of the districts of Tahiti, Moorea, Maiao and Makatea.

[12] *J.O.E.F.O.*, 1887, p. 139; *J.O.E.F.O.*, 1903, p. 283; *J.O.E.F.O.*, 1948, *Arrêté* 664 reorganized the Chamber of Agriculture.

Nevertheless a distinction has always been drawn between the *services d'état,* under the control of the Ministries in Paris, in which the higher posts are held by metropolitan French and local *cadres* or *services territoriaux* which are recruited from the citizens of French Polynesia. Allowing for the existence of the professional colonial civil servants who come from France, the citizens of the colony can obtain posts within both kinds of department, the extent to which they do so being controlled by the system of examinations and promotions which follows civil service practice, but the former, as they offer greater security of tenure and greater opportunity of promotion, are the harder to obtain. There are also local posts in the villages and districts, as *agents de police,* although here again the higher posts in the police department are filled by *gendarmerie* of the metropolitan colonial service; such local posts are of relatively little authority or executive opportunity. Since the war, it has been the policy to open as many posts as possible to local residents, with a corresponding reduction in the number of metropolitan officials who, however, still occupy the senior posts.

Assimilation in practice has meant in Tahiti that the institutions through which political advancement can occur are distinctively French. Except in certain island groups, like the Tuamotus, from the early stages of colonial government the French have ignored traditional institutions; certainly they have not attempted to use the old system of rank and authority, and where they have preserved something of a formal position, like a district chief, the office has in fact been a modern administration one and not at all traditional. The *loi-cadre* represents administrative assimilation to the metropolitan French institutions which have been provided for the whole of the Union or Community, with the corollaries that the society within which these institutions exist is dominated by French values, French education and French culture. Plainly it assumes that the Tahitians are French; that, as in France, the Government shall be highly centralized in the capital; that political advancement shall be distinctively French and not Polynesian.

CHAPTER VI

POLITICAL ADVANCEMENT IN TAHITI

All colonial practice is in one sense assimilationist: it presupposes that colonial institutions must embody at least some of the attitudes and values of metropolitan society. Thus, in Fiji, the structure of the Fijian Administration assumes that democratic processes of discussion and decision making are a desirable end and that from the hybrid institutions provided there will emerge some kind of responsible government. French practice differs from this, not so much in the ends it seeks, for the *loi-cadre* is also a step in development towards responsible government, but in the means. Unlike Fiji, the institutions of political advancement are assimilated not merely to values and attitudes but to precise metropolitan forms. Moreover, because of this assimilation, there is no separate advancement for the Tahitians: there is but one set of institutions for all French citizens. Thus it becomes harder in the operation of these institutions to separate distinctively Tahitian characteristics from French ones, more difficult to examine the survival and the influence of Polynesian custom in their working.

One of the cruder tests which can be used to distinguish Tahitian custom is the nature of elections to the Assembly and of the parties which fight them. The first elections for an Assembly took place in December 1945 and January 1946; a predominantly conservative Assembly was returned. Very few of the twenty members remained in political life in subsequent Assemblies, and of the four who did, three belonged to the later right-wing party and only one to the left; of three others who stood again, unsuccessfully, in later years, all stood as right-wing or independent candidates.[1] It is impossible to know how many of the electorate voted because the published figures provide only the votes cast for the candidates actually elected, which numbered 11,628, but a rough comparison with the total of votes cast for the winning candidates at the next elections in 1953, allowing for the differ-

[1] *J.O.E.F.O.*, *Arrêté* 67 of 1946; *J.O.E.F.O.*, of 9 February 1953, *Avis Officiels, Résultats des élections pour l'Assemblée Territoriale.*

ences, suggests that the poll was low. There was no organized political conflict, for there were as yet no parties, and the election was rather a matter of personalities than a conflict of policies or organizations; it also reflected a lack of preparation in the electorate called upon to provide the first Assembly, although Papeete returned a group of members, including the mayor, who represented the commercial interests of the town and who have continued to represent the capital in each subsequent Assembly. The lack of preparation was more important in the outer electorates. For, when the next elections took place, a very different result was produced. The poll was held on 18 January 1953 and declared on 9 February following, with the result that a left-wing party gained a large majority. The *Rassemblement Démocratique des Populations Tahitiennes (R.D.P.T.)* obtained eighteen of the twenty-five seats; the former conservative group retained only Papeete, and the commune of Uturoa returned an independent who was also its mayor. In fact, as soon as political life became organized, with parties contesting the elections, it was clear that there was a Tahitian party distinct from the commercial interests of the town, and this party was the party predominantly of the countryside and the villages. Subsequent elections merely confirmed that it was so. The first election under the *loi-cadre* with proportional representation was held in November 1957.[2] The method of voting gave greater weight to Papeete where, under the constituency system, a large vote for the right-wing party had been wasted,[3] but the general result confirmed that of the second Assembly election of 1953. In the 1957 election, the *R.D.P.T.* secured seventeen seats, the right-wing group nine, and a miscellaneous collection of parties styling themselves Independent, Independent for Social Action, the Union of Cultivators of the Tuamotu-Gambiers, held the balance of four seats. Even

[2] *J.O.P.F.*, 1957, p. 668 ff.; where the party lists were published, together with the voting by *circonscriptions*; and by districts in *J.O.P.F.*, 1958, p. 26 ff.

[3] In the first two elections, Papeete returned a solid group of right-wing members, and Pouvanaa, whose constituency of domicile it was, failed to gain election. For example, in 1953, the right-wing group presented five candidates who polled from 1,559 to 1,521 votes each; the *R.D.P.T.* group of five candidates polled from 1,236 to 1,210 votes each. In 1957 the *R.D.P.T.* list for the *circonscription* of the Windward Isles (which included Papeete) polled 5,319 and the right-wing list 4,589, in a total poll of 11,862; proportionately, therefore, the *R.D.P.T.* got eight seats (of which Pouvanaa at the head of the list held one) and the opposition seven, an advance of two on the former constituency of Papeete, while an independent who polled 829 votes was also elected.

when these independents later joined the right-wing group, the *R.D.P.T.* still had an overall majority of four. Moreover, in 1949, the leader of that party, Pouvanaa a Oopa, was first elected Deputy to the National Assembly in Paris with seventy per cent. of the votes cast, a proportion which did not change substantially in any subsequent election by which he was always returned until he went to prison in 1958.[4]

Voting results clearly indicate the extent to which the countryside has supported a distinctive Tahitian political party, and the actual campaigning reveals issues which have a peculiarly Tahitian quality. The *R.D.P.T.* was the outcome of a committee, formed in 1947, during the life of the first conservative Assembly, under the name of Pouvanaa.[5] Pouvanaa a Oopa, now a man in his sixties, who was leader of the party and later Deputy to the National Assembly, is a Tahitian with a fair proportion of European ancestry: blond hair (now grey) and blue eyes. He had a primary education, and followed a variety of trades, being at times a carpenter and a vendor of fried potatoes on the waterfront at Papeete; he is also an ex-serviceman of the First World War, and the head of a Protestant sect, a religion to which the majority of Tahitians still subscribe. The *Comité Pouvanaa* of 1947 was formed to organize a political party to fight the next Assembly elections. At first its activity was confined to Papeete where private meetings were held and tracts and pamphlets circulated. On 9 May 1947 it published the first issue of its newspaper, *Te Aratai*, in French and Tahitian, which carried the statute of the committee, its programme, and a project for modifying the constitution bearing the date 16 March 1947. This political programme was published under the heading '*Tahiti d'abord et pour les Tahitiens*'. No demand for political independence was made, for Tahiti was to continue within the French Union, but the plan was to achieve local autonomy by a sovereign Assembly and a Council of Government wielding executive power elected by the Assembly; a French governor should ensure liaison with France, especially in matters of justice, foreign affairs and national defence, assisted by a *corps* of metropolitan officials.

[4] *J.O.E.F.O.*, 1949, *Avis* of election of 23 October; ibid., 1951, *Avis* of 2 September; ibid., 1956, *Avis* of 29 January.

[5] There are two published versions of this committee and its history, one by the *R.D.P.T.* in its newspaper *Te Aratai* of 6 and 13 December 1958, the other in an opposition newspaper, *To Tatou Aveia*, of 6 December 1958, a date at which Pouvanaa's history assumed some importance with his arrest and imminent trial.

'Nationalist' is not quite the right word to apply to this programme, in the sense that only local autonomy was demanded within the framework of French sovereignty, but it was a word which, together with an adjective like 'Leftist', was applied to Pouvanaa and his movement, particularly by those who asserted that he was in private anti-French. In support of such descriptions they could point to some overt violence which could be interpreted to justify such adjectives.

In May 1947 the Secretary-General of the Government and his wife were to leave the colony, on completion of their tour of duty, in the S.S. *Waitemata,* a New Zealand ship which was sailing to the United States; the official and his wife would thus return to France via America. Tahiti was having credit and exchange problems at the time, and the control of dollars had been in the hands of the departing official. It is hardly necessary to say that gossip spreads very easily in any tropical colony, and more easily in Tahiti than most. Rightly or wrongly, the wife was supposed to have said that she and her husband intended to buy an American car, a fur coat, and various other things in the dollar area. The *Comité Pouvanaa* reasoned that the official could not have dollars of his own since that was illegal, nor could he have an account in the United States since he was not engaged in trade; the suggestion was, therefore, that he had reserved some of Tahiti's much-needed dollars for his own use. Indignation was roused to fever pitch; deputations waited on the Governor to inform him that the couple would not be allowed to embark; and, no satisfactory assurance being received, a demonstration was arranged on the eve of the vessel's sailing. In the face of a large crowd, the Governor is alleged to have said: 'All right I've decided they won't leave', and then to have added: 'You see, I've made a nice gesture. It's up to the crowd to make another and let them go'.[6] In fact he capitulated to the picketing of the ship, and the couple left for France via New Zealand. A month later there was a further demonstration when the *Ville d'Amiens* arrived in Papeete harbour with some new metropolitan officials. The wharf was again picketed in an organized manner, but on this occasion the Governor took a stronger line. In a situation where feelings were running high, with the Tahitian police and militia waiting on the outcome of events, the Governor declared a state of siege, and the officials landed under the cover of machine guns. On 1 July Pouvanaa and some of his principal colleagues were arrested

[6] *Te Aratai*, 13 December 1958, p. 3.

for 'an attempt on the internal security of the state'. They were later acquitted by three French judges and four Tahitian assessors, and released.

To those who feared that Pouvanaa was a Tahitian nationalist and ultimately anti-French, this violence must have seemed a confirmation of their opinion. In fact, the demonstrations were not so much anti-French as anti-metropolitan French. Their major significance, however, was the revelation of the kind of support Pouvanaa could get. As the leading figure in the incidents, he was clearly a man of wide popularity and oratorical appeal; a new kind of leader whose strength rested on a mass following in the electorate and whose leadership was based not at all on the old qualifications for rank and authority but upon distinctively French institutions: the church, the veterans' association, the trade unions. At the same time, Pouvanaa's appeal to the electorate had to make itself felt through its relationship with certain Polynesian traits; his oratory, for example, which with its Tahitian dialect and Biblical quotations evoked a great response in the villages where mission education and the church are still strong;[7] his party, which looked at times more like a kinship group than a modern political one; his generosity to those dependent on him. And he also, of course, served as a focus for the social and economic discontents which the war had exacerbated in Tahitian society, with a programme which emphasized local autonomy, symbolized by his revival of the old Tahitian flag which was presented to Queen Pomare by the British more than a century ago.

The *R.D.P.T.* was formally constituted as a party in 1949, and its institution forced other groups to organize also. When the elections of 1953 took place, the major opposition party was the *Union pour la Défense des intérêts de l'Océanie,* although in certain islands another party styled *R.P.F.* also fought and lost, together with some independents.[8] The main opposition to

[7] An example may be quoted from his campaign against General de Gaulle in the referendum of September 1958. In the villages, a standard speech of Pouvanaa's may be summarized thus; 'In the Bible there is the Book of Genesis, and in that book the story of Adam and Eve. Eve tempted Adam with an apple, and Adam said, "Yes", and look what happened to him. So you say "No" to General de Gaulle.'

[8] The strength of the opposition to the *R.D.P.T.* varied. Its centre was Papeete, but it made some showing in the island of Tahiti, in Moorea-Maiao, in Huahine, in Bora Bora-Maupiti, the North Marquesas, the Tuamotu-Gambier *rattachées* and Tuamotu Central and East. Elsewhere its support was insignificant.

Pouvanaa centred on Papeete and the commune of Uturoa which regularly returned their mayors. In 1957, when proportional representation was introduced, the main opposition party and other groups did a little better[9] and, together with the small party representatives who were then elected, it formed, in April 1959, a united opposition party calling itself the *Union Tahitienne démocratique*. Party organization was loose, as indeed it was with the *R.D.P.T.* (of which Pouvanaa was not an Assembly member until 1957) which at one time maintained discipline over its members by a system of *lettres de démission* supplied to the leadership in advance by each office-holder. Still, weak as the *R.D.P.T.* party apparatus was by European standards (and complicated as it was by Pouvanaa's absence from the Assembly and the power of his lieutenants), it held together until the events of 1958, when on two occasions the opportunity arose for a statement of the clash of party aims.

The first of these was in April-May 1958 over the introduction of an income tax by the majority party.[10] This proposal was hotly contested by the right wing, although there is some reason to believe that the contest was to some extent an artificial one because the relations between some *R.D.P.T.* leaders and the right-wing party were neither so strained nor so divergent as some public utterances implied. In the opening session of the Assembly which voted on the income tax law, the leader of the right-wing group had said that his newly formed Tahitian Democratic Union would co-operate for the general good with the majority, but that on one point they were firm: the French presence in the colony and the error of any idea of a Tahitian republic; what was wanted was slow and normal evolution. Jean-Baptiste Heitarauri Céran-Jérusalémy (who had always led the *R.D.P.T.* in the Assembly) had replied that the *R.D.P.T.* wished to lead Tahiti to the status of a republic within the French Union in accordance with 'the new tendencies of modern politics', but not to reject France outside the boundaries of the territory, rather to seek the most cordial and comprehensive links with '*cette généreuse Métropole*'. Co-operation broke down almost at once when the *U.T.D.* refused to accept the proposed lists of office-holders for the Permanent

[9] In the *circonscription* of the Windward Isles, the *R.D.P.T.* had a total of less than fifty per cent. of the votes, in the Leeward Isles more than fifty per cent., in the Marquesas scarcely more than one-third, in the Australs two-thirds, in the Tuamotu-Gambiers rather more than one-third.

[10] *Session Administrative de l'Assemblée Territoriale*, 3rd Session, 29 April 1958.

Commission of the Assembly which included two of their own members; in consequence a purely *R.D.P.T.* bureau was elected with the *U.T.D.* abstaining from voting.[11] Thus, when the *U.T.D.* demanded on 29 April that the deliberation of the Council of Government of February 1958 in favour of an income tax be abrogated, there was an apparent clash of political principle and the machinery of the Assembly represented only the majority party. The strength of the minority was extra-parliamentary, for while a stormy debate went on, a crowd of right-wing supporters demonstrated against the proposed law outside the building, necessitating police protection for some members of the Assembly. A bombardment of stones through the windows and a threat to knock down the walls of the building with a bulldozer, caused the majority to abstain from voting, and by a minority vote the Assembly transmitted to the Council of Government a resolution, which was acted upon, favouring suspension of the tax.

The precise occasion for this conflict is less important than its effects. The *R.D.P.T.* split into two factions, the one headed by Pouvanaa and the other by Céran-Jérusalémy,[12] with the result that unless the two voted together in the Assembly the *R.D.P.T.* majority disappeared. The Council of Government remained a predominantly *R.D.P.T.* one, but the new bureau of the Assembly, which was elected following Céran's resignation as president upon the defeat of the tax proposal, consisted of a right-wing president, an *R.D.P.T.* vice-president of Pouvanaa's faction, and an equal division of the other offices between the same two groups. Thus, when the next occasion of sharp conflict arose, the right-wing party was in a position to dominate the Assembly if the two left-wing groups declined to co-operate with each other. This occasion was the de Gaulle referendum of September 1958. Pouvanaa campaigned for a 'No' vote against de Gaulle on a platform of 'Tahiti for the Tahitians and the French into the sea', using an appeal to the electorate which was compounded of Biblical quotation and analogy and naïve promises of economic aid from the United States to replace French.[13]

[11] ibid., Session of 24 April.

[12] A split not solely one of policy or principle, for there was some personal jealousy over the filling of ministerial offices and perhaps some commercial influence involved.

[13] Pouvanaa's campaign has often seemed inexplicable, because under the de Gaulle constitution he could have secured autonomy within the French Community. The probable explanation is that, with the split in his party, he could not be sure of a majority in the Assembly which should vote on the choice before Tahiti.

The Tahitians voted 63·7 per cent. in favour of de Gaulle's constitution, after which Pouvanaa was accused of having plotted to burn the town of Papeete, subsequently tried, and convicted. When the Assembly, therefore, came to vote upon its future under the terms of the new constitution, the extreme left-wing group was imprisoned or discredited, and the Council of Government suspended by the Governor's order during the disturbances.[14]

The constitution of the Fifth Republic offered to the Assemblies of French Territories a choice under Article 76 which lay between maintaining their present status, or becoming departments of metropolitan France, or *état-membres* of the French Community (the new style for the Union). The absence of Pouvanaa and the circumstances in which the Assembly met precluded the third possibility: the Assembly in effect agreed with, or at least did not dispute, the statement of the *rapporteur* that the territory was too weak to be autonomous under the provisions of Article 77, which gave to *état-membres* power to administer themselves except for foreign affairs, defence, money, common financial and economic policy, strategic matters, justice, higher education and external communications. The choice, therefore, lay between departmentalization and the maintenance of the *status quo*.[15] The former was supported by a number of people, drawn from both right- and left-wing groups, part of them at least because it was felt that the problems of population growth and economic strain would be cured. The *rapporteur* argued, using the examples of colonies like Guadeloupe and Réunion, that departmentalization did not work well, that local interests were sacrificed, that control from Paris did not really solve local problems, and that no assurances for the particular welfare of Tahiti were forthcoming. Thus it remained only to maintain the *loi-cadre* in operation with some modifications. An attempt was made to abolish the individual functions of ministers, but a compromise was reached that although individual functions should be retained they were to be exercised collegially and no minister might by himself give a direct order to an administrator except as specifically charged for a year at a time. Behind this issue lay that of the *politisation* of the administration by ministers, as well as the more general question of experience and efficiency. The number of the Council of Government was to be reduced to five since its functions were

[14] *J.O.P.F., Arrêté* 1090 of 1958.

[15] *Session Extraordinaire de l'Assemblée,* Session 14, November 1958.

to be largely collegial for a trial period of four years. With these relatively slight modifications, the Territorial Assembly voted to maintain the present status of French Polynesia under the *loi-cadre,* with only two abstentions (one an independent, the other left-wing) and five absentees, including Pouvanaa who was in prison.

This brief history of party conflict in French Polynesia points up, perhaps in rather dramatic form, the degree to which French institutions operate in a Polynesian context. Leaving aside for the moment the actual working of the Assembly, and looking at the electoral campaigns and the organization of the *R.D.P.T.*, it is clear that both Tahitian history and custom still work within the French framework of government. Pouvanaa's appeal to the Tahitians had many of the elements which elsewhere in the Pacific would be called a cargo cult: the promise and expectation of the arrival of a cargo, the messianic flavour which came from Pouvanaa's own headship of a Protestant sect and the Biblical cast of his Polynesian-style oratory, the reliance on kinship ties for party and political organization. The electoral campaigns have also depended on the resentment which exists against the metropolitan French officials who, during the war (and after in the case of the dollar allocation), sometimes discriminated against the Tahitians with scarce goods. In this sense Pouvanaa expressed something which can loosely be called Tahitian nationalism if it be remembered that the local French shared some of its attitudes. Nevertheless, Pouvanaa's appeal was also to the Polynesian elements in Tahitian society, to the Tahitian Protestant pastors whose influence in the village was enormous, and to the general *malaise* which exists in consequence of the policy of assimilation which has abolished the traditional system of rank and so eliminated any rival authority to the new leadership which Pouvanaa represents. Electoral success which relied on its appeal to Polynesian survivals was, however, only the means by which Pouvanaa and his party controlled the Assembly; once there, they worked in recognizably French ways through French institutions, and they worked too, of course, in an urban situation which was different from that of the Tahitian countryside. The means of gaining power may have been partly Polynesian; the end result was more distinctively French.

The parties, the electoral system, and the clash of opinion, of institutions, and Polynesian custom, provide the setting in which those institutions operate, and some of the conflict of attitudes and custom occurs precisely because in French Polynesia the *loi-cadre* afforded the opportunity for Tahitian citizens to discuss policy and, within limits, to control it. Every Tahitian can express himself by voting for a party contesting an election, and his representatives exercise some real power in local affairs. Final power rests with the Governor, but the political framework which has been created since the war imposes on that official the necessity for co-operation with the Assembly and, latterly, the Council of Government of the kind which a Prefect must achieve with the *conseil général* in a French metropolitan department.

Under the constitution the Assembly has formal power in local matters which are executed by *arrêté* of the Governor. Its exercise of these powers has, on the whole, been restrained. A right-wing member who was also a Senator of the Fourth Republic elected by the Tahitian Assembly, claimed during the debate on the status of the territory in 1958 that its powers had not been abused, and that it had done good work in dealing with local *fonctionnaires*, forestry matters, the regulation of fishing and pearl-shell industries and mineral resources, and his claim is the more significant if it be remembered that the Assembly has been controlled, since 1953, by the left-wing party. All the matters named are local economic ones, and such affairs have always constituted the bulk of the discussion in the Assembly. During a sitting of the administrative session of the Assembly in May 1958, for example, the proceedings opened with a question for debate concerning the introduction of a water supply at Auatonu in Raivavae, and the credits under the plan for economic and social development (FIDES) which were necessary for this.[16] It was unanimously agreed that the question be discussed and the proposal was therefore sent to the committee of the Assembly which was concerned with economic, financial and social matters. The report of the Permanent Commission was then discussed, together with the relevant correspondence. The latter comprised copies of the Governor's orders which made decisions of the Assembly effective, rates in the local budget, communications about tourism and exchange problems, correspondence about the suppression of the income tax proposal, the minutes of the Chamber of Commerce and various other letters dealing, for instance, with the admission of a motor car to the administration garage for repair. There followed letters directed to the Assembly itself requesting reimbursement of the tax on copra paid by an individual grower,

[16] *Session Administrative*, 7th Session, 31 May 1958.

or dealing with the demolition of the old *chefferie* of Mahina, or the price of petrol. All of these were matters within the Assembly's power to decide, but in addition it received letters which did not involve debate but simply information. Such were the communications from ministers of the Council of Government about education and domanial lands. Other than letters for information only, the Assembly might debate the questions before it. The matter of the demolition of the *chefferie* of Mahina was discussed and the Assembly's approval given. Other matters it might transmit to the Council of Government. There was a long debate, for example, over the purchase of a new flying-boat to replace one which had crashed in the service from Bora Bora to Papeete. An equally long debate occurred over the abolition of a sub-division of public works at Uturoa. These matters may in themselves be trivial, but they are the stuff of the Assembly's control over local affairs, and their very triviality ensures that the Assembly will behave responsibly in discussing and deciding them since no great issues or matters of principle are raised.

Party politics do, of course, enter into the Assembly's deliberations and even a matter like the public works sub-division of Uturoa can lead to accusations of political manoeuvring and personalities, yet the claim that the Assembly has worked effectively is broadly true. Meeting in two ordinary sessions a year on the summons of the Governor, it has regularly discussed and taken decisions on matters within its competence. It has regularly fixed the taxes on vanilla, commercial licences for foreigners and Asiatics, the *octroi* and customs duties.[17] Such ordinary sessions of the Assembly have produced party politics and rhetoric similar to that of the National Assembly in Paris, but the histrionics of debate should not obscure the work done by the committee system of the Assembly which has in private discharged its powers and duties efficiently. A number of committees elected by the representatives has been set up: of Rules and Accounts, Administrative Business, Financial, Economic and Social Business. Under Administrative Business, one committee has dealt with questions like territorial waters; under the last heading, with questions like tariffs, the *cabinet* of the Vice-President of the Council of Government and the regulation of mineral industry. Within the face-to-face relationships of such small groups, representing both political parties, the representatives have been able to discuss and decide

[17] *J.O.E.F.O.*, 1948, *Arrêtés* Nos. 120, 585, 831, 1482; ibid., 1949, *Arrêtés* Nos. 98, 348, 404, 656, 663, 769.

policy within the competence of the Assembly without the public conflict of party debate.

Most obviously, the Permanent Commission of the Assembly has demonstrated the value of the committee system. Elected by each session of the Assembly to sit in the intervals between sessions, the Permanent Commission of five members, with perhaps others added in a consultative capacity, meets for a few days each month, unless convoked in extraordinary session by the Governor, and works from nine to eleven each morning.[18] Its method of working is by the appointment of *rapporteurs* to deal with the business before it, who prepare a report on the matter in hand which the Commission discusses and decides upon by virtue of its delegated power from the Assembly (to which it must, of course, report decisions and recommendations in each of the two annual sessions). Procedure usually, therefore, takes the form of consideration of correspondence under several headings and, where necessary, the designation of a *rapporteur*. The Governor transmits to the Commission copies of the orders which put the decisions of the Assembly or the Commission into effect, and others may seek the advice of the Commission or petition it, as in the case of a protest about the price of petrol. When the correspondence has been classified and *rapporteurs* appointed, the Commission will proceed to discuss such reports. Since the creation of the Council of Government, many of the matters on which the opinion of the Commission has been sought have been passed on to the Council, but the Commission has discussed the decisions of the latter. For example, the funds available from the European economic community for overseas development were allocated by decision of the Council under certain priorities, one of which was the construction of a quay for schooners at Papeete; the Commission appointed its Vice-President, a member of the left-wing party, to report upon the matter.[19] Again, when the question arose of creating a cost of living index for French Polynesia, the Commission regarded one of its members as a specialist in such matters, although in fact he designated another member to report in his place. Like the Assembly itself, the heads of administrative departments could be

[18] *Commission Permanente, Session ordinaire* of August 1958, 1st Session, 12 August. The members were then President (an Independent), Vice-President (*R.D.P.T.*), Secretary (*Union*), two members (one *R.D.P.T.*, the other *Union*) and two members *à titre consultatif* (both *Union*).

[19] ibid.

asked to attend to give specialist advice, as the head of the Department of Education was when the question arose of the erection of a school in Papeete rather than scholarships to France for the same standard of education.[20] The Commission decided that the results of the scholarship system were deplorable and agreed on the transformation of the course into an *Ecole Normale des Instituteurs* by three votes, not on party lines, with one abstainer who thought that, on procedural grounds, the Assembly itself ought to have discussed the matter. The Commission is, of course, a delegate of the Assembly, but it, together with the committees which operate while the Assembly is in session, provides the technical basis for the effective working of the machinery. Each member of the Assembly serves on one committee or another, and in doing so is trained to discuss administrative questions and matters of local policy under conditions which impose some responsibility upon him. Many of the members of the Assembly have performed this work well, although there have been obvious exceptions. Within the limits of local decisions and local conditions, the Assembly has generally risen to the responsibility conferred upon it under the constitution.

There have, of course, been failures. In part these arise from the attitudes and the conflicts which have characterized elections to the Assembly and party organization. The programme of the majority party has naturally raised some suspicion among the French officials who have had to co-operate with it, but the conflicts due to Tahitian 'nationalism' have been much less than one might expect from the example of other colonial areas; indeed, in the African sense, such 'nationalism' belies its name because of a general awareness of the economic dependence of Tahiti upon France or upon other metropolitan countries. The more serious failures in co-operation have been conflict between different economic interests and the administration; a conflict between local business men and the Government which has seemed to frustrate them. Public statements by left-wing members suggest a substantial agreement between them and right-wing members on many local economic questions, as opposed to the interests of metropolitan France and its officials. Indeed, the relations between the first 'conservative' Assembly and the Government were probably worse than those of later 'left' Assemblies, although increasing practice and experience of power has no doubt helped to smooth away some of the earlier frictions.

[20] ibid., 2nd Session, 13 August.

That the possibilities of serious friction are economic rather than political can be shown from the occasions on which it occurs, which are usually budgetary ones. The distinction between obligatory and optional sections in the budget still causes trouble, as it always did in the past, whenever the Governor has felt it necessary to exercise his right to reduce the optional expenditure to make adequate provision for the obligatory items.[21] Such action has caused tension between the Governor and the Assembly which would be of minor importance if there were not suspicion on the part of the representatives, fostered by memories of the kind of officials stationed in the colony throughout its history, that the administration may be neither impartial nor competent. The general effect of 'nationalist' or 'anti-administration' feeling is to magnify what are in themselves trivial disputes or technical deficiencies in the structure of government.

Leaving aside any frustration felt because final power is in the Governor's hands, the actual means by which that power expresses itself can cause difficulty. The delay, for example, between a resolution of the Assembly on matters within its competence being taken and being put into effect can be considerable. When such a resolution requires only the approval of the Governor and his Privy Council, it may not be excessive, but if the need arises to refer the matter to Paris, months can go by. On 28 January, 1949, the Assembly passed three resolutions effecting the remission of import duties and customs on certain articles of medical research which were to the general benefit of the public; these resolutions were put into effect by a Governor's order of 18 July.[22] A delay of six months is exceptional, but one to two months is common enough. There is no need to suppose any lack of good will or a deliberate policy of frustration, but technical necessities may have much the same appearance. No doubt they are inevitable under the constitution: when final power does not rest with the Assembly some such procedures of approval must be gone through and some expert advice may be required before it can well be given; but it certainly provides the occasion for co-operation to wear thin and for suspicion to flourish when trust is required to make the institutions work. And trust is a matter of personalities. The *loi-cadre* imposes co-operation on the Governor and the Assembly and because it does

[21] *J.O.E.F.O.*, 1953, *Arrêté* 907 of 22 June promulgating an act of the central power.

[22] *J.O.E.F.O.*, 1949, *Arrêté* 769.

so it places a heavy premium on the personalities of both. Governors have changed rapidly, and so have many senior officials; the Assembly changed, too, in the elections of 1953, although its personnel has been remarkably constant since then. Very little time has been available for the growth of confidence with such a transient administration and an Assembly whose members have sometimes appeared to officials as both naïve in their appreciation of wider issues than the local affairs of Tahiti, and perhaps corrupt in their dealings with business interests or their friends and relations. Technical difficulties and general atmosphere notwithstanding, the Assembly has worked, and it has promoted the political advancement of Tahitian citizens towards control of their local affairs. The growing pains from which it has suffered have become less severe, especially since the creation of the Council of Government has obviated some of the delays and some of the problems of technical advice.

Like the permanent Commission, the Council of Government is dependent on the Assembly for its election and must account to the Assembly for its decisions, although the minutes of its proceedings and its discussions are confidential. The first Council of Government was established in December 1957, and it consisted of Pouvanaa a Oopa as Vice-President, three other members of his party, and two other ministers drawn from outside the Assembly, one of them being a former member of the right-wing groups and one an unsuccessful *R.D.P.T.* candidate in the 1957 election.[23] The territorial services were divided between these six ministers. Pouvanaa as Vice-President dealt with the Interior and with Information, which made him responsible for general administration of territorial interest.[24] The other Ministries were those of Finance and Planning,[25] Economic Affairs of the territory,[26] Public Works, Agriculture and Fishing,[27] Public Health

23 *J.O.P.F.*, 1957, *Numéro spécial* of 15 December; *Numéro spécial* of 19 December.

24 Including liaison with the *services d'état* through the Governor as President of the Council, prisons, information of territorial interest, excluding the radio *service d'état,* the Government printing office and the personnel of territorial services.

25 Including the financial system, the budget, *matériel*, pensions, and FIDES excluding the *service d'état,* direct and indirect taxes, domanial lands and industrial affairs.

26 Including resources and their development, tourism and production.

27 Including inter-island transport, bridges, wharves, ports and aerodromes, forests and forest waters, fishing and pearl diving.

and Social Affairs,[28] and Education, Youth and Sports.[29] The three members of the Assembly of the *R.D.P.T.* held the Ministries of Economic Affairs, Public Works and Health, under Pouvanaa. This composition of the Council thus gave the opposition party representation, although not proportionately to numbers, while it gave to the majority party control of the economic territorial services.

The Council of Government began to discharge its duties in December 1957. Sitting on 30 December, the Council advised on the creation of a modified committee of inter-island maritime transport and, on the proposal of the Minister of Economic Affairs, the order of 1955 which originally set up the Committee was altered to make the minister its president.[30] The *arrêté* which embodied this decision was signed by the Governor as President of the Council and Pouvanaa as Vice-President. The next sitting was held on 8 January 1958 when the Council advised, through the proposal of the Minister of Finance, on the amount of the tax on employers intended to pay the indemnity of salaried women in child-bed, and, following an opinion of Assembly of the preceding 26 December, further advised on the question of family allowances for workers, both of these being modifications of the orders which implemented the Labour Code in French Polynesia.[31] Such decisions were implemented through an individual minister acting on the opinion of the Council as a whole. A different class of decisions was those heard but not taken by the Council. On 30 December provisional credits on the local budget for the following year were opened by the Governor under his authority conferred by the *loi-cadre*, and the *arrêté* was taken in the Council. In the next session, the order which set up a council for programmes of Radio Papeete, which was not a local service but a State one, was also taken in the Council of Government because two of its members were appointed to the council for programmes.[32] All of these decisions reflect the collegial capacity of the Council of Government, acting within its own powers or with the Assembly or with the Governor. As part

[28] Including the Labour Code, family benefits and social assistance.

[29] Public and private education (primary and secondary), professional and technical education, except syllabuses, examinations and qualifications for teaching.

[30] *J.O.P.F.*, 1958, p. 5.

[31] ibid., pp. 14, 15.

[32] ibid., pp. 12, 13.

of the *loi-cadre*, the Council has operated in close co-operation with the two latter, and the decisions which it has taken or has listened to have been the routine ones of territorial government. On the details of administration and economic and social life, the Council has worked well. A dispute, such as the income tax trouble of April 1958, has been exceptional, and most of the matters dealt with have been divorced from the game of party politics.

There was general agreement in November 1958 among all parties that the Council should be retained in its collegial functions, and that it represented an effective measure of decentralization of power from Paris, which gave to local ministers the opportunity to take and advise upon decisions affecting the interests of the territory while it also provided a necessary training in executive control of the territorial services, partly because the Governor himself presided over the Council and could guide or influence its deliberations.

What was not agreed was that the individual functions of ministers controlling departments had worked well. A number of criticisms was made of this part of the *loi-cadre*. One was the alleged incompetence and lack of experience of ministers which damaged the efficient operation of the services under their control. Another was the degree of corruption, styled *politisation*; it was alleged that territorial services were being staffed by political or personal adherents of ministers. A third was the expense of maintaining the secretarial apparatus of individual ministers, which was said to be beyond the resources of the territory. Undeniably there is truth in each of these criticisms, but they can be overstated. The choice of competent ministers was plainly limited by lack of experience and education and the dominance of the *R.D.P.T.*, but it is difficult to see how this situation can be avoided in the initial stages of any new constitution, although it may be controlled by the existence of a department and its officials to advise a minister. It is, of course, the contention of critics that this departmental advice was precisely what had been sapped by bad ministerial control. It is very doubtful if this is actually the case in the higher ranks of the services. In January 1956, for example, a head of the accounting office for the purchase and sale of tobacco was appointed, and on the proposal of the Vice-President of the Council and the Minister for Economic Affairs he was confirmed in his duties in December 1957 under the authority of the chief of territorial economic affairs.[33] There was, in general, no sudden influx of political appointees in the higher ranks of the territorial services which were, in any case, very much influenced by their association with the services of State. The real basis of the charges of inefficiency, incompetence and *politisation* was not the territorial services but the ministerial secretariats. On 31 December 1957 a number of appointments was announced.[34] M. Jacques Drollet was replaced as director of the school at Papeari because he had become the *chef du cabinet* to the Minister of Education. M. Drollet was a leading figure in the *R.D.P.T.* in the Assembly, and in this sense his appointment was political, but he was also a schoolteacher and a man of ability and experience whose appointment was a reasonable one, as was that of Dr Florisson, a former Senator of the Republic and a member of the *R.D.P.T.*, to be the director of the Vice-President's secretariat. Similarly, M. Alfred Grand, the director of the school of Hitiaa, was replaced when he was seconded to the office of the Vice-President. M. Claude Valot of the *cadre supérieure* of education was placed at the disposal of the Minister of Education to ensure the direction of his secretariat, just as Madame Annette Swenson, who had been serving in the administrative division of the Leeward Isles, was placed at the disposal of the Vice-President of the Council to serve in the territorial personnel section. There was certainly some appointment of relations of both Pouvanaa and Céran-Jérusalémy to ministerial secretariats, but the same is true of the ministries held by the right-wing party member. When in October 1958 the Council of Government was suppressed, a number of officials within these offices reverted to the services from which they had been drawn.[35] The degree to which *politisation* affected the ministries has probably been exaggerated; certainly it principally affected, in an inefficient form, the lower reaches of those secretariats, not the higher ones; and it is sometimes difficult to distinguish what is called *politisation* from nepotism. There was undoubtedly some evidence of both, but it is difficult to find proof that it was extensive. The more general charge that the whole idea of individual ministers each with his *cabinet* was expensive has more substance, but any judgement

[33] ibid., p. 4.

[34] ibid., *Extraits*, p. 16 ff.

[35] ibid., p. 635 ff.

that these disadvantages outweighed the advantages of executive training is one inevitably coloured by party attitudes. There is not much indication that the inefficiency or corruption that was talked about was more than one might normally expect, and have to accept, as a consequence of the implementation of a system like the *loi-cadre* in such a society as Tahiti.

Some at least of the difficulties which the institutions of the *loi-cadre* have encountered in their operation arise from the effects of assimilation upon Polynesian custom. The most obvious survival of that custom–kinship ties and attitudes–plainly influences both the electoral machinery and the Assembly, and the executive organs of central political development. An Assembly and the equivalent of a cabinet, which in theory provide the opportunity and the training to discuss and execute policy, are institutions conceived in European terms: they imply standards of behaviour which, in Tahiti, are modified by custom and by past history. Thus the critics of the *loi-cadre* believed that some approximation to those European standards of honesty and efficiency which at a minimum are necessary for European political institutions to work at all, would be encouraged by a more rigid separation of legislative and executive power: that the behaviour of people who retain some of the Polynesian attitudes of their ancestors would be controlled if the possibilities for kinship, for example, to influence their actions were limited in scope by limiting the institutions in which they operate. The root of the matter is that the old system of rank and its sanctions has vanished and therefore the new political leaders have no rivals, but the new criteria of leadership are not solely French. Pouvanaa has certainly gained influence through characteristically French institutions: the trade unions, the veterans' association, a church sect, as well as the *loi-cadre*; but to the content of those institutions he has given a distinctive Polynesian flavour. His electoral campaigns have looked like a cargo cult movement; his followers have adhered to him through Polynesian superstitions, kinship and neighbourhood, as well as for the more obvious economic or political reasons of a European kind. Tahitian society is not yet French; Tahitians are not yet Frenchmen in fact as well as theory, although French culture has deeply influenced both. The result is that French Polynesia is in one sense a vacuum: nothing has yet completely replaced the old order, although the framework of a new order which is distinctively French has been set up. There is thus a competition, not between the old order and the new, but between the new and a curious French-Polynesian mixture. The *loi-cadre* itself slowly asserts influence towards the French order, but its operation is conditioned by the heterogeneous characteristics of Tahiti, which will probably always give some scope for the survivals of a Polynesian society which has, on the surface, completely broken down.

Because political advancement in Tahiti has been so much central development, the clash of custom and of values is most dramatically shown in the institutions of the *loi-cadre*. Still, the Tahitians who play their part in the centre of the stage are those least easily distinguishable from the French, at any rate from those of local families. The more profound difficulty for French institutions in Tahitian society exists in the districts, but it is, of course, of less immediate political importance since the chief and district councils have little legislative or executive power. Indirectly it is of great importance because opinion in the districts can influence central politics, and any kind of tension may reflect itself in the political attitude and programmes of the parties; it exists as the major pressure upon the *R.D.P.T.*, just as the merchants and traders of Papeete and the Chamber of Commerce exist as the major pressure upon the opposition party. Pouvanaa's political strength was drawn primarily from the districts. The existence of a conflict between the district administrative structure and Polynesian society obviously varies in degree, particularly with the distance of any area from Papeete; probably no general picture would be really accurate, although certain general features undoubtedly exist.

One of the most widely spread attitudes in the villages is a common complaint of peasant or farming communities at large: 'the Government neglect us; the Government interferes with us'; and on this point Polynesian custom and French attitudes agree. The Tahitian villagers, like French peasants, want to be left alone by the Government. On the other hand, they want some of the services and goods a Government can provide, and blame the Government when there is not enough of either. This attitude is reflected in the elections to the district councils. The men elected are usually those who will do nothing, and so please their electors. In any case, no ambitious or able man would be tempted by the office of chief or councillor because neither has much power or responsibility, and the path of ambition lies through central political structure. For these reasons, the chiefs and district councils play little part in any process of political advancement, even when they work at all. At most, they contribute to a political atmosphere in which the electorate blames the Government equally for doing something or for doing nothing. The real agent of authority in the districts is the *gendarme*, a member of the *service d'état*, or, by extension, the *mutoi*, a member of the territorial service; it is upon these two officials that any real resentment against the Government descends, although the council may suffer by being turned out of office on the strength of any such feeling. The fact is that all organs of Government are lumped into one generally suspected group by the Tahitian villagers, and although they may respond to the electoral appeal of the *R.D.P.T.* and regard Pouvanaa as a kind of hero-figure, members of the Assembly itself tend to be looked upon as part of the apparatus of government which is beyond their experience to the point of being regarded with distrust.

The real loyalties of the Tahitian villagers are given to the pastor and the church: that Tahitian Protestant church which derives from London Missionary Society work in the early days and is now part of a French Protestant congregation in Paris. And it is the village church which enshrines Polynesian traditions and customs, which serves as a focus for kinship groups, social life and social ambition. Thus the real centre of authority in a village is often the Tahitian pastor, who is very little controlled by any central organization, but who works with the deacons of his village, in effect, to replace a vanished system of rank and authority which has not really been replaced by local government institutions. Of course, there is not necessarily any conflict between local government and local church: the pastors may reinforce the administration, and they may influence their people (as many suspect they did in the de Gaulle referendum) to support the Government. The district chief and council may be substantially indentical with the deacons of the church, and so gain a prestige and authority which does not inhere in the institutions themselves. Thus the Tahitian church represents what is now Polynesian custom, a fact recognized by Pouvanaa, who was head of a Protestant group and whose enormous political appeal rested on this basis in the countryside; he failed when some of the missionaries took a different line from his in the de Gaulle referendum. And if this Tahitian institution of the church can influence central politics in this way, in the districts it is probably decisive, except in those villages very close to Papeete. Whether the local institutions work badly, or at all, depends upon their correspondence with the power structure of a village resting upon the pastor and the deacons (who may, of course, now be politically divided), the degree to which the Tahitian church affects the traditional indifference of Tahitian villagers, and the degree to which the deacons and pastors support the Government or one or other of the political parties.

The central institutions of the *loi-cadre* are indirectly affected by this situation in these villages, for the Tahitian countryside is a pressure upon the Assembly and the Council of Government; it was the strength of Pouvanaa's position, and the weakness of Céran-Jérusalémy's who represented essentially an urban, trade union outlook.[36] The two men may stand as symbols of the complicated situation within which the *loi-cadre* works. Pouvanaa illustrates both the connection and the gulf between those institutions and the Tahitian villager. The latter is at once the source of Pouvanaa's political strength but is indifferent to affairs outside his local interests; a situation which creates a gap between leadership and people, which makes for both irresponsibility in the leader who uses his electoral power knowing that his electorate is not thereafter much interested in what he does except in so far as it has local effects, and *naïveté* in the leader whose horizon has this local boundary. Such a state of affairs will slowly be altered by the existence of the *loi-cadre* itself, and it is already influenced by growing party political divisions in the villages, but in the early stages its institutions are rooted not in the Tahitian countryside and people but in the more urban section of the population. The districts are the background to political life, but the more immediate pressures are the trade unions in Papeete, and the commercial interests of the town represented by its mayor and the Chambers of Commerce and

[36] There are a large number of unions in Tahiti which have grown rapidly since the war. Thus there is the *Syndicat des Travailleurs des Quais* (affiliated to the *Confédération Général du Travail* in France), *Syndicat des Dockers Chrétiens* (affiliated to its Christian rival in France), *Syndicat des Gens de Mer Chrétien, Syndicat Général du Personnel des Entreprises Industrielles et Commerciales des E.F.O., Syndicat des Fonctionnaires Chrétiens, Union Territoriale des Syndicats Chrétiens de Tahiti.* Céran-Jérusalémy, who was manager of a Co-operative of Tahitian workers, was General Secretary of the Christian Dockers, while his brother was Secretary of the Christian *Fonctionnaires.* Pouvanaa was President of the *Union Nationale de Combattants.*

Agriculture.[37] The pressure groups reinforce the centralized character of political advancement, and in a sense the *loi-cadre* works because of them. They provide that outside opinion, that clash of policy which breathes life into representative government; they provide that relatively educated independent opinion, outside the administration, which is so lacking in Fiji and Samoa.[38] The danger is that they will widen the gap between the centre and the districts at a greater pace than the latter come to accept this kind of political organization.

Assimilation in colonial practice creates a gap between the Government and the governed, although a different one from that which opens between traditional leaders and their people in such a system as the Fijian. There is no conflict between the old and new, for the old has long since disappeared in Tahiti. Instead, the major issue is the acceptance of metropolitan institutions as representative by people who are in theory the same as metropolitan citizens and in practice only partly so. The strength of this colonial practice is that these are the only formal political institutions; they have no rival. But their effective operation depends upon the extent to which education and economic attitudes produce the desire and the ambition to use them; and upon the degree to which informal institutions which have been built up in the absence of the traditional system of authority are prepared to supplement them rather than compete with them. Assimilation has provided part of the solution by creating an educated, politically conscious, *élite*, but success depends upon closing the gap between this *élite* and the mass of the population. More than the Fijian system, the Tahitian approach to political advancement requires greater resources for education and development because, lacking an alternative traditional basis, there is nothing else to build upon.

[37] Members of the *R.D.P.T.* are represented in both, but the elected leadership is right-wing, for example, *J.O.P.F.*, 1957, p. 673.

[38] In its most obvious form, this clash of opinion occurs in the newspapers which political groups and individuals publish in roneoed form: *Te Aratai*, the paper of Céran's faction of the *R.D.P.T.*, *Te Mau Opuaraa*, edited by Edwin Atger, an *Indépendent d'Action Sociale* member, *Les Vrais Débats*, edited by Franz Vanizette, an Independent member, *Les Débats*, published 'with the participation of elected democrats', and *To Tatou Aveia*, 'an independent and democratic organ'. Only *Te Aratai* has a long history.

CHAPTER VII

THE SAMOAN BACKGROUND

1. *Physical Description*

Eastern or American Samoa comprises the islands of the Samoan archipelago between latitudes 13°30′ and 14°32′ south and longitudes 168° and 171° west.[1] There are six islands in the American group, divided from the eight islands of Western (New Zealand) Samoa by the 171st meridian, of a total area of seventy-six square miles. By far the largest of the islands is Tutuila, measuring fifty-two square miles, followed by the Manuʻa group of three islands (lying sixty miles to the east of Tutuila), Taʻu, Olosega and Ofu, which make up twenty-one and a half square miles of the remaining land surface. The other units in the group are the islet of Aunuʻu at the eastern tip of Tutuila, and Rose atoll which is uninhabited. Swain's Island, geographically not part of the Samoan group but of the Tokelaus, is included in the administrative sphere of American Samoa. The colony is thus very small compared with its neighbour, Western Samoa, and much smaller of course than Fiji; and Tutuila dominates the group to a greater extent than does Viti Levu. The main island possesses in Pago Pago one of the best deep-water natural harbours in the south Pacific which was, until 1951, a United States naval base; it is now a port of call for liners on one leg of the trip from North America to Australia, but it is not a centre of sea traffic as Suva is: vessels call relatively infrequently. There is also on Tutuila an aerodrome at Tafuna which, it is hoped, when developed may rival Nadi because it lies on a straight route from Hawaii to Australia or New Zealand. At the moment, both Pago harbour and Tafuna are backwaters out of the main stream of south Pacific traffic.

Rose and Swain's islands are low coral atolls of no significance, and the major islands of Eastern Samoa are all high volcanic ones. Tutuila is about eighteen and a half miles in length, and its greatest width is seven miles. The shape of the island is irregular

[1] The islands lie on a direct line between Hawaii and New Zealand, which are respectively 2,600 and 1,300 miles away.

for it is nearly divided in two by Pago harbour which occupies a huge, ancient, breached volcanic crater. Tutuila has a backbone of high volcanic mountains which are considerably eroded, with an extremely rugged landscape covered with dense, luxuriant, tropical vegetation. The mountains rise up very steeply from the coast and there is little flat or level land other than a plain of about five square miles in the south-west of the island; elsewhere the shore is formed of low rocks and blocks of lava projecting into the sea. There are many small rivers which cascade from the steep slopes, but many of these are absorbed by the porous soil before they reach the sea. The island is surrounded by coral reefs, but the harbour of Pago itself is a well protected deep-water anchorage. The islet of Aunu'u is also a volcanic cone about 200 feet high, and roughly elliptical in shape; it is about 1,800 yards long and 1,300 yards wide, with a flat plain in the north-west. The Manu'a group consists of three high islands on which there is little level ground. Ofu, which consists of a hilly ridge, has a small, narrow strip of flat land on the west coast; Olosega rises to a pyramid peak of 2,095 feet with two small level strips of ground on the north-west and south-west sides; Ta'u has a high peak of 3,056 feet in its centre, with small patches of level ground along the east and west coasts. The soil of all the islands is fertile, but so little of it is flat that there is severe erosion on all the slopes. It has been estimated that only fifteen per cent. of the land is arable, and the bulk of that only a few degrees off perpendicular. On none of the islands other than Tutuila is a landing easy or an anchorage good.

The group is about 1,000 miles south of the Equator, closer than either Fiji or French Polynesia, and in the absence of neighbouring large land masses it has a purely oceanic climate. The south-east trades which are the prevailing winds, tend to be easterly, but the northern and westerly winds from December to March produce a wet season. The average annual rainfall at Pago Pago is 200 inches, and the humidity averages eighty per cent.; temperatures range from 70° to 90°F. The group is exposed to severe storms and hurricanes. The climate is less bearable for Europeans than either Fiji or Tahiti, being in general hotter and more humid.

2. *Resources*

The natural resources of Samoa are, like those of Fiji, primarily agricultural, but in fact only one crop has any economic significance so far as trade is concerned: copra. More than any of the islands under discussion, copra dominates the Samoan economy. It is possible to grow bananas and citrus fruits, but these are grown only for local consumption, and cocoa, which is also a possibility, has not achieved any significance to the present date. Nevertheless, although copra is the dominant Samoan crop, the major part of the export trade is fish. Prior to 1954, copra and some handicraft work were the sole exports of American Samoa, but the establishment of an American company's fish cannery in that year made fish an important item in exports, and it is now the largest single one. Thus the picture of the Samoan economy changes after 1954, but the change is the imposition of a fish industry on a one-crop economy which remained unaltered. In 1954, the total value of exports was 788,973 dollars, of which copra made up 385,735 or 49·1 per cent.; fish constituted 42·4 per cent. or 332,970 dollars.[2] In that year there was an excess of imports over exports of 310,429 dollars, which was an improvement over previous years when there was no fish cannery and copra was seventy per cent. or more of the total export value. Since 1954 there has been a favourable balance of trade of more than 2,000,000 dollars for which the fishing industry has been responsible.[3] This is apparently a dramatic change but it is to some extent a deceptive one, because the fishing industry impinges on the local Samoan economy only through its labour force:[4] the capital is American and the fishing fleet Japanese. The old copra economy is left virtually untouched, and the withdrawal of the fish cannery would produce a reversion to the familiar pattern of a one-crop economy and unfavourable terms of trade. The development of a fishing industry in Samoa, however, gives its economy a rather different aspect from the other island groups by exploiting other than agricultural resources, and potentially it is a very important factor of change in a traditional economy. There is one other difference which must be mentioned. Since the American Samoans are American nationals, there is no restriction on their movement to Hawaii and the United States, nor on their enlistment in the armed forces, and the dependants' cheques which come into Eastern Samoa from these expatriates

[2] United States Department of Labour, *Economic Report on American Samoa*, March 1957, p. 18.

[3] In 1956 the total export value was 3,527,639 dollars of which the fish was worth 3,377,943 and copra 154,130 or only 4·3 per cent. of the total.

[4] Usually numbering from 300 to 400 Samoans, mostly women.

is a very considerable addition—estimated at from one to two million dollars a year—to the *per capita* income of Samoans. By comparison, therefore, with the other island groups under discussion, the Eastern Samoans are economically well off and their *per capita* income is probably higher than that of any other group in the south Pacific. It is, moreover, augmented by a Federal grant from the United States towards the cost of government and public works.

Such additional sources of income are very necessary to the economy of American Samoa because, unlike the other colonies, there is considerable pressure of population upon the land. The total population is not large—in 1956 it was only 20,154—but it is great in proportion to the cultivable land in the group, and it is increasing at a phenomenal rate: it has doubled since 1930. The bulk of this population—87·8 per cent.—is Eastern Samoan, and another 8·5 per cent. are Samoans from the New Zealand islands of the group, although their total includes 1,518 part-Samoans.[5] The European population numbers only 173 and other Pacific islanders 347. Thus there are no communal or racial problems in the colony, nor is it necessary to make the reservation which must be made in the case of Tahiti that part of the economy is controlled by a resident foreign group: the labour of the fish cannery is Samoan, its capital American. American Samoa is a homogeneous society, but one which, unlike the Tahitian, has preserved its own social organization.

3. *The People of Samoa*

Samoan society was distinctively a society of villages *(nu'u)* which were largely autonomous units consisting of a group of related households, settled in a formal and organized pattern of well-built houses around the *malae* which was, unlike the Tahitian *marae*, a village green rather than a sacred enclosure.[6] The household was an extended family *(aiga)* consisting of the titled head of the family, the *matai*, his untitled brothers, wives and children.[7] The *matai* was a patriarch who directed all the activities of his household, both economic and social, whose members obeyed him and served him. A village, made up of a number of families, varied in size from some tens to some hundreds of people; and

[5] *Census of American Samoa*, 25 September 1956.

[6] Williamson, op. cit., vol. ii, p. 82.

[7] J. W. Davidson, 'Scholarship and the Government of Colonies', *Historical Studies*, vol. 7, No. 28, pp. 407-8.

the *matai* of the families made up the ruling council or *fono* of a village which governed the community under a ranking *matai* who had precedence. Within the village there were also institutions which linked families together and organized the workaday life of the community.[8] Within each of these groups there were differences of status and function, and perhaps some specialization with a type of guild, for example, of carpenters. The village was thus the important social and political unit of Samoan society and although the family under its *matai* had economic functions, especially in regard to land which he controlled on behalf of his family group, a village was a unit which had considerable autonomy under its own *fono* in economic or daily affairs, its identity asserted by the *fa'alupega,* a formula of genealogy and precedence which was in effect an order of rank prestige; a kind of community history and *Who's Who* rolled into one.[9] For the *matai* titles were carefully graded in relation to each other: some were better than others and conferred greater prestige on the family and the village which possessed them, a prestige which was important when villages combined into wider political units like the districts or *itu.* Within the district or sub-district a *fa'alupega* crystallized the order of precedence among *matai,* and a *fono* dealt with the less mundane functions of war, marriages, political alliances and high ceremonial. Both this wider organization and the village were, therefore, preoccupied with questions of rank and precedence.

Broadly speaking, Samoan society had the two basic groups of those who possessed titles and those who did not, but the organization of the system of rank was much more complex and elaborate than in the other societies under discussion.[10] Within the titled class there were not only various ranks and various preeminences, as there were in Tahiti, but two quite distinct kinds of chief: the *ali'i,* and the talking chief or orator, *tulafale.* The two types were not ranked in relation to each other, but within each there was a system of rank and precedence. Each important chief had at least one orator chief of high rank who acted as a sort of advisory executive, but both acted, more often, within

[8] The *aumaga* was a work and ceremonial group of the young men who had no *matai* title, who did most of the heavy manual work, cooking and serving food and *kava* for the *matai,* with equivalent female organizations, the *aualuma* whose members were the unmarried girls, the wives belonging to the *tausi* and *ava taulele'a.*

[9] F. M. Keesing, *Modern Samoa* (London, 1934), p. 48.

[10] Sahlins, op. cit., p. 29 ff.

a *fono* of other lesser chiefs, and the actual power wielded by the one in relation to the other varied with place and circumstance. The precedence of different titles reflected the changing balance of power in Samoan society, the dominant party for the time being called the *malo* which held one or more of the four high titles which conferred ceremonial precedence in the whole of Samoa (except Manu'a which was distinct)[11] as well as actual political force. Hence the election by a district to one of the higher titles might be, and usually was, accompanied by tension and strife between different areas and parties, between chiefs and orator chiefs. Throughout the system of rank there might be a struggle to combine the power or *pule* of various titles, culminating in the struggle between two rival groups of orator chiefs, the *Tumua* and the *Pule,* each associated with a particular district and group of families, to achieve the political and ceremonial headship of Samoa expressed in the four titles of supreme quality.[12] The impression created by this pattern of rank was, therefore, one of inherent instability, which was reflected in the changing *fa'alupega* of all Samoa.

This instability was due to the fact of election to the higher titles, and while in the lower levels of *matai* in the village there was less of the political manoeuvring which accompanied the election to the higher ones, there might still be competition even within the kinship group which controlled the lesser titles. A *matai* could never be sure who his successor would be, for there were descent and supernatural considerations involved as well as suitability.[13] The higher chiefs derived authority from their direct descent from the gods, and were supported in this authority by ceremonial *tabu* connected with their bodies and their personal possessions. Punishments for breach of these *tabu* could be inflicted by the chief or by the chiefs in the *fono,* but the main sanctions were supernatural ones as they were in Tahiti. And the position of the chiefs, so obviously symbolized by the ceremonial respect of prostration before them or the use of chiefly litters to carry them or food privileges, were one side of the relationship which was reciprocal; the chiefly position satisfied certain social and economic needs of the Samoan people, and at its best it was a patriarchal relationship. The relationship was

11 M. Mead, *Social Organisation of Manu'a* (Bernice P. Bishop Museum Bulletin 76, 1930).

12 Keesing, op. cit., p. 49 ff.

13 Sahlins, op. cit., p. 36.

most obviously reciprocal in the villages, while the high titles were primarily matters of authority in warfare and ceremonial, and the system was flexible enough to secure the election of able leaders or to secure the gradual eclipse of titles held by non-entities.

4. *Historical Factors*

American Samoa cannot be treated separately from Western Samoa for much of its history because its islands have often been overshadowed in European perception and importance by their larger neighbours. The whole Samoa group was discovered by Roggeveen in 1721-2, although he did not land there. La Pérouse landed on Tutuila in 1787 but left after an attack by the Samoans. It was not until 1830 that Samoa was really affected by European contact when missionary influence made itself felt with the arrival of John Williams.[14] As in Tahiti, this European impact coincided with a shift in political power inside Samoan society. The four highest titles had been combined in the person of a woman within the Tupua family, but in the early nineteenth century one of her successors had nominated in his will—a death-bed pronouncement of great importance in determining the succession to titles—a member of the rival Malietoa family to succeed him. Upolu was ravaged by a long war in consequence, and when Williams landed, Malietoa had just secured a complete victory over the Aana and Atua districts which supported the Tupua family in resisting his title. Malietoa received the Europeans hospitably and accepted Christianity, with the result that his importance as the receiver of European goods, including firearms, enhanced his traditional importance, as that of Pomare and Cakobau had been or was to be increased in the other islands. He was treated, in fact, as if he and his party were the national Government, and himself the 'king'. In 1839 a set of Commercial Regulations was promulgated by British and American naval commanders through the *malo* party, which were largely ineffectual, and by 1860 Britain, America and the city of Hamburg had consular representatives to control the relations of Europeans and Samoans. Malietoa's position had never been unchallenged, and in spite of foreign mediation there was revolt in 1848 and 1869; disputes in which Britain and America tended to support Malietoa against German support for Tupua. The disputes themselves were the more bitter because with European recognition the 'kingship' had

[14] Keesing, op. cit., p. 60; Morrell, op. cit., p. 53 ff.

itself acquired more than the traditional significance. In 1873 an American called Steinberger attempted to formulate a constitution and code of law for all Samoa, with an upper and lower house and district governors, which came to grief in the traditional rivalry of *Tumua* and *Pule* within the houses, quite apart from the general question of rivalry for the higher titles.[15]

The Malietoa-Tupua squabble continued throughout the 'seventies, with requests to Britain and the United States to annex the islands, which were refused, although a series of treaties between these two powers, Germany and the Samoan Government established rights to naval coaling stations: the Americans in Pago Pago, the Germans in Upolu and Britain in a never-defined site; Apia was established as a neutral municipality. The Samoan faction fighting was still, however, supported by these rival nations, until the Germans deported Malietoa, installing Tamasese Tupua in his place and obtaining recognition for him from the other two Governments. Samoan custom reasserted itself when the Malietoa title was transferred by election to a third chief, Mata'afa, who headed another opposition. A German naval force supporting Tamasese caused a similar American fleet to be despatched to protect their interests and, together with a British ship which escaped by good seamanship, these vessels were lying in Apia harbour when the hurricane of 1889 destroyed them. In 1889 a Samoa Act, signed in Berlin by the three powers, established a tripartite supervision under which the islands became neutral territory in which the citizens and subjects of the three powers were to have equal rights of residence, trade and personal protection, at the same time recognizing an independent native kingdom with its own Government, Malietoa being proclaimed king with the consent of the Tamasese party. Ten years of this arrangement reproduced the friction between Europeans and the rivalry between Samoan factions expressed by Mata'afa's rebellion in 1893. When Malietoa died five years later, *Tumua* and *Pule* both supported Mata'afa, with the support of the Germans, but a minority backed by the British and American residents recognized the son of Malietoa. Mata'afa's supporters overran the municipality of Apia which, early in 1899, was bombarded by American and British warships. A temporary solution was reached when both claimants were dispossessed by the abolition of the 'kingship' itself, and a more permanent one when a commission of representatives of the three powers re-

[15] Keesing, op. cit., p. 64; Morrell, op. cit., p. 215 ff.

commended partition of the group among themselves. Britain withdrew in return for compensation elsewhere, and the islands of Western Samoa became a German colony while Eastern Samoa became an American possession.

These events by which the Samoa group was divided between European powers affected Samoan life by breaking the unity of society, although Manu'a had always stood outside the normal area of Samoan political order. In themselves, however, they had little effect on the day-to-day life of the islands. Tupua and Malietoa might dispute the high titles with European support, but in the villages the Samoan was affected by missionary teaching and by European trade goods in much the same way as the other island groups. This European influence was most marked in the large islands of Savai'i and Upolu, much less in Tutuila and Manu'a. Pago Pago had a fine harbour which attracted ships but it was relatively unimportant compared with the anchorages which drew their trade from the large European plantations and companies in the islands where land was available.

The sheer physical smallness of the Eastern Samoan islands meant that trade and commerce were severely limited, and that the major influence upon Samoan life there was missionary. The villages each had their church and their native pastor whom they were called upon to support. Obviously the wholesale conversion to Christianity, which happened relatively rapidly, struck at the divine basis of high chiefly authority and the supernatural sanctions by which the old order was sustained. Williams brought Tahitian mission teachers and, within a decade of his arrival, there were some twelve European missionaries of the London Missionary Society throughout the group, covering the islands with a network of mission stations and schools; in the 'forties a training school was also established for native pastors, the *faife'au* who came to constitute a distinctively Samoan church. A Catholic mission began work in 1845, with primarily French personnel, and in 1888 the Mormon church obtained a small following. Nevertheless the extensive organization of religion was perhaps less destructive of traditional society than it was in Tahiti or even in Fiji. There was in Samoa no powerful priesthood nor institutionalized religion which, when it crumbled, carried society with it. The Samoan chiefs and orators tended to take over a new set of beliefs which they interpreted in terms of the existing social order.[16] The *matai* who had been the mediator with the

[16] Keesing, op. cit., pp. 217, 396 ff.

old gods now became the deacon of the church and the mediator with the new; and his patriarchal position tended to be bolstered by the Old Testament society of the Hebrews. Still, the passing of the old *tabu* did loosen some of the bonds of the old society, while at the same time creating new ones. The Samoans are Christians, but the London Missionary Society especially has retained the structure of Samoan life, organizing its church through the *matai*, the *fono* and the district, and supporting the traditional patterns of authority while substituting a Christian theology for the old deities; and even more has the Christian theology of devils and angels maintained many old Samoan superstitions, especially in medical practice.

The general reinforcement that mission activity has lent to the preservation of Samoan society, relatively unaffected in Eastern Samoa by European traders and planters, has been further supported by the American form of government. Pago Pago was viewed primarily as a naval base, and when in 1899 a warship was despatched there to establish one, the settlement of traders and commercial exploitation was severely discouraged. By order of President McKinley on 19 February 1900, the possession was placed under the Department of the Navy, and a further order established a naval station under a Commandant, to whom the detailed government of the station was committed.[17] In 1902 the Department stated that 'it does not consider it necessary to give formal approval to the station regulations that have from time to time been issued, preferring to indicate such as need amendment. This will be necessary until such time as Congress shall see fit to legislate for the islands'. Nothing more than this was ever done during the period of naval control. In fact the first Commandant, Captain Tilley, had not merely to establish a government but to persuade the chiefs to accept American rule. On 13 March 1900 Tui Manu'a, the high ranking chief of the group, gave Tilley a letter accepting the sovereignty and protection of the United States, and in April the high chiefs of Tutuila ceded that island and Aunu'u, although Manu'a's formal act of union did not occur until 14 July 1904.[18] (The Manuans were hesitant about the cession primarily because they had stood aside from the general political framework of old Samoa and, therefore, suspected the Tutuilans.) The Government which Tilley estab-

[17] *Administration of the Government of American Samoa 1900-1951* (Department of the Navy), p. 1.

[18] *Code of American Samoa*, Basis of Authority section.

lished was clearly based on chiefly authority. As he said 'the Government which I propose for these islands is a Government of the chiefs who are to receive additional appointments to their positions from the Commandant of the station', with the result that purely local matters were left in the hands of the chief with whom the central Government was rarely called upon to interfere. Three districts were established, representing the old Samoan districts, and within them fourteen counties which also represented old political affiliations, and the fifty-two villages which were the primary units of Samoan life. And the chiefs of highest rank, except in one or two instances where they were not judged the most capable men, were in general appointed to the governorships of the districts and the chieftainships of the counties. This local government system was supplemented by a series of councils in the districts and the counties, and by village councils which assisted the *pulenu'u* or village chiefs who, unlike the higher chiefs appointed by the Commandant or Governor, were elected annually by the village council. The village councils were empowered to make regulations about roads, sanitation, personal conduct and other matters for the benefit and protection of the people, and to enforce them with punishments through the village magistrate. Such regulations did not need previous approval although they had to be recorded and reported. Between the legislative and executive functions of the officials and the councils no line was clearly drawn, nor was it at the highest council level in the annual *Fono* which was held after 1905. To this came the district governors, county chiefs, *matai* elected by the district councils, and the Governor and his departmental officials who were serving naval officers, with the exception of the first Secretary for Native Affairs who was a white resident of long standing. The *Fono* had purely advisory functions, but its advice covered executive as well as legislative matters.

This was the structure of the Samoan Government which rested on the policy that 'the customs of Samoa, not in conflict with the laws of the United States concerning American Samoa, shall be preserved unless otherwise requested by the representatives of the people'. There were, however, executive agencies, run by the Navy, which dealt with Samoan affairs. The Governor, as the Commandant became, had complete power, and he was a serving officer carrying out an eighteen-month tour of duty. The central executive machinery, staffed by naval personnel on similar short terms of duty, consisted of departments which, other than the

Secretary for Native Affairs who from the beginning dealt with local Samoan affairs, began in 1913 with those for judicial, financial, interior, agricultural and public health affairs, with a public works department created in 1919. By 1930, however, the Secretary for Native Affairs was also the secretary to the Governor, district judge, registrar of titles, supervisor of district governors, chiefs, judges, magistrates, of the copra industry, taxes, passports, police, sheriffs and statistics. The judicial functions of this office were then split up between an attorney-general and a chief justice. Apart from the secretary's office, the executive departments were linked to the Samoan Government by a system of Boards which, originally three in number, for the execution of policy (which included district governors), the Samoan hospital, and auditing, later proliferated. These, too, like the *Fono,* were advisory and, like the departments, carried out the will of the Governor.

The naval administration was naturally principally concerned with the conduct of the station. It provided for the material needs of the Samoans within the limits of its resources, but its general concern was to provoke as little trouble as possible. Hence local government was left to the chiefs, and Samoan custom left as far as possible untouched, to be administered by the *matai.* The Code of American Samoa, first promulgated in 1917 and revised in 1937, gave legal sanction to the system of local government and Samoan custom so far as it did not conflict with the laws of American Samoa; in particular it preserved the land to the Samoans under the old system of *pule.* Nevertheless, the naval administration had its troubles arising from native policy and organization, and also from the small European population.[19] The latter, as early as 1902, were claiming that taxpayers should have some share in the absolute authority of the Governor, and in 1904 a petition was carried to Washington which claimed that the Samoans were sick of Navy rule. These were minor irritations which, however, reflected the indeterminate status of the possession. For Congress did not accept the cession of islands by formal Act until 1929, and it failed to provide a form of government when a proposed Organic Act was rejected in the House of Representatives in 1933, and a similar Act failed to pass in the Senate in 1937, so that a naval officer continued to rule under the executive order of the President.[20] White discontent with this

19 Keesing, op. cit., p. 130 ff.

20 *Congressional Record,* 75th Congress, 1st Session, S 1095.

absolute naval rule also had its effects upon the Samoans who, naturally enough, were affected by the clash between naval government and Samoan custom. In 1909, for example, Tui Manu'a died, and a typical struggle occurred over the election to the high title of the kind which had regularly occurred in Upolu and Savai'i. The authorities persuaded the rival factions to leave the title in abeyance, but in 1924 the death of the district governor who had exercised authority on Manu'a revived the dispute.[21] An election to the title was made, thus creating a potential rival to the appointed successor to the district governorship. The new Tui Manu'a was banished to Tutuila by the Governor who declared there could be no such title-holder, although petitions suggested that the fact was never really accepted by the Manuans.

This clash of custom in Manu'a was the result of the conservative character of society: it was less affected than Tutuila by European contacts. The latter place produced troubles of a different order which were in part due to the clash of custom and modern government but also to the direct influence of European ideas upon Samoan perception. The *Mau,* or opinion movement, which began in 1920 took the form of demands for civil government, although the similar movement in Western Samoa which took a different form suggests that the underlying causes were more important than the precise demands.[22] In 1921 seventeen chiefs and orators were arrested for conspiring to kill the high chiefs who had signified their loyalty to the Governor, a situation partly prompted by the fact that the orators, as a matter of policy, had been ignored in favour of the *ali'i* in appointment to the offices of district governor or county chiefs; they were imprisoned and then paroled in 1924. Throughout 1927 and 1928, the Governor continued to meet *Mau* leaders, and to be confronted with demands for civil government and American citizenship, demands which were echoed and supported outside the islands. A Commission, appointed by Congress, collected evidence in Samoa in 1930, and its proposals formed the basis of the abortive Organic Act of 1933, the expectation of which slowly caused the *Mau* to fade, although the strains and tensions underlying the movement certainly remained. Some of them were economic. For example, the *fita fita* guard of about seventy young Samoan men enlisted for local service had much the same conditions and pay as the United States personnel, but within their villages

[21] Keesing, op. cit., pp. 131, 207.
[22] ibid., pp. 177 ff., 205 ff.

and under their *matai* they represented an economic threat to the old subsistence agriculture. Similarly, apart from economic attitudes, the political assumptions of Americans about self-determination and human rights influenced Samoan attitudes to modify custom. The *Mau* was in fact a result of the changing order of society which, because of the nature of American government and the form of its institutions, was still preserved within the framework of Samoan custom.

Under naval control the Samoans were governed by a benevolent paternalism. Their material wants were taken care of within the limits of naval resources, and their wishes were respected so far as they were consistent with the smooth and efficient running of the station. Nevertheless, the Samoans were always incidental rather than central to the main concern of government. This situation had its advantages: Samoan society was protected from the most destructive effects of European contact which elsewhere in the Pacific produced a breakdown of society or an apathetic situation, and it retained its vitality, living in its villages under the traditional system of authority. Such changes as there were, like the conversion to Christianity, were adapted to Samoan life, and whatever strains and stresses they may have set up, when the time came for civilian control and political development which was not possible under Navy rule, the traditional Samoan society was still functioning and vigorous.

CHAPTER VIII

THE STRUCTURE OF SAMOAN GOVERNMENT

The Second World War demonstrated that as a naval base Pago Pago was of limited value, and after it was over there began in the United States and in Samoa a movement to transfer the island territories to civilian administration. On 18 June 1947 the Secretaries of State, Navy and Interior, agreed that responsibility should be transferred to the last, their decision being approved by the President in February 1948. He subsequently ordered, in a letter of May 1949, that the Secretaries of the Navy and the Interior should prepare a plan for the transfer of control. By joint memorandum of 31 August 1949 the two set the date 1 July 1951 as the occasion for Samoa's becoming a civilian concern.

An official statement of policy which was made in 1956 declared that the general objective was to provide for the orderly and progressive development of people towards self-government and to assist the people to obtain the maximum possible self-support. In political terms, this meant a territorial government which separated legislative, executive and judicial branches, with appropriate checks and balances, but, within this framework, a government in accordance with the desires of the Samoan people, adapted to Samoan customs, traditions and land ownership. As part of this policy, there was to be increased delegation of authority to local Samoan officials, as well as to the legislative body when it demonstrated its ability to legislate effectively and continuously. More generally, the policy was stated as a desire to respect the Samoan wish to retain the *matai* system, and to consult fully with the Samoans, but also to encourage such non-indigenous social concepts as would be beneficial, and to provide such social regulations and benefits as necessary in local conditions. There was, in fact, a change in emphasis from naval days; a change from a policy basically concerned with preserving the *status quo* to one which looked forward to change.

1. *The Executive Institutions and Councils*

The institutions which served this policy were not, however, wholly the creation of civilian government. The first Samoan legislature was set up by the Navy in 1948 to consist of two houses: a Senate or House of *Ali'i* of twelve high chiefs whose titles were designated by law in the Code of American Samoa, and who held office so long as they held their titles, and a House of Representatives of fifty *matai,* one from each of the villages of the territory, together with two non-*matai* members. The initiative was not wholly the Navy's; it came from a meeting of the hereditary leaders of Samoa in April 1945 in a *Fono* which discussed the form of making law, and which formulated a Bill, known as the Samoa Act of 1945, principally under the inspiration of High Talking Chief Tuiasosopo.[1] The *Fono* resolved that a legislative body of accredited representatives of Samoa be created. The Governor returned the answer that he was not exactly clear as to the meaning of the resolution; legislation had in the past been discussed in the annual *Fono,* and there had been close co-operation between it and the Governor; he thought, therefore, that a legislative committee of three should be set up to discuss with the Governor any matters of legislation which came up in the *Fono*. The annual *Fono* of the same year again resolved in favour of a legislative body, and the Governor in reply expanded his point. Power, he said, had been placed by the President of the United States with the Navy Department which authorized the Governor to act; he could not therefore delegate power without the approval of the President and Congress. The Samoan people, he continued, had in the past advised the Governor through the annual *Fono* and had made their desires known in this way; in effect it was an advisory legislative body and many of its suggestions had been adopted into law or had influenced policy. Nevertheless, he agreed to pass the resolution on to Washington. In the following year, a similar resolution was passed by the annual *Fono* in identical form, receiving the answer that the Governor doubted if American Samoa could afford the expense of a legislature, and that the present annual *Fono* was commensurate with the needs and abilities of the people. Tuiasosopo nevertheless pressed the point by presenting the proposed Samoa Bill, and it was followed up in 1947 with a resolution asking for

[1] 'Roads Leading to the Founding of Our Present Legislature' (typescript in the Legislative Office of American Samoa).

the establishment of a legislature of two Houses, one of nobles to conform with Samoan custom, and one of representatives to maintain fully the principles of democracy. Neither House was to interfere with appointed native officials, and the whole body was to act in an advisory capacity for ten years until it was clear that it could fully and competently make law. A further meeting of Samoan leaders in 1948 approved a final draft of the changes desired in the Code of American Samoa by which a legislative body of this advisory kind could be erected, and to these the Governor agreed, no doubt in the light of the Hopkins Report which had expressed a similar view in March 1947, after resolutions in Congress in January and February 1948 had proposed a government for American Samoa, and a declaration of President Truman in June 1947 that organic legislation should be prepared.[2]

The Code of American Samoa, as amended in February 1948, provided for a House of *Ali'i* composed of the holders of the titles Faumuina, Fuimaono, Lefiti, Le'iato, Mauga, Misa, Satele, Sotoa, Tufele, Tuitele and Tuiolosega, all of whom had to be more than thirty years of age.[3] The House of Representatives was elected, composed of members who were at least thirty years of age, able to read and write Samoan, of at least three-quarters Samoan blood, born in American Samoa, and resident in the village which they represented for five years. No person holding public office was eligible, but representatives might sit on another council. The method of election to the House of Representatives was by Samoan custom in the village on the first Monday in November in even-numbered years beginning with 1948, the two non-*matai* members, however, being elected by secret ballot on the same day. Once elected, the legislative body met on the third Tuesday in November of each year as a Committee of the

[2] *Congressional Record*, 80th Congress, 1st Session. In January 1947 Representative Cole of New York introduced House Joint Resolution 70 to provide for an office of External Possessions inside the Navy Department, headed by an assistant-secretary; it was lost in the Committee on Public Lands. Jackson of Washington introduced H.J.R. 80, seven days later, to establish civil administration, a resolution which was also lost in the Committee on Public Lands. Both of these proposals related to all island territories, not just to American Samoa. In May 1947 Bradley of California introduced House Resolution 3564 to provide a government for American Samoa and confer citizenship, which was also referred to the Committee on Public Lands. The Hopkins Committee Report was prepared by the Institute of Ethnic Affairs at the request of Samoan chiefs, and it was on this basis that Representative Bradley, a former Governor of Guam, introduced his resolution in Congress.

[3] *Code of American Samoa*, 1948, Section 76.

Whole of both Houses to propose resolutions to be considered at the next session, which were then forwarded to the Governor for comment. The regular session met on the second Tuesday in January, although the Governor might call a special session of not more than two days' duration for a specific purpose. The Governor might also submit resolutions to the legislature and attend its sessions in person or by deputy, as well as addressing both Houses, in joint session at their opening, on the affairs of government. Each House elected a president, appointed its own clerk and made rules for the conduct of its business. The procedure was for a resolution first to be considered by the representatives and, if passed by an absolute majority, to be sent to the House of *Ali'i* which, if it also passed the resolution by an absolute majority, would then send it to the Governor. If the upper House failed to vote on such a resolution by the end of the day following its receipt, it still went to the Governor. Failure to secure an absolute majority in the upper House involved the return of such a Bill to the lower, which might then convene a joint session for reconsideration. A resolution which was sent to the Governor, either in its original form or as amended after a joint session would, if the Governor approved, be effective within thirty days; but the Governor had also the power of veto.

In May 1949 a resolution was introduced into the House of Representatives of the United States by Mr Redden to provide for civilian government in American Samoa, which envisaged an executive council of district governors and county chiefs to consult on economic and social policy, a *fono* of one or two Houses, as the *Fono* might determine, with legislative power; if a Bill passed and was disapproved by the Governor and returned, it might be passed over his objection by a two-thirds majority of each House, upon which it might go to the President for signature or not, as he decided.[4] Provision was also made in House Resolution 4500 for a Resident Commissioner to sit in the House of the United States Congress to debate but not to vote. The judicature was linked to the federal district of Hawaii. A commission of seven persons, at least three of them residents of American Samoa, was to be set up by the President to survey the application of federal statutes. The Resolution was referred to the Committee on Public Lands, which heard testimony from the Secretary of the Interior and high ranking naval officers in favour of it, and the Miles Committee reported upon it in November-December 1949, having

[4] *Congressional Record*, 81st Congress, 1st Session, H.R. 4500.

held hearings in American Samoa itself where the Resolution had been circulated in advance. The *Fono* also had the opportunity to suggest amendments which were, in substance, directed towards the maintenance of Samoan custom. They sought, for example, to have the prohibition against 'involuntary servitude' amended to read 'slavery' in order to avoid any assault on the *matai* system, which in another amendment they desired to be the basis of voting; elections ought to be by Samoan custom not universal suffrage. The *Fono* also expressed itself in favour of two Houses, which the amendment of the Code in February 1948 had already established. The Miles Committee had reservations about these amendments. It frankly stated that it regarded the '*matai* system as undemocratic and inconsistent with American principles, but at the same time it recognizes the upheaval that would follow if so ancient and strongly rooted a tradition were legislated out of existence'; especially, it thought, Samoan land must for the present be protected. Nevertheless, the Committee concluded that 'the *matai* system will fall of its own accord, as the people become more exposed to American ways, and therefore recommends that nothing be included now in the organic legislation which would directly and instantly destroy it'. Nothing was; for, like previous reports, no organic legislation followed.

This legislative arrangement set up in February 1948 lasted for four years. In a special session of June 1952 the *Fono* passed a joint resolution calling for a reorganization and corresponding amendments to the Code, asking also for full legislative power and the delay of any organic legislation in Congress until the Samoans were sure that their customs and their lands would be safeguarded.[5] The Secretary of the Interior refused full legislative power, but agreed to the reorganization, which was then proclaimed by the Governor.[6] A Council of Paramount Chiefs was set up, consisting of the former members of the House of *Ali'i*, which was transferred to the executive branch of the government 'to maintain the dignity and prestige of Samoa from ancient times', for 'the maintenance and preservation of their traditions and customs'. A Senate of fifteen members was substituted in the legislature, representing the fourteen counties of American Samoa, plus one extra member who represented in turn each of the four Western District counties. A senator must be at least thirty years old, of

[5] *Legislative Record*, 2nd Legislature, Special Session, June 1952.

[6] Office of the Governor, GAS/8B(1)/8E, Serial 958, JCE-GHG/jan.

at least half Samoan blood, living in American Samoa for at least five years, and a bona fide resident of at least one year, the registered *matai* of a Samoan family who maintains his *monotaga* (custom of reciprocal furnishing of goods and services between a chief and the villagers), unconvicted of any crime or of treason and not holding appointive office in the Government of American Samoa. He was elected by Samoan custom, which involves a village council selecting a candidate who is then presented to the county council which decides between village candidates; no vote being taken in either case but there being discussion until unanimous agreement is reached. A senator thus elected held office for four years. The House of Representatives was made up of seventeen members plus one delegate,[7] whose qualifications had to be the same as those of a senator with the important exception that they need not be *matai*, and with a lower age limit of twenty-five. They were elected by universal suffrage and a secret ballot for a term of two years by an electorate consisting of all eighteen-year-olds living in American Samoa for five years and bona fide residents of the constituency for one, unconvicted and registered as voters. Both senators and representatives were paid a small salary of 180 dollars per year, and the President of the Senate and the Speaker of the House were paid 1,800 dollars per year.

The 1952 legislature was to have a trial period of two years, while the Governor promised that successive grants of legislative authority would be made as rapidly as the legislature demonstrated its ability to exercise it.[8] A special committee was set up in 1954 to consider the results of the trial period. It recommended that the House be elected by direct and secret ballot and universal suffrage from political counties on the basis of population; one representative for each thousand persons within a county, providing that, regardless of population, no county should have less than one and none more than three members. There should be no further representation of the non-*matai* community as such; and Swain's Island should continue to have a delegate but not a

[7] Being elected by constituencies: one from Leone village (the old capital), one from the county outside Leone, one from the villages Faga'alu, Utulei and Faga Toga, one from the villages of Pago Pago and Satala, one from the villages of Leloaloa and Aua, and one each from the other counties (with the exception of Lealataua and Mauputasi in which these villages stand) to a total of twelve members; the delegate comes from Swain's Island and has no right to vote.

[8] *Legislative Record*, 2nd Legislature, Special Session, October 1952.

representative. The term of the House should be retained as two years. No changes in the qualifications of members were proposed, but every county, the committee thought, should be allowed to impose such qualifications as they deemed in the best interest of the county in addition to those prescribed by the Government. The Senate was said to be functioning effectively, and no changes were proposed. To replace the Council of Paramount Chiefs, however, a Samoan Ceremonial Council was recommended, composed of the members of the Council of Paramount Chiefs and open to all traditional chiefs of the counties, new members to be admitted by majority vote if they were otherwise qualified. Membership should not preclude the holding of public or private office, and they should, in fact, be given prior consideration in the selection of officers of the local government organization provided they were otherwise qualified. It was intended that the Council should act in a ceremonial capacity upon the request of the Governor in such matters as greetings to distinguished visitors and other customary practices, but it should have no executive, legislative or judicial authority, nor should its members be paid anything except their actual expenses. More generally, it was recommended that the sessions of the legislature should remain at thirty days per year, although budgetary provision should be made for emergency sessions not exceeding fifteen days in all at the discretion of the Governor on the recommendation of the President of the Senate and Speaker of the House. An increase in compensation to ten dollars per day was suggested. Following a legislative training programme to be conducted in December 1954, a regular drafting session of the legislature should be held in June each year, after the elections in May. The Governor's comments on such draft resolutions should be returned to a regular session not later than August in each year. A final recommendation was made for full legislative power (subject only to such veto as the President of the United States exercised over the Congress) in matters of Samoan land and titles, levying of local taxes, appropriation of local revenue for local government and such other matters of strictly local interest as did not affect the funds and welfare of citizens of the United States.

Not all of the committee's recommendations were accepted. In September 1954 the Governor commented that the proposal to allow the counties to impose additional qualifications for membership of the House was unacceptable; that senators should be elected for four-year terms with half of them being elected every two years, since this would give the councils better control over senators than six-year terms, the next Senate to decide the length of term of its elected members by lot, and geographically; that the Ceremonial Council must have a limit placed on its membership at eighteen, having no intrinsic claim to high office other than merit; and that increased pay for legislators was beyond the scope of the committee, as was the suggestion of full legislative power. The Governor was in agreement with the general findings of the committee, and he pointed out that when the two-year period ended, both Houses would be dissolved and the Council of Paramount Chiefs would disappear, the two former being brought back into existence simultaneously on 1 January 1955, and the Ceremonial Council being recruited by nominations from the traditional councils of their respective district to hold office at the Governor's pleasure. He further recommended that each district select one high orator chief for membership of the Ceremonial Council.

The effect of these proposals of 1954 was essentially to leave the constitution as it was. A special committee on territorial and insular affairs, appointed by the 83rd Congress, visited Samoa in November 1954 and expressed the view that considerable progress had been made by the legislature within the trial period as an independent and responsible law-making body to which authority could be relinquished as soon as it was deemed ready.[9] The invitation to district governors to attend meetings of the legislature was thought to have raised debates from a petty or local level. No immediate steps were taken towards an Organic Act, but a constitutional committee was established in American Samoa in 1954 to assemble material. There was general agreement that the trial period had worked well, but the steps taken were only intermediate ones.

After five years, during which the committee assembled some material and then lapsed and the legislature had some heated discussions and debates, a drafting committee was set up in late 1959 to prepare a constitution for American Samoa. The text of this was presented to a Convention gathered in April 1960 which, after long discussions and some high feelings, approved it. The constitution of American Samoa included a Bill of Rights which,

[9] The committee was set up by the special sub-committee on Territorial and Insular Affairs of the Committee on Interior and Insular Affairs, pursuant to House Resolution 89 of the 83rd Congress; *Congressional Record*, 83rd Congress, 2nd Session.

in addition to the safeguards provided in the American Constitution itself, also protected Samoan land and social organization, and it ratified what had been political practice in the colony since 1952. The Senate was retained in its existing form, while the House was to be elected on a basis of population, providing that a county should always have at least one representative, and the total number of the House should not exceed twenty-four, representation to be reapportioned at not less than ten-yearly intervals. The specific reference to 'at least half Samoan blood' was dropped from their qualifications which now required them only to be American nationals and left the other qualifications as they were in 1952. The qualifications of an elector were redefined to raise the age limit to twenty, reduce residence to two years in American Samoa and one in the constituency, and to provide that he or she be an American national or a person of at least half Samoan blood owing no allegiance to any foreign state.

The general form of the legislature was thus maintained, but its power was greatly increased. Under the constitution it became a law-making body, meeting for this purpose in one regular session of not more than thirty days in March of each year, with provision for a special session of not more than fifteen days at the call of the Governor. It was provided that laws might be enacted, originating in either House or from the Governor, by a Bill obtaining a majority in each House and receiving the Governor's assent. His control was maintained by a veto within twenty days of receiving a Bill, after which a measure became law without his assent unless the legislature had adjourned. Such a vetoed Bill might be repassed in the next session, and if the Governor then failed to approve it, the Bill went to the Secretary of the Interior in Washington who might approve it within ninety days, after which it lapsed. A further control was the Governor's power to promulgate urgent legislation without the assent of the legislature. Under these safeguards, the legislature was transformed from an advisory to a law-making body in 1960, when the Secretary of the Interior signed the new constitution after four Samoan delegates, from each of the seventeen electoral districts, and the Governor had also signed. Apart from this major change in the status of the legislature, the other changes wrought by this constitution were minor technical ones relating to the form of legislation, payment of legislators (raised to 300 dollars a year), and the provision of a Legislative Counsel to assist with technical details. The constitution in essence confirmed the structure of government which had existed since 1952; it had already been tested by experience, and it satisfied a constant Samoan demand for a law-making body while reserving final control to the Governor and the Department of the Interior.

The creation of a law-making body to replace the advisory one did not effect the separation of powers which had been introduced into the Samoan Government with civilian control. The Code debarred, and the present constitution debars, appointive officers from membership of the *Fono*. The executive structure consists of the Governor in whom all executive power is vested, who is appointed as the laws of the United States provide.[10] He is assisted by the Secretary of American Samoa, and various specialist officers and departments which were reorganized when naval personnel withdrew, but which cover the range of colonial government: health, education, public works and so on, the number of departments being limited to eight.

The Samoan Affairs Office, which is the local government executive, has, on the other hand, remained virtually unchanged, the Secretary for Samoan Affairs now being appointed by the Governor from among the leading chiefs. American Samoa is still divided into the three districts of Tutuila and Aunu'u which make up the Eastern and Western districts, and Manu'a, further sub-divided into their five, four and five counties respectively, containing the fifty-two villages or settlements.[11] Each of these is an administrative unit under a graded series of officials. The district governors are appointed by the Governor on the recommendation of the district council, to hold office for four years.[12] Their duty is to preside at the district council, and to take responsibility for the welfare and good order of the district; they may be removed for misconduct. The district governor is assisted by a clerk appointed by the Governor of Samoa on the former's recommendation, to assist with correspondence and records (the clerk is a paid official removable at the Governor's pleasure) and a secretary of the district council who, like his superior, is required to take an oath of office. The district council over which the district governor presides is charged especially with the cleanli-

[10] *Constitution of American Samoa*, Article iv, Section 1; *Review of Civil Administration*, 1956; *Annual Reports* of the Governor to the Department of the Interior.

[11] *Code of American Samoa*, Section 61.

[12] ibid., Section 63; *Constitution of American Samoa*, Article iv, Section 11.

ness of the district, planting of lands, roads and all local matters, and it may make regulations on these local concerns. The county reproduces this organization at a lower level. A county chief is appointed by the Governor, on the recommendation of the district governor and county council, for four years, and he presides over the county council under the supervision of the district governor.[13] He is responsible for the welfare and good order of the county, and he must report upon all meetings of the county council to his superior. A county chief is removable only by the request of the majority of the chiefs of the county for cause shown. He also has duties as a member of the district council. Both the district governor and the county chief are paid officials.

The district and the county represent the old political groupings of Samoa, but the villages were largely autonomous units and the grass-roots of the local government system lie there. Annually on the second Wednesday in December the village nominates from the ranks of its resident *matai,* a chief to be styled *pulenu'u.*[14] The nomination is referred to the county chief and the district governor who shall approve or disapprove and forward the recommendation to the Governor, who may confirm or reject it. The *pulenu'u* receives such compensation as fixed by the Governor. He is required to obey the district governor, to preside at all village meetings, which he must report upon to the county chief, to be responsible for the state of the village, roads, sanitation and the carrying out of the regulations. He may be removed for cause shown. The village council which assists him consists of all chiefs and heads of families whose titles and their succession are legally registered under the Code, and who, sitting together, are the village guardians; but the *pulenu'u* shall point out to them the measures for discussion, expect obedience and watch the observance of the laws.[15] He and the council may make regulations for cleanliness, planting roads and local matters, and may provide penalties for the district court to inflict. Such regulations come into force when the chief proclaims them publicly, but the penalties may not exceed ten dollars or thirty days' hard labour and they must be inflicted by the court. Any such regulations, and matters discussed in council, must be reported to the county

[13] *Code,* Section 64; *Constitution of American Samoa,* Article iv, Section 11.

[14] *Code,* Section 65.

[15] *Code,* Sections 66-71.

chief who passes them on to the higher reaches of local government.

These higher reaches were joined together by an Executive Council which, when it was set up in 1956, included the President of the Senate, the Speaker of the House, and the three district governors who met to assist the Governor in a purely advisory capacity at regular intervals, by the discussion of policy affecting Samoan welfare and liaison with different bodies. The Local Government Council, which was part of the executive branch with a permanent office in the Executive Building, was just as important, however, as this link of legislative and executive branches. This Council, also created in 1956, and composed of the district governors and the fourteen county chiefs nominated for four years by their respective councils, gradually assumed the role of a policy-making body within the Department of Samoan Affairs, including all local government business normally dealt with in conference with the Governor. By appointing its own officers who, for a yearly period, form an executive committee, it maintains constant liaison with the Governor and the Secretary of American Samoa, co-ordinating all matters pertaining to local government and reporting all its decisions to the Secretary and the Governor. This Council had its origin in the irregular meetings held by the Governor for the district governors and county chiefs, at which it became apparent that these officials were able to assume a more important role in the direction of local government; a more formal organization, therefore, was thought to be desirable, which had permanent headquarters in the Executive Building to ensure that consultation was permanently available. As a body within the executive branch it was effective, unlike the abortive Council of Paramount Chiefs which did not distinguish between advisory and executive functions. The policy was intended to develop a greater measure of responsible administration among Samoan leaders by continually pressing increased measures of responsibility upon them and, especially at the village level, developing a self-sustaining formal political organization for executive purposes.

2. *The Judiciary*

The separation of legislative and executive branches of government which came with civilian control also distinguished the judicial branch. The laws set out as applicable in American Samoa were defined in the Code as 'those parts of the Constitution and

Laws of the United States as shall by their own force be in effect in Samoa', the laws defined in the Code itself and the executive orders promulgated by the Governor, so much of the common law of England as was suitable and not inconsistent with either of the preceding two, and Samoan custom which was not in conflict with any of them.[16] To enforce the law, the Navy had set up three kinds of courts: a High Court, district and village courts which, since 1931, had been presided over by a judge independent of the executive.[17] Under civilian control the village courts, in which the *matai* who was an executive official also sat as judge, were abolished. A Chief Justice, whose position was confirmed by Article iii of the new constitution, now supervises the judicial branch, presiding over the High Court and selecting Samoan associate judges to sit with him in the trial division of that court and in the district courts; he makes the final decision if there is any disagreement and establishes the rules for business in all courts. The Chief Justice is appointed as provided by the laws of the United States. His associate judges are four, appointed by the Governor on the Chief Justice's recommendation during good conduct. They sit in the appellate division of the High Court, unless disqualified on precise grounds of family or professional involvement, and in the district courts as assigned by the Chief Justice. The High Court has three divisions: appellate, trial and probate. The first is constituted by the Chief Justice and all the associates to hear appeals from the other divisions and the district courts. With two associates, the Chief Justice constitutes the trial division, although in cases of treason, murder, manslaughter and intent to kill there must be four associates, two of them temporary ones nominated from a 'panel'. Civil cases (including land and *matai* titles), and criminal cases involving punishment of more than a ten-dollar fine or one month's imprisonment, are in the original jurisdiction of the High Court. In the probate division, the Chief Justice sits alone. The High Court staff is appointed by the Chief Justice, and one of them, the clerk, is charged not only with keeping the records of court business but birth and death registers, Government archives,

[16] *Code*, Section 1.

[17] The Bingham Congressional Committee in 1930 recommended that the office of judge be separated from the executive; at the same time an attorney-general's office was created. The court system in Navy times is that described in Section 5 of the *Code of American Samoa,* 1948. Some amendments were made under civilian control to the effect described in the text.

register of land and *matai* titles, deeds, mortgages and leases and the issue of marriage licences and records.

American Samoa is divided into five judicial districts, called by their respective numbers. Each has a district court made up of the Chief Justice, if he is present, and an associate assigned by him to the particular district. They possess original jurisdiction in all civil cases of debt or injury of less than 1,000 dollars (but all land-right cases must go to the High Court) and in criminal cases where punishment involves a fine of less than ten dollars or a sentence of less than one month. In addition, the two judicial districts of Manu'a (4th and 5th) have original jurisdiction over all cases of divorce, separation, adoption, probate, and annulment of marriage and all except the serious criminal cases. The unappealed decisions are reviewed by the Chief Justice in cases of debt or injury to property or people, criminal cases of more than a ten-dollar fine or one month's imprisonment, and the cases tried by the Manu'a districts; he can uphold, change, reverse, set aside or return any case. Death sentences may be reviewed by the Secretary of the Interior, but there is no provision for appeal beyond the High Court of Samoa to any other United States court.

This structure of government in American Samoa has affinities with both British and French practice in the colonies under discussion. It reveals on the one hand marked assimilationist tendencies, and on the other a paternalistic tradition of protection of customary society. The form of its central institutions, the Senate, the House of Representatives and the High Court is precisely modelled on metropolitan institutions, enshrining the principle of the separation of powers. The institutions of local government employ the traditional authorities. The Governor, whose internal power is more absolute than that of the President of the United States because it is based on external authority, is both a check and a balance in the constitution. Samoan political advancement is thus expected to occur through both characteristically American and characteristically Samoan institutions. The Samoans are not expected to become American as the Tahitians are to become French, but it is assumed that, while remaining Samoans, they will add some of the values enshrined in American institutions.

CHAPTER IX

POLITICAL ADVANCEMENT IN AMERICAN SAMOA

Because the American Government distinguishes so sharply between legislative, executive and judicial branches, political advancement in Eastern Samoa is the easier to describe in terms of the two questions which have been asked in each of these colonies. It is easier for another reason, too. American Samoa does not have the complicated communal situation of Fiji, nor the incredibly mixed situation of French Polynesia; its population is still Samoan, its life still deeply influenced by traditional forms and values, and its population and area small enough to present the administration with a far less formidable task; not, however, a less complicated one. The same issues which arise from the operation of European-conceived institutions and values in a non-European society are present, perhaps in an even more acute form, because the Samoans among the peoples of South Pacific islands have been notoriously difficult to rule.

The legislative body of American Samoa, unlike the Tahitian Assembly, was not a new body in the post-war period; like the Council of Chiefs in Fiji, it had a long history behind it, and it is necessary to examine one or two of the salient characteristics of the *Fono* before discussing the present operation of the Senate and House of Representatives. The annual *Fono* contained all the high title-holders of Samoa, both *ali'i* and *tulafale,* whether or not they held executive offices; indeed, the most constant element in the gathering was the district governors, county chiefs and judges, who were much the same group of men in succeeding years.[1] The delegates from each of the three districts varied, but some delegates reappeared in each session. The composition of the *Fono* thus gave the old leaders of Samoa a dominant voice in its proceedings, and they were, of course, the leaders primarily by Samoan custom. Lower ranking title-holders spoke seldom in

[1] The record of the annual *Fono* preserved in the Governor's Office, American Samoa.

the meetings and, if they spoke, spoke timidly.[2] The *Fono* enshrined conservative Samoan attitudes; an advantage when the body was purely consultative and the Navy looking for tranquillity. Under the circumstances, it is not surprising that the resolutions and advice of this body showed more concern with Samoan custom than familiarity with the needs of modern government, and that successive governors doubted the Samoan capacity to rise above their traditional feuds, jealousies and preoccupations.

It must be admitted that, looking at the resolutions passed by the *Fono,* the governors had good grounds for their doubts. There were recurrent motions for the reductions of the poll tax, the reduction of dog licences, reduction in the number of schools and reduction of bus fares, while side by side with such resolutions it was urged that a passenger vessel should be built, that salaries be increased, that new roads be made and new classes started. Such attitudes are not, of course, peculiar to Samoans, but they existed in the *Fono* in a much more open and glaring contradiction than they do in more sophisticated assemblies, and the blatant attempt to pay less and get more struck all the governors as evidence of the failure to grasp the economic situation of American Samoa or the failure of responsibility in taking decisions. Alone, such incompetence may have seemed susceptible to experience and training, but, in the governors' eyes, it was coupled with attitudes rooted in Samoan custom which suggested that not much could be hoped for. Time after time, the *Fono* wanted authority given back to the family to remove the *matai,* to abolish the registration of *matai* titles, to allow the old authority represented by the *fa'a Samoa* fines to be resumed, to enable a *matai* who failed to pay him taxes to continue in his position and to enable the family to divide *matai* titles. To all such requests, the Governor had to reply in effect that such resolutions would impair the efficiency of the Government and throw it into confusion, and there was always the strong suspicion that the instability of traditional Samoan politics lay just below the surface of the *Fono* resolutions. In 1938, for example, the Eastern District presented a motion that *fita fita* guards should be recruited from the

[2] For example, in the *Fono* of 1938, the tendency was for one high title-holder to speak for a district. Thus, most resolutions were spoken to only by Tufele, Leoso, Le'iato and Tuiasosopo; with occasional intervention by others. On the general question of 'weighted voices' in Samoa, see F. M. and M. M. Keesing, *Elite Communication in Samoa* (Stanford, 1956), p. 98 ff.

district to which their predecessors had belonged; since the figures were then Eastern District forty-three, Western fifteen and Manu'a eighteen, the resolution was intended to secure an Eastern monopoly. It is not surprising, therefore, that in 1946 the naval Governor was convinced that the advisory *Fono,* which had no legislative powers nor any clear distinction from the executive branch, was commensurate with the abilities of the Samoans. The legislature which was set up in 1948 began to work in the shadow of this conviction born of past experience.

Whatever the defects of the annual *Fono,* however, it did avoid one consequence of the separation of powers in a society like that of Samoan custom, and so did the first legislature. The House of *Ali'i* contained, as had the *Fono,* the high ranking title-holders of American Samoa, even when they held executive office. In the Code of 1948, Le'iato, Tufele and Tuitele, who were district governors, were by title members of the upper House, and Mauga, Misa, Lefiti, Tuiolosega, Letuli, Satele and Fuimaono were county chiefs; between them they constituted five-sixths of the House.[3] Plainly there was no separation of executive and legislature in the upper House, but there was one important difference from the *Fono:* since the lower House was elected, the possibility occurred of rivalry between the traditional title-holders and leaders of Samoa and the representatives of the villages. In the *Fono* the delegates had been very quiet: in the House of Representatives they were not so overshadowed. Nevertheless, the possibility of friction on this score was reduced by the method of election to the lower House by Samoan custom, which gave the powerful chief the opportunity to influence selection. Thus the conflicts which arose were not those of traditional leaders against the new men, for both were part of the traditional order, but, as was the case with the *Fono,* between different districts and title-holders and their supporters.[4] The conflicts were due to Samoan custom itself and not to the emergence of new attitudes.

[3] *Code of American Samoa,* Section 76.

[4] *Legislative Record,* 1st Legislature, Special Session, November 1948. Tuitele, for example, spoke about the political relationship of Sua and Vaifanua with Fofo and Aitulagi counties, which had been agreed upon in earlier *Fono* but which was now challenged by High Chief Mauga and the leaders of Mauputasi county; both groups had petitioned Washington. In the Regular Session of the same Legislature in January 1949 the question arose of the representation of Ituau county in the Eastern District, where three chiefs had been nominated for one seat by the four different village councils; on the motion of Satele a choice was made between two of the three nominees. But then Sotoa wanted another

A different situation arose when the third legislature sat in 1953. The Senate elected by Samoan custom and the House elected by universal suffrage then began to represent the old and the new, and to produce a much more obvious conflict between modern institutions and Polynesian custom. The separation of powers applied to the new Senate, which contained only a few of the high title-holders of the House of *Ali'i* (who were instead confined to their executive functions as district governors and county chiefs or to a ceremonial position in the Council of Paramount Chiefs), although they were presided over by Tuiasosopo, the most outstanding of the Samoan leaders who was one of the leading orator chiefs of the group. In traditional terms, therefore, the Senate had little standing in relation to the executive branch, a situation which was recognized when the Governor made provision for the district governors to attend sittings, and later by the formation of an executive council to bring executive and legislature together. A similar gulf began to open not only between the House and the executive but between the former and the Senate. When the first elections by secret ballot were held, twelve of the eighteen representatives, including two women, were not holders of *matai* titles. The standing of the House was thus prejudiced in terms of its authority, with the additional result that few of the members were experienced in debating even within the village, and certainly not for taking issue with the higher title-holders. The separation of powers, in the context of Samoan custom, meant an unbalanced division of power between two of the branches of government and, depending upon the degree to which the *matai* system broke down or was modified by social and economic change, rival depositaries of power.

But the absence of any very serious conflict has also been due to that Samoan context. The influence which the high title-holders still wield, and the fact that in subsequent elections to the House a high proportion of the members have been *matai,* has provided a general agreement on the maintenance of Samoan custom which has hardly as yet been challenged by the non-*matai,* and which

seat for High Chief Galea'i of Fitiuta, Manu'a, while the Ituau representation was strongly opposed by High Chief Mauga of Tutuila on the grounds of Ituau's being socially under the jurisdiction of his own county. Mauga also attacked the idea of another seat for Manu'a on the grounds that it would cause discontent in Tutuila. This latter dispute concerned the House of *Ali'i,* but the former is an example of the upper House deciding the membership of the lower. The relationship of Sua and Vaifanua with Fofo and Aitulagi is an old dispute, which came up again in 1956.

has worked in terms of personal influence and standing to smooth away difficulties which the formal structure of power might have promoted. The *matai* system has proved adaptable enough to enable the American type of constitution to work, because anyone ambitious for a political career can probably obtain a *matai* title, either from the dormant ones or from the splitting of titles; he can, in other words, find scope for his ambition within the traditional system which is itself strong enough to impose Samoan standards on him. At the same time, a *matai* title ties a man to place and to kin, with the general result that political parties in a Tahitian sense do not exist, and the divisions of opinion and rivalry which do arise between groups, individuals and institutions are also Samoan ones, not merely in terms of prestige and standing but of districts, villages and families. The strength of Samoan custom which controls one possible set of conflicts in the operation of American institutions produces yet others; and as that custom weakens or crumbles conflicts which are now controlled may break out. Indeed, if the institutions serve their purpose of promoting political advancement they will break out.

The individual units of the legislature work inside this general framework of attitudes which controls the extent to which the Samoans can take the opportunity to discuss policy; by definition the same people cannot execute it. The Senate, or the former House of *Ali'i,* has always been the body in which Samoan custom has been most strongly upheld; the present Senate, representing less important title-holders, still adheres to that position in contrast to the House of Representatives. During a debate in special session in October 1953, the President of the Senate, High Talking Chief Tuiasosopo, formerly a Speaker of the House, stated:[5]

> It is an opinion of the Chair that everything concerning the rights of the people is the direct responsibility of the House of Representatives because of its election by secret ballot and universal suffrage. We were not elected by such ballot or suffrage, no, but by custom and usage. But the protection of custom and the people is our direct look out. It follows, therefore, that the subject of the rights of the people must necessarily be looked into first over there while that of protection of custom must be examined here in all that, in the opinion of the *Fono,* would not extend to it such protection.

Such a view, which was no doubt a practical one, was not necessary to the House of *Ali'i* up to 1953 because the proposals

[5] *Legislative Record,* 3rd Legislature, Special Session, October 1953.

of the Legislature originated in a Committee of the Whole of both Houses, but that practice was discontinued under the 1953 reorganization when a conflict arose between an elected Senate and an elected House. Disagreements had occurred under the earlier arrangement because, after the Committee of the Whole had made proposals originating in the villages, the Governor commented upon them, and these comments were considered in separate session, first by the House of Representatives which put them into the form of Concurrent Resolutions which the House of *Ali'i* might then amend or disapprove. In the first legislature of 1949, of twenty such House Concurrent Resolutions, the House of *Ali'i* amended one and disapproved four, of which one was the budget resolution, for which the House of *Ali'i* wished to set up an investigating committee, another was the question of shot-gun licences which would cause the *matai* trouble to control, and the remaining two concerned the sale of six per cent. beer and the appointment of Samoan officials by the Governor with the consent of the House of *Ali'i*, both of which were deferred to the consideration of a joint session.[6] All of these matters related directly or indirectly to the power and influence of the high title-holders in the Government and in Samoan life, and the movers in each case were a small group: Mauga, Tuitele, Sotoa and Satele who between them represented the higher titles of Tutuila and Manu'a. In each case the House accepted the amendments and no conflict arose. The same high titles, however, were not represented in the later Senate, although the one or two remaining tended to dominate the proceedings, and Tuiasosopo, the first President, regarded the Senate as the trustee of Samoan custom, if necessary against the House.

The House of Representatives, when it was elected by Samoan

[6] *Legislative Record*, 1st Legislature, Joint Session, January 1949; the amended resolution concerned the legislative budget, and although three members of the Representatives opposed the *Ali'i* amendment, it was accepted by forty-six to five with thirteen abstentions. The resolution on the Government budget was disapproved because the *Ali'i* did not like some of the items, and a compromise was reached by which the resolution was approved but the *Ali'i* committee of investigation went on working. The resolution on the appointment of Samoan officials was disapproved because the *Ali'i*, according to Mauga, wanted full power to appoint and no authority to remain to the Governor. Sotoa proposed an amendment that the Governor should appoint district judges, chiefs of police, and heads of departments where Samoans are nominated with the consent of the *Fono* of American Samoa, and gained fifty-five for, to nine against. Such opposition as there was in the House was headed by a non-*matai* and an orator.

custom, might disagree with the upper House on procedure or on specific issues, but it, too, had a vested interest in the society from which its members took their standing, an interest symbolized by the election of Tuiasosopo as Speaker over two lower title-holders. His dominance of the House was part of the process by which harmony was in general maintained with the *Ali'i*, the other part being the general acceptance of the authority of traditional leaders displayed by the fact that it was two members of the House who proposed to make the *Ali'i* the Governor's advisers in the appointment of Samoan officials. Many of the representatives themselves were *pulenu'u* whose offices reinforced their subordination to the higher title-holders who filled the higher offices. Such tendencies as there were towards conflict or disagreement with the House of *Ali'i* might find a focus in the non-*matai* representatives, but they arose principally from the old rivalries between districts and villages and rival groups of title-holders, and they were held in check by anti-administration feeling reflected in such motions as those which sought the discontinuance of the appointment of non-Samoans in the Government, the investigation of all such non-Samoans and the return of alienated *matai* land. None of these motions got much support, but they represented a feeling that lay behind the well-supported demand for civilian government, a demand which kept the old Samoan feuds in check.

Civilian government, however, introduced universal suffrage, and thereby the possibility of the House taking a different attitude from the Senate when the majority of its members were no longer *matai*. This actually occurred in the elections in January 1953, when the first House was elected by universal suffrage for a trial period of two years. When the session of the Committee of the Whole met on 3 February, the first symptom of a move away from the dominance of Samoan custom represented by the Senate was evident in the motion of Pritchard, a part-Samoan.[7] Tuiasosopo, the chairman of the Committee of the Whole, stated that proposals would be accepted and then directed to a *Fono* committee on rules and administration to be classified and referred to the relevant committee for study and action; this, he said,

[7] *Legislative Record*, 3rd Legislature, Special Session, February 1953. Keesing, *Elite Communication*, p. 111, regarded the lower House as marking a possible major breach in the Samoan pattern, but they were writing before subsequent elections demonstrated the influence of the *matai* under the electoral system.

would take three to four weeks, and then the *Fono* should meet in separate Houses to hear the committee reports so that either House could initiate action. Pritchard thereupon observed that this procedure was not right, that each House should meet separately to put forward proposals, too, and when he divided the joint session he was supported by fourteen members of the House and three members of the Senate, to gain an overall majority of three. After this vote a formal resolution was moved by Pritchard and Mrs Mabel Reid, another part-Samoan representative, that there should be no more Committee of the Whole. By another joint resolution of the same session, a conference committee was substituted in case of differences between the two Houses. The attitude of the House was quite clearly that all matters of a political nature should originate there, and the Senate should confine itself to matters of custom and tradition, a view which was a more extreme version of that enunciated by Tuiasosopo in the Senate; as such it was unanimously rejected by the Senate when it came before them in the form of House amendments to a joint resolution. Even so, the conflict was largely a theoretical one which did not, in practice, lead to any violent disagreements over particular resolutions; the House certainly made no attempt to attack the *matai* system or Samoan custom, although members of it were certainly impatient of some of its effects, and the Senate in particular was criticized by one member as 'an unfair thing, because we all know by learning Samoan traditions that there was no such thing as a Senate'. Both Houses could agree, however, in their desire for full legislative power, and this desire, combined with a disturbed political situation because of a rapid turnover in governors and officials, held them together.[8] Indeed, in March 1954, the committee of the legislature appointed by the Governor to consider the results of the two years' trial period reported, through the very representative who had criticized the Senate, that the constitution should in essentials be retained as it was, and the committee so far took account of Samoan custom to propose a Samoan Ceremonial Council open to all traditional chiefs of counties, the members of which should

[8] The symptoms of this disturbed situation were petitions and counter-petitions to Washington about the appointment of a new Governor, which led to a special session of the third Legislature to consider the right of petition and the rights of alien nationals to participate in the political life of American Samoa; ibid., Special Session, October 1953.

be given prior consideration for high offices in the local government.

The non-*matai* members of the House no doubt expected that they would continue to be re-elected under the ballot system, but in fact they were disappointed. In the elections of November 1954 only seven members of the previous House were returned, Mrs Reid and Pritchard who had led the non-*matai* element not being among them, while the proportion of *matai* title-holders increased markedly. One of the defeated non-*matai* candidates blamed the division of the larger counties on a population basis, which was said to have split the non-*matai* vote, but alleged also that the electoral machinery was defective and offered too great a scope for the operation of Samoan custom. This latter condition was certainly true. Since political titles carry great prestige, there was no shortage of candidates; in the first election there were sixty-two for eighteen seats. The registration of voters, however, was a different matter; in 1953 only sixty-five per cent. of those eligible registered in the three weeks' period before the election, and many of those failed to vote.[9] There was no general grasp of the implications of the ballot, but under the circumstances the response was reasonable. An attempt was made, through the schoolteachers especially, to prepare the Samoans for an electoral system, but the campaigning had a distinct Samoan flavour. Some of the candidates in 1953 tried to use the radio, but a lack of receiving sets limited this approach. More usually, a candidate relied on ceremonial or informal visits to local *matai* who controlled family groups, and at such meetings most of the discussions followed custom by leaving speeches to the orators whom candidates tended to use as the equivalent of campaign-managers. In the first election, the strangeness of the proceedings no doubt helped the election of non-*matai* candidates, but later elections, following the same general method of campaigning, showed a growing awareness by *matai* of the political possibilities, aided by the attitude which the non-*matai* House had displayed towards the Senate. Accordingly, in November 1954, it was alleged that one powerful *matai*, in whose house the voting booth was established, campaigned for a candidate against a non-titled per-

[9] *Report on the Election* (Samoan Affairs Files), 15 January 1953; *Election Statistics* 1956, 1958 (supplied by the Attorney-General's Department). In 1956 out of 7,673 who were registered, only 4,659 cast their ballots, and two years later the registration had decreased to 6,040 of whom 4,973 voted.

son, telling his people who to vote for, remaining near the voting booth, taking ballots from voters to deposit them himself, and actually accompanying some voters into the booth.[10] This particular man had formerly been chief clerk of the legislature before he was convicted of perjury. In 1956 an adult male of a family received the voting cards for three other members of it, and attempted to use them all himself.[11] After the first election the electoral system has been accepted by the Samoans in accordance with their customs, and has in fact worked to reinforce the authority of the *matai* and the orators who have in effect begun to control the elections in the absence of any party organization or active campaigning of a European kind. Hence the relative harmony between the House and the Senate, which is likely to be disturbed only when economic development begins to produce the kind of distinctions which exist in Tahiti.

Both the Senate and the House, therefore, have tended to conduct debates along Samoan lines, and their resolutions have had some of the same elements of what earlier governors had regarded as irresponsibility. In the first legislature the Samoan preoccupation with road-making by the American Government was demonstrated by several resolutions, of which one asked for the construction of motor roads in Manu'a which had no motor vehicles. Similarly the motion for the consumption of alcoholic liquor reappeared, as did the request that *fa'a Samoa* fines be restored.[12] There were, of course, resolutions which were both practical and desirable, but there was an underlying current of ignorance of the financial situation and irresponsibility in the suggested use of the funds. After three years of experience of the legislature, the resolutions were displaying a clear appreciation of the problems of government. When an extended electrification programme was requested in 1954, it was accompanied by an offer of assistance with labour, but the road-making programme asked for would have cost 600,000 dollars, with no suggested scheme for raising the money by increased taxation.[13] Although

[10] Statement to Governor, 29 December 1954.

[11] Election Commissioner to Chairman Election Board of Appeals, 7 January 1957. He was probably influenced by the Samoan tradition of public unanimity; Keesing, *Elite Communication*, p. 114 ff.

[12] *Legislative Record,* 1st Legislature, Special Session, October 1948.

[13] ibid., Third Legislature, Session January 1954. In the new constitution it is particularly provided that any legislation involving expenditure additional to the budget shall include revenue measures to provide the money; Article ii, Section 1 (d).

a copra fund had been established for years, it was apparent in 1954 that the *Fono* regarded this as a surplus fund which could be used by the Samoans, although it was in fact a revolving fund to enable producers to be paid in cash upon delivery. Apart from financial ignorance, there was also an apparent lack of information about the activities of the Government, reflected in the legislature's attempt to request an executive appointment and a misinformed resolution about the provision for tuberculosis patients. The lack of information was not solely the fault of the legislature but of the Government in providing information, but the general impression persisted that the *Fono* had not yet demonstrated capacity for leadership or the responsibility which went with it.

So far as this is due to Samoan custom, the grasp of the implications of modern government will plainly be of slow growth, although there are signs that such an appreciation is growing more rapidly than one might suppose. Many of the young *matai* are alive to economic possibilities, and their political attitudes are being influenced by this.[14] There is, too, a growing section of the population which is involved in a Western-style economy. And the organization of the legislature itself promotes these changes (as well as reflecting the speed at which they occur) by the introduction of a legislative training programme for the newly elected members before the opening session. In December 1958 a conference on procedure was organized which explained the structure and working of the legislature to those just elected.[15] More important, however, was the actual experience members obtained through the committee system of both Houses, and in the fifth legislature there were nine committees in each House which gave every member the opportunity of serving on at least two and usually three. In addition, the Legislative Council which was a permanent joint committee meeting periodically between sessions to study and review Government policy, programmes and statutes, and which consisted of five members from each house (the President, Speaker and chairmen of the Rules committee *ex officio*), and the Legislative Liaison Officer appointed by the Governor, advised the Administrator of Legislative Services on rules and procedures, and approved the legislative budget. This, too, contributed to the experience of some members who could

[14] As an example, one may quote Mr P. Lauvao, the present Speaker of the House of Representatives.

[15] *Orientation Course for the Legislature,* 1958, prepared by the Legislative Administration Officer.

then provide a better informed nucleus in each House. A subcommittee of this body was also set up for information and reference, including the Legislative Liaison Officer who co-ordinates legislative and executive work (and who was in 1958 the Attorney-General, although there had previously been a special office) and the Legislative Administrator who is either the President or the Speaker, assisted by a permanent secretary. Such institutions modified the influence of Samoan custom by bringing the members into contact with executive officers of the central Government in small groups, obviating some of the public attitudes taken in the Houses and the influence of high ranking titleholders in public debate. These committees are probably more effective than the Senate and the House in producing that awareness of modern government which Samoan custom translates into customary terms, but, like the economic changes which operate outside the legislature, they work slowly.

The strength of Samoan custom is thus clearly shown in the elections, the debates and resolutions and the operation of the legislature, quite apart from the conflict it produces between the legislative and executive branches. It has a vitality which causes European-conceived institutions to work in its own terms quite as much as in American ones, to the point at which their effects in the process of political advancement may be frustrated. The successive delegations of authority to the legislature have led to its gaining authority to make law on matters of local interest, but in the period discussed this power was withheld. How much difference this new authority will make is a matter of speculation. In each of the other colonies dealt with, the heart of an elected body's power has been its control of the budget. In Fiji this was a Native Administration budget within the general budget of the colony, in Tahiti it was the colonial budget itself, but in both cases the control of revenue raised by direct or indirect taxation has been the basis of responsible decision-making, of deciding priorities and allocations and, therefore, policy. In American Samoa the legislature has hitherto not had this control. The colony has depended upon American subventions, and the small Samoan contribution has been a poll tax at a flat rate of some five dollars. Budgetary control, therefore, has always been in the hands of the Governor who may or may not listen to the legislature's advice after its discussion of the accounts. Under the new constitution, the legislature has to face the issue of raising money itself, but the budget is still prepared by the Governor largely from United States funds. In the past the legislature has not displayed any considerable grasp of the financial implications of government and Samoan custom has obviously prevailed in the attitude to money. The question is whether the new law-making body will be influenced by its powers to accept modern attitudes to financial responsibility. For the crux of the issue of political advancement lies in this linking of power and responsibility of which the concrete symbol is finance. The legislature must represent traditional Samoa, but it must also discharge the duties of modern government. The past operation of Samoan custom in the legislature suggests that the latter will happen slowly.

Nevertheless, whatever the attitudes of the legislature, the operation of modern government depends on the executive, of which Samoan local government is the vital part. As a matter of policy, the achievement of local self-government has often been regarded as more important than the development of the legislature; indeed, there has been some feeling among officials that political advancement has been tackled from the wrong end with the legislature, and that the real contact with the Samoans should be made at village level. It is claimed that the local government organization, growing out of traditional social organization and based on the authority of the *matai,* is the meaningful part of government to the Samoans. That system has existed in essentials for sixty years, being little altered by civilian control with the major exception that the 'separation of powers' isolates it from the legislature as it did not from the pre-war *Fono*. Thus *a priori* one might expect the local government to work more efficiently than the newly created legislature.

Yet Samoan custom works just as strongly in the ranks of local government officials as it does in the ranks of legislators. The district governors and county chiefs have always been selected from the high *ali'i* of the counties, and usually from the same few title-holders.[16] Whatever considerations of merit may have entered into appointments, in practice the district governor was usually the holder of a particular title, and so, although not to such a

[16] Records of the *Fono* preserved in the Office of the Governor. In 1938 the district governors were Tufele, Le'iato and Tuitele, and the only change by 1945 was that Tuitele had been replaced by Toomata. In 1958 the governors were Le'iato, Tuitele and Lefiti, although another high title-holder, Mauga, had held office meanwhile.

marked extent, were the county chiefs.[17] The range of choice for a county chief was greater than for a district governor, but in general there has been a high stability of personnel which is necessary both to satisfy any desire to maintain the traditional leaders in office and to give the experience in executive government. Of course, the instability which was due to disputed elections to high titles affected such appointments, although the registration and High Court decisions in disputed cases controlled some of this unrest. Nevertheless, the method of appointment, by which the Governor receives a nomination for office from a district or county, ensures that the nominee has traditional standing, even though disputes may break out afterwards as they did in old Samoa. Where there is disagreement on such a nominee, the Governor exercises his discretion. In 1929 the Eastern District could not unanimously support a candidate for the district governorship, and the Governor had to choose between two nominees, both high title-holders; he appointed Le'iato, and the other candidate, Mauga, was sent off to Hawaii for study purposes. Similarly in May 1956 the *ali'i* and *tulafale* of Lealataua county could not agree upon a single candidate as county chief, and the Governor responded by placing a time limit upon their deliberations at the end of which they should forward to him the names of all those eligible and qualified who were still being considered by the county council.[18] An obviously unsuitable candidate would, no doubt, not be appointed, but merit is less important than acceptance by Samoan custom, and this custom has in general tended to secure the appointment of the same title-holders.

The length of tenure of office in theory means that the executive branch is staffed with experienced men, but that experience is not solely or even primarily in the ways of modern government. The method of appointment tends, in fact, to place a premium on the ability to translate the demands of government in terms of Samoan custom. Two county chiefs who retired in 1955 had been in office for a long period but their departure was regarded as being a great help to the progress of local government. There

[17] In 1938, for example, the county chiefs of the Manu'a District were Misa, Lefiti, Asoau and Tuiolosega; of the Eastern District, Mauga, Faumuina, Logo and Savusa; of the Western District, Letuli, Satele and Fuimaono. In 1945 the only changes had been in the Western District where two of the chiefs had been succeeded by others. Thirteen years later five of these chiefs were still in office, a sixth had become a district governor, and a seventh had been a district governor.

[18] Governor to the Chiefs and Orators of Lealataua County, 25 May 1956.

is the need for constant pressure on both district governor and county chief to carry out the duties the Government imposes on them. When the maintenance fees of Junior High School students, for instance, were not used for the purpose for which they were collected, the Government suggested to all the district governors that sufficient should be released to carry out repairs to the schools. Financial matters are notoriously those most affected by the prevalence of Samoan custom and, like Fiji, there have been a considerable number of cases of misuse of public money under the control of Samoan officials.[19] In general, however, those officials' executive duties were confined to the minimum ones required to maintain public health in the villages, and their chief importance was the adjustment of Samoan affairs themselves.

Custom may inhibit the growth of modern executive responsibilities, but the district governors and county chiefs who work within its framework can cope with the quarrels which arise out of it and so avoid friction which the Government would otherwise have to smooth away. In September and October 1952 the Eastern District governor informed the Adviser on Samoan Affairs, an American official, that he had issued orders in two cases of land dispute which he had settled by agreement between the parties, in one case from his own knowledge. Similarly the county chief of Tualata notified the Adviser that a land dispute had been settled amicably in accordance with the boundaries decided by the county chief's office. Such an official, appointed because of his traditional high rank, can plainly save the Government a great deal of trouble, but he can also himself become involved in it. In Iliili village the district governor reported that the county chief had had a dispute with another man and had agreed to settle the matter amicably in the district governor's office, but that later he had destroyed the crops of his opponent; the district governor recommended that his subsequent planting on the disputed land should be removed. The same county chief, a week later, wrote to the Adviser that his county council had decided to withdraw recognition from certain chiefs and orators of the county in view of their wilful, high-handed and insubordinate conduct. Such an official having traditional rank may be encouraged to behave in this way because of the additional prestige which accrues to him through his Government office. Because of this prestige he will be able to settle some disputes,

19 Of which the most notorious was the embezzlement of more than 40,000 dollars by officials of the Bank of American Samoa.

although he may also cause others. Thus, the executive Government also faces the dilemma created by the need for modern standards of government which it must try to insist on in a customary society, and their execution by a man whose standing derives from that society as much as from the Government. The chiefs cannot be ignored because of their independent authority which could frustrate any direct action by American officials, but to use them means some compromise in the standards which the Government deems necessary. The Samoan official faces the reverse of the same dilemma: conflict between what his people expect of him and what the Government expects. In the present state of Samoan society, the former is likely to be his principal consideration.

Slowly this state of affairs will alter. The changes in Samoan society will no doubt lead to an acceptance of the Government's standards, and pressure is kept up upon the district governors and county chiefs to carry out the policy the Government wants: disinterested administration, public health measures, agricultural and economic development. The chief means of pressure is the monthly meeting of these two groups of officials with the Governor and his advisers which was formalized into the Local Government Council. In these meetings matters of policy were discussed. In 1955 one meeting considered tuition in schools, Japanese fishing techniques, the system of local government inspection by rewards and prizes for clean villages, and the employment questions raised by the building of a dock and roads in Manu'a.[20] In June of the same year it was agreed to assign to certain county chiefs particular responsibilities in each district, so that one of them in each was responsible for agriculture, another for education, another for public works and another for sanitation. Such regular monthly meetings, in contact with the specialist officers of the central Government, no doubt help to make the Samoan officials aware of what the Government expects, but are no real substitute for specialized training. The officials are still concerned with Government action principally as it affects the day-to-day life of the Samoans, and any more specialized activity, such as agricultural extension work, has to be specially urged on them as something worthy of help for the good of American Samoa. Many of the topics brought up in the monthly meetings reflect concern with their own status. In August 1957 the questions of free

20 *Minutes* of 3 February 1955 in the Samoan Affairs Office.

transport for local government officers, free hospitalization and retirement pension deductions were all raised as they had been regularly in the past,[21] and they suggest very strongly that the district governors and county chiefs still look upon their offices in terms of the standing they give in Samoan society rather than the duties which are involved in a Government appointment.

High officials can be subjected to the pressure of regular meetings or the Governor's circulars, but the lower official, the *pulenu'u,* upon whom the effectiveness of the system ultimately depends, is much farther removed from this kind of pressure, especially when it is moderated by its passage down the executive channel. The *pulenu'u* is nowadays a title-holder of low rank and, since there are a number of *matai* in a village, he is never without rivals.[22] Thus he, more than the other officials, faces the conflict between his traditional authority in the village, his responsibility to the higher ranking title-holders who hold Government office and those who do not, and the Government itself. The *pulenu'u* is responsible for seeing that the work involved in the sanitation, planting, road-making, water supply, school construction and insect control regulations, is actually carried out. His salary is low. Since he is most obviously caught between modern government and Samoan custom for little reward and not much dignity, the office is not sought after, and usually goes to a man of no great calibre who will not push the village too hard. Still there is some pressure upon him to discharge his duties, partly through his superior officers who inspect the villages and partly through an annual meeting with the Governor and the central Government officials. At such a meeting there may be discussion of such things as the listing of taxpayers, the parcel post, dog licences and other matters of village duties.[23] One meeting a year, however, is not enough to train such officials or even to make sure that they have a clear grasp of their duties, and the position is complicated further by the fact that the ranks of *pulenu'u* change, that any ambitious or well-educated man looks to other offices and branches of the Government for his prestige and power. Regular inspections and local meetings may help, but their success is also limited by the difficulties implicit in the office and the calibre of its holders. In 1953 an attempt

21 *Minutes* of 30 August 1957.

22 Keesing, *Elite Communication*, pp. 63, 95-6.

23 *Minutes* of 2 November 1955.

was made to remedy at least one of the failings by providing that a satisfactory *pulenu'u* could serve for two terms of two years each to achieve stability and continuity at village level, but 'satisfactory' to a village and to the Government implies different things, making 'stability' merely the maintenance of the *status quo*. With the *pulenu'u* the executive government of the islands really slows to the pace of *fa'a Samoa.*

These executive officers are not alone; they are linked to the councils of district, county and village, which in theory unite the executive officers to their people and incorporate the elements of advice and consent in the executive branch. The councils are all charged with responsibility for good government and welfare, but the district and the county councils are probably more significant as political bodies in which the ranking Samoans can indulge in their oratory and precedence but which, more practically, select both senators and executive officers. The legislative and executive branches are linked in these councils which probably serve to maintain some harmony between *ali'i* and *tulafale,* which might become strained by the virtual exclusion of the latter from executive office, thus diminishing the old orators' power. They also ensure, of course, that both the Senate and the executive are rooted in Samoan custom as expressed by themselves, and they have an effective veto and control over lower appointments. If these councils tend to be of political and ceremonial significance, the village council is much more concerned with actual administration. The *matai* of a village exercise immediate influence upon local matters, and the *pulenu'u* must cooperate with them. Thus it is in the village council that the best medium for training in local government exists, although it, too, of course, is as much concerned with Samoan custom as Government duties; and its authority may weaken from two causes. One is the absence of *matai* from the village which attracted the attention of the Local Government Council in July 1956, when eighteen *matai* were listed as having lived away from their villages for at least a year, thereby infringing the Code. The second is the reluctance of a council to act on its own initiative but rather to appeal to the central Government. In July 1952, for example, the *matai* of Pavai'ai' asked the Attorney-General to 'improve' the village laws with his power, especially those prescribing fences against pigs damaging plantations, the presence of all people over eighteen for work or a fine in default, and the taking of anything to market without knowledge of the *pulenu'u* to prevent stealing. Such a request shows awareness of genuine local difficulties, but they are difficulties which are occasioned by the attempt to preserve Samoan life. There is in the village councils a lack of initiative in any modern sense, which its structure does nothing to remedy: an acceptance of the *status quo* which is encouraged by an action of the Government such as the introduction of a standard set of village regulations, to produce greater uniformity and legal enforceability, which come into effect on approval by a village council, thereby reducing still further the initiative it might be expected to show, even within the limits of Samoan customary society.[24]

The long tradition of this executive government in American Samoa no doubt plays a considerable part in the slowness with which the system changes, unlike the newer legislature which is making its own conventions as it goes along. Thus there is created the obvious imbalance between the legislature which enthusiastically demands full power, and the executive which retains the attitudes and the pace of Navy days. Both are rooted in Samoan custom, but the House of Representatives provides a possible outlet for more radical attitudes. As the agencies of political advancement they promote slow and not rapid growth, although this situation could change with the present economic and social forces at work in American Samoa of which one of the most important is the community living in Pago Pago. Here are people who are not controlled by the social sanctions which still operate strongly in the villages; there is a growing number not living under the *matai* system. No comparable situation with Papeete exists, but the settlement has received notice since 1953, and the urgency of providing a municipality which would be formally distinct from the rest of Samoa has been recognized. Such a non-*matai* unit would be a pressure group and perhaps a source of radical leaders rather than a serious modification of Samoan society. Radical leadership would not, however, necessarily be any better trained than the traditional leadership. The same case can be made for using traditional rank as in Fiji: in a customary society it is a useful expedient where the Government's resources in men and money are lacking, and it avoids the grave risks of social disorganization. Unlike Fiji, the Samoans are not competing with other social groups in their own island, so that there is none of the pressing urgency of Fijian develop-

[24] *Annual Report,* Samoan Affairs Office, 1953.

ment. Unlike Tahiti, there is no social vacuum because the old society and rank still functions in modified ways. But there is an even greater lack of trained leadership in both legislature and executive, accentuated by the tendency of the educated to leave for Hawaii and the United States, and not to return, and in American Samoa the separation of power spreads what leadership there is more thinly, tending to produce conflict and rivalry within its ranks. American institutions which in theory seem to combine old and new in Samoa, and to be accepted by the Samoans, demand circumstances for their effectiveness which have not yet arisen; they imply an assimilation which has yet to occur while supporting a society which retards it.

CHAPTER X

COMPARATIVE COLONIAL PRACTICE

Colonial practice not colonial policy has been the subject of this book because colonial policy is moulded by all kinds of forces which for the present purpose must be taken for granted. Still, there are other reasons for concentrating on practice. Too often, in writings on colonial topics, colonial policy has been discussed to the general neglect of what actually happens when Western institutions are set up in colonies. Nor would a comparison simply of colonial policies be very significant. There may seem to be all the difference in the world between assimilation and association or federation; the difference, as the *rapporteur* said at Brazzaville, between empire in the Roman sense of the word and in the Anglo-Saxon. Assimilation apparently denies the validity of colour distinctions by recognizing that a man is either civilized or uncivilized with no reference to his colour. In practice, nevertheless, it may be hard to distinguish assimilation from another view which frankly recognizes colour differences if part of the definition of civilized means giving up, for example, the Mohammedan religion; the kind of distinctions which exist in an assimilated colony may easily be equated both by the inhabitants and by outsiders with racial differences. Significant comparisons must, therefore, be those of colonial practice, not policy, but they must also be comparisons of different practices in similar conditions. Fiji, Tahiti and Samoa belonged to a common Polynesian system of rank and authority; they experienced a similar history of European contact; but their political advancement has been moulded by three different colonial practices. They afford, therefore, a rare opportunity to make comparisons, employing the standards that were set out in the Introduction. Having examined each colony in some detail, it remains to draw together some of the contrasts and comparisons which have emerged.

Taking first of all the formal political structure, certain differences readily appear. In Fiji, the Fijians have been isolated within their own 'communal system', living in their villages under their chiefs, and being thus separated from the general Government of the colony the Fijian Administration is primarily an organization for local not central Government. Tahiti, by contrast, has a well developed central Government which rules the whole colony, and its local government has been generally neglected to the point at which it is largely inoperative. The Samoan Government tries to give equal emphasis to both central and local institutions. These differences can be explained partly by colonial traditions. The British, whether or not they have used the techniques of 'direct' or 'indirect' rule, have always preserved a separation between indigenous people and themselves which, if the word were not nowadays emotive, one might call apartheid. The French, with a Roman conception of empire, have followed a practice of assimilation which has reproduced the features of centralized government in France. The Americans, who have not accepted the fact of their being a colonial power and, therefore, have never evolved or admitted to evolving a theory of colonial rule, have proceeded on an *ad hoc* basis, considering each case on its own merits, to reproduce the equivalent of a federal structure balancing central and local interests. National traditions, however, although they may broadly determine the form of colonial practice, are not a sufficient explanation of the differences to be found in these colonies; this must also be sought in local conditions.

Once again the differences are not difficult to perceive. Fiji has a plural society in which the Fijians are both a minority and economically the weakest group, while they retain, modified but resilient and vigorous, their traditional society. Tahiti has no plural society in the Fijian sense but one assimilated to French culture and united by it in the absence of any traditional bonds, and in which social distinctions are largely French ones. Samoa is a homogeneous society which is still traditional, unchallenged by other resident racial groups, living in its villages under its chiefs and, although modified by European contacts, vigorous in its assertion of Samoan values and attitudes: 'Samoa is Samoa'. Quite apart, therefore, from the disposition of a colonial power to use standard models which have been tested elsewhere for its colonial practice, it has to take into account local circumstances if its institutions are to stand a chance of working, and if it is committed, as these powers are, to promote political advancement, it must be prepared to modify the structure of government to achieve at least a minimum acceptance of it. Thus, for example, the British must meet the Fijian demand for protection from

Indian competition, the French meet the growing demand of Tahitian 'nationalism', and the Americans meet the Samoan demand for the retention of the *matai* system. The extent to which the powers acknowledge local circumstances may vary: the British and the Americans have done so deliberately, the French incidentally with the rest of the community by recognizing the 'personality' of individual colonies within a common framework; but in each case local circumstances have helped to shape the forms through which political advancement takes place.

Differences in the structure of government in each of these colonies, therefore, represent compromises between metropolitan and local requirements, because colonial government must meet both the demands of the colonial society and those of the outside world. Government in Fiji, Tahiti and Samoa differs because each of the colonial powers has attempted to make this compromise in the light of its own traditions in the particular circumstances of each territory. Those circumstances have arisen from other causes than the action of colonial rulers; they are the product of every kind of European contact, of which in the earlier part of the nineteenth century the unofficial element was the most important. Nevertheless, if the structure of government must be bent to fit them, it is also true that it moulds them. The institutions of government which have been described in this book serve two functions: they attempt to provide a Government which is accepted as representative of them by the people for whom it is intended, and they provide a channel which guides the way in which that popular demand expresses itself. In the detailed examination of political advancement in the three colonies, two questions were asked: what were the institutions available for deciding policy and executing it? How did they work in non-Western societies? The answers which have been given may now be compared in terms of the premisses upon which they were based: that the structure of government must be accepted as representative of them by the people, and that it must also satisfy the requirements of efficiency, law and order demanded by the outer world.

The first of these two criteria, acceptance of the formal government, is one aspect of what has been called by Furnivall and some sociologists the 'common social will' or the 'majority social demand'.[1] In terms of the organization of government, this means

[1] J. S. Furnivall, *Colonial Policy and Practice: A Comparative Study of Burma and Netherlands India* (Cambridge, 1948), p. 506.

that its institutions must be accepted as those through which political aspirations will naturally and normally be satisfied.[2] In Fiji this is true of the Fijian Administration. The traditional authority which it incorporates is probably still accepted by much the greater number of Fijians. They may, and do, grumble at some of its workings or feel frustration over the paternalistic attitude which regulates their behaviour, but the alternatives of individual peasant holdings and economic competition with Indians and Europeans, perhaps with risk to their lands, causes them to accept the Fijian Administration. The situation in Tahiti is not so clear. With the disappearance of the old system of authority, there is no rival to the *loi-cadre,* and plainly it is accepted by a sufficient number of Tahitians to make it work, but the extent of this acceptance is much harder to determine. There are indications that in the remoter villages of the main island and in the outer islands of French Polynesia where contacts with Papeete are neither close nor frequent, there is no great understanding of, nor enthusiasm for, the central Government. Certainly its structure is not generally or equally accepted throughout French Polynesia, but since it is the only system of authority, there is no alternative to eventual acceptance. Samoa, by the test of representative institutions, resembles Fiji. A traditional system of authority has been absorbed into the Government and it is, therefore, representative of Samoans. Because the history of the legislature has been short, there may be ignorance of its working or confusion over its functions, but the long history of the executive branch has accustomed even the remote villages to Government authority and no doubt the whole structure is either accepted for this reason or not too difficult of acceptance in a relatively short time.

It would be tempting but wrong to conclude that the first criterion of acceptance of Government institutions was fulfilled in the two colonies where the indigenous authorities were employed for Governmental purposes and unfulfilled in the third where it was not. In the former colonies there is a conflict within the structure of the Government between the demands of traditional society and those of modern government, a conflict which it is the hope of the colonial powers to resolve in favour of the new. The Government which uses traditional authority is therefore transitional: it supposes, as the American committee of

[2] Francis X. Sutton, 'Representation and the Nature of Political Systems', *Comparative Studies in Society and History*, vol. ii, no. 1, p. 1.

inquiry wrote in Samoa, that the traditional system will eventually disappear of its own accord to be replaced by the new. So far as acceptance of the institutions of government is concerned, it follows that this may also be transient because as modern demands increase, a gap may easily widen between the Government and the governed. In the last colony, where the old system of rank has been ignored and has disappeared, there is no such transitional quality about government which has a form already tested by the requirements of modern government in metropolitan France. If its institutions are not completely accepted in Tahiti, if there is some present distance between the Government and the governed, this is not because of the conflict with a traditional and alternative political order, and for this reason the gap may rather be narrowed than widened: the reverse of the tendency in the other colonies. By the criterion of acceptance of the structure of government, each of these colonies has a half-measure of achievement.

Each, moreover, is weakest at the same point: in the villages. From the detailed analysis of the three colonies, one major similarity appears: that the village authorities are the weakest unit of the Government because they are most exposed to conflicting claims. There may be, as in Fiji and Samoa, conflicts between traditional and modern duties which are resolved largely by inaction, or there may be, as in Tahiti, conflicts of local interests centred on the Tahitian church against the claims of the central Government, or of countryside versus town, but in each colony the executive functions of government are often frustrated in the villages. For the same reasons of tradition or local interests the legislative institutions are in some degree alien to village life. The executive has an immediate impact on the population, whether or not they understand it or try to avoid it, but the legislature is a much more remote phenomenon. An elector may vote without comprehension: in Fiji he will vote for the *turaga-ni-koro* of his village to go to the *tikina* council, in Tahiti he will vote for a party list, in Samoa for the *matai* of his family; but a vote does not imply the comprehension of either institutions or issues, and a candidate once elected tends to vanish into another world which he may or may not try to make intelligible to his constituents. Tradition or local interests may easily make a villager desire nothing more than to be left alone, bounded by familiar horizons. This situation is probably characteristic of large areas of each colony: it is more obvious in the remoter villages of Vanua Levu, or the Marquesas, or Manu'a, than it is closer to Suva, Papeete or Pago Pago. Nevertheless, this village attitude is an important modification of any statement that the structure of government is accepted by the people as representative.

Yet there is a sense in which this village acceptance of institutions is irrelevant. One of the difficulties in using terms like 'common social will' or 'majority social demand' is the doubt: how 'common' or how much of a majority? How many people must accept the institutions of government before they start to become representative? Plainly in both Fiji and Samoa they are accepted by the majority of the traditional leaders who derive part of their power and status from their Government authority and have a vested interest in accepting their sources, and if the traditional leaders are acknowledged by their people, it follows that indirectly the Government structure is generally accepted; this is the current situation in Fiji and Samoa. A weakness of this position is that the conservative outlook of the chiefs, their adherence to the *status quo,* may lead to a separation between themselves and their people who are exposed to new economic attitudes and, therefore, to a separation of the Government from the mass of the people; for this reason a chiefly acceptance of the structure of the Government is a transitory stage in the general acceptance. There is the further risk that the chiefs, the people and the Government may all three be separated from each other to produce a general breakdown in government. Nevertheless, at the present stage of Fijian and Samoan political development the traditional system of rank covers the distance between the Government and the governed.

Tahiti is a different matter. There are no traditional leaders to commit their people, and those who do accept the *loi-cadre* are a diverse group of men: merchants, lawyers, doctors, schoolteachers, trade union officials and charismatic leaders like Pouvanaa. They are relatively few in numbers and essentially urban in outlook. Among them, only Pouvanaa has attempted or had much success in gaining a mass following. As a group, such men have accepted the *loi-cadre,* have filled the Assembly and the Council of Government, but they can do little or nothing in their position to bring the countryside to the same acceptance unless they produce leaders of Pouvanaa's type. Nevertheless, the *loi-cadre* works because the most economically important and well-educated groups in Tahiti accept it, and if there is a transitional quality about this situation, it is a transitoriness which looks forward to acceptance by an increasing number of Tahitians rather than a widening gulf. For there exists in Tahiti this class which is both educated and independent of the Government; an educated Tahitian does not look exclusively to the Government service as his goal, unlike educated Fijians or Samoans, with the result that there is a middle class between the Government and the mass of the people in Tahiti which is lacking in Fiji and Samoa, a class which, participating in political life, fills some of the gap between the Government and the governed.

In each colony the institutions of government are accepted by leaders who enable them to work, but there is a critical problem of extending this acceptance to include the bulk of the population before the first of these criteria of political advancement can be satisfied. These leaders also carry the chief burden of satisfying the second criterion: that the Government should be modern, accepting the standards which the outer world holds up and which are immediately impressed upon them by the presence of colonial government and the requirements of its institutions.

Modern standards imply the acceptance of change in society, not reliance on traditional practices or desire for the *status quo*;[3] they imply a commitment to social, economic and educational advancement which the United Nations Charter particularly links with political advancement. At the very least, this means acceptance of Western science and technology, and the provision of the social and educational conditions in which these can be used, primarily for the exploitation of economic resources, so that eventually the colonial people will be able, as the League of Nations put it, 'to stand on their own feet under the strenuous conditions of the modern world'. It is unlikely that any of the three colonies will ever have anything other than a dependent economy, but it is clear that much greater economic exploitation of resources could occur, especially in Fiji, because all of them still have, so far as the indigenous people are concerned, an essentially subsistence economy with a small margin for exchange. Economic, social and educational advancement are necessities in any colony, but it is their relationship to political advancement which is the concern of this book.

Independently of political institutions or of leadership, modern attitudes slowly spread among Fijians, Samoans and Tahitians because of their day-to-day contacts with Europeans. Their

[3] Edward Shils, 'Political Development in New States', *Comparative Studies in Society and History*, vol. ii, no. 3, p. 265 ff.

desire for European goods set these changes in motion from the first day that Europeans traded with them, and they began to be transformed by what has been called the 'magic of the market'. In Tahiti this transformation was part of the general destruction of the old society, for assimilation implied encouragement of the process not protection from it, but in Fiji and Samoa, the traditional society was shielded by official action. Whereas in Tahiti it has always been assumed that Tahitian society accepted modern standards because Tahitians were French, educated in French schools, and living in a French society not a traditional one, in Fiji and Samoa it has been assumed that any changes must be interpreted in traditional ways, through the 'communal' or *matai* system; but whatever the part played by independent agencies such as traders and missionaries in promoting modern standards and modern needs, either assumption implies Government action. Because of the general recognition that economic, social and educational advancement is closely connected with political, it follows that if the political institutions are to work and to gain acceptance, the other changes must be controlled. It is equally true that the political structure itself is part of that control; that it influences the acceptance of modern economic and social standards as well as shaping political demands.

Executive departments, like Agriculture, Education, Health and Public Works, are the technical instruments by which modern standards may be established in the colonies, but their achievement is conditioned by political factors. Most obviously, their effectiveness depends on money. So far as this comes in the form of subsidies from a metropolitan power, it is dependent upon political circumstances beyond the control of the people themselves, but the amount which is raised locally and its allocation are determined by political circumstances in the colony itself. In the first place, its raising depends upon the general recognition of the benefits of Government activity in the technical field of the departments, in the second upon the local government's perception of urgent needs. Both of these conditions are essentially political. The first implies that Government action is recognized by the people as desirable and efficient; the second that the Government itself recognizes its duty to the people; and both are part of the acceptance of the structure of government as representative of colonial society. The executive departments' success in promoting social, economic and educational advancement is thus dependent on the way in which the legislative or representative branch of the Government functions. This proposition is an inversion of the usual colonial formula that 'economic development is a condition of welfare, and welfare a condition of autonomy, because self-governing institutions cannot be built on a foundation of ignorance and ill health', but it seems amply demonstrated from colonies like Burma and Netherlands India,[4] and it provides a major contrast between Tahiti where, with the disappearance of the traditional political order, social and economic measures simply contributed to the disappearance of the old society as a whole, and Fiji and Samoa where the preservation of the traditional order has helped to control the effects of social and economic change. In all three cases the political structure must promote these modern standards for it is as much the prerequisite for other kinds of developments as the ultimate result.

In Fiji, one of the chief purposes of the Fijian Administration is economic and social development; a similar pressure is exerted through the institutions of government in American Samoa. Since these Governments are largely accepted because of the traditional authority they enshrine, this pressure has considerable force behind it, but it also contains the dilemma of any system of colonial rule of its type. The basis of traditional authority depends upon the preservation of traditional society and if the latter is changed by modern social or economic attitudes, the basis of traditional leadership is altered, and the Government which relies upon it must, therefore, adapt itself or face a growing distance between itself and a changing society. The chiefs have a vested interest in the old society unless they are educated and prepared to translate their authority into new terms. Sukuna, in Fiji, urged them to do this, and influential voices in Samoa raise the same cry, but it has not generally been heeded. Most traditional leaders, naturally enough, would rather not make the great effort required, and whatever encouragement of modern social and economic standards they are prepared to offer, they commit the Government to slow progress. As in the case of acceptance of the structure of government, so in the case of acceptance of modern standards, the essence of the problem in Fiji and American Samoa is educated leadership. So it is in Tahiti, too, but in a rather different sense. The leaders who occupy positions in the structure of the Government have no traditional basis of

[4] Furnivall, op. cit., p. 459.

authority but a modern one: the electoral system. The majority party which controls the legislature, and through the Council of Government the territorial services as well, has a vested interest in the system that elects it. Its leaders are men who have some knowledge of modern government and local needs, but they also face the question: can we afford social and economic changes which may make the basis of our power less certain? If the Tahitian electorate were to become thoroughly assimilated to French values and attitudes, it would be necessary to use a more sophisticated, reasoned appeal for election, which would make greater demands upon the leadership. This effort is no doubt easier for them to make than that required of a traditional leader in the other colonies, but it may still be shirked if possible. The dilemma of Tahiti is the reluctance of leaders with a vested interest in parish pump politics to see a broadening of their constituents' horizons.

Whatever the differences between these three colonies, therefore, by the second criterion of meeting modern standards of government, they are alike in having a partial measure of success, just as there is a similar comparison using the first criterion of acceptance of Government institutions as representative. The weaknesses in the structure of government come at the same points: leadership and village government. This is not primarily the fault of the metropolitan powers or the colonial Governments; it is an inevitable consequence of the operation of Western institutions in non-Western societies whose unity, such as it is, is a Western creation. The weaknesses tend to disappear with the passage of time. It may be argued that greater resources in men, money and material would speed the process, but there is a rate beyond which it is impossible to travel without running the risk of outstripping acceptance of what is being done which is vital to any political advancement. The weaknesses are often ascribed to ill will or bad faith on the part of the colonial powers, but the detailed examination suggests that they are rather produced by an inescapable clash of custom, and by technical difficulties or inadequate techniques, than by malevolence. In none of these colonies can Western institutions be expected to work as they do in metropolitan societies, and some failures, some loss of efficiency, must be accepted. The colonial powers are still there to exert pressure towards good government, and to supply some of the resources to achieve it. The present difficulties are not the end of colonial rule, but part of a continuing process of political advancement which, granted the responsibilities of Britain, France and the United States, rests as much upon the indigenous leaders who have certainly not been denied the opportunity to lead the political advance in the years since the Second World War.

INDEX

N.B. Abbreviations used in Index: (F.) = Fiji, (S.) = American Samoa, (T.) = Tahiti

9 780313 245336

Printed by Libri Plureos GmbH in Hamburg,
Germany